ܐܠܦ ܒܝܬ

ܡܒܠܝܐ ܠܠܫܢܐ ܐܬܘܪܝܐ

ܠܗܘܪܐ ܬܚܝܬܐ

ܐܘܪܚܐ ܐܠܝܬܐ ܝܡܝܐ

ܝܡܝܐ ܐܪܝܐܝܬܐ ܕܦܘܡ

ܬܠܬ - ܩܡܐ

ALAP BETH

An Introduction To Modern Syriac

Eastern Dialect - 3rd Edition

Mahir Awrahem

© 2021 - Michigan

Printed in the United States of America/Michigan

Chapters Video/Audio Recordings URL: https://www.aramaicstudies.org

Third Edition. © 2021
ISBN: 978-0-578-83976-9.

ܐܢ

ܣܥܕܐ ܘ ܦܪܚ، ܪܝܡ

ܩܘܝܣܐ ܠܟܘܢ ܣܘܣܬܐ ܟܦܘܢܐ ܩܘܠܟܘܢ ܩܘܠܟܘܢ

ܝܘ ܦܐܠܐ ܝܘܡܐ ܟܠܐ ܩܕܡ

To Farah, Mariam, and Jacob.
Thank you for all your support and encouragement.

Acknowledgments

There are several people I wish to thank, especially those who helped in the editing, providing resources, and meeting with me to finish this book: my father Deacon Ilya, my aunt Najwa Dallo, my brother Deacon Matthew, my sister Dr Marwa, my father-in-law Deacon Edward Hanna, Deacon Khairy Foumia, Deacon Yasser Hannawi, Jamil Mansour, Lawrence Mansour, David Enochs, to my first teacher Deacon Nameer Loussia and to my mentor Fr. Manuel Boji.

Notice to the Readers

ܒܫܝܢܐ B'shayna! Welcome to Modern Syriac Language (Syriac – for short), also known as Sooruth ܣܘܪܬ, Chaldean language ܠܫܢܐ ܟܠܕܝܐ, or Assyrian language ܠܫܢܐ ܐܬܘܪܝܐ. The grammar of this book represents the fundamental of Syriac language to assist you learn to pronounce the sounds of Syriac, vocabulary, simple grammar, and some Syriac culture.

The language represent in this book is the most widely spoken dialect among the Syriac people which is called "Dashta D'Ninweh – ܕܫܬܐ ܕܢܝܢܘܐ (The Nineveh Plain) dialect.

You might want more; other will want less. Nevertheless, this is our best judgment of what constitute a basic, one course in Syriac language should. We know that a big number of those who study Syriac do so in preparation for some type of pastoral or serving as a deacon at the church. Chapter 6 - The Basic Grammar, Chapter 7 - The Verbs , Appendixes C, D, E, and F will help pastoral students to know more about basic Syriac grammar.

In the meantime, this book will help other people never had chance to learn the language especially Syriac people in diaspora. In general, the design of this grammar reflects both its basic and its primary audience.

What is New in this Edition?
More grammar and verbs added and discussed in chapter 6:
- The Adjectives possessive.
- The Pronominal prefixes.
- The Absolute possessive.
- The Demonstratives.

And the following verb tense added and discussed in Chapter 7:
- The past continuous tense.
- The present perfect tense.
- The future perfect tense.
- The modal verbs: Could, Should, Used To verb, May and May have.
- The conditional, unless/if not, and in case forms.

iv

And more:-

- Practice exercises added at the end of each chapter for learner to practice his or her acquired knowledge from that chapter..
- Examples of conversations and illustrations were added in Chapters 8 for more practices on the spoken language. More reading paragraphs and stories were added in Chapter 9 for understanding the concept of the spoken language and learning how to use grammar.

To help enhance the readers experience we have recorded chapters 1 to 9 content of this book. This will hopefully guide the reader for better pronunciation and to simplify the navigation of this book. To access the recordings video/audio chapters and for any questions or comments, please visit www.aramaicstudies.org.

Table of Contents ܦܶܢܩܺܝܬ݂ܐ ܕܣܶܕܪܐ

vii

viii

ix

Chapter 1

The History of The Aramaic and Syriac Languages
ܟܬ̈ܒܐ ܕܠܩܬܐ ܐܝܪܢܝܐ ܐܪܡܝܐ ܘܣܘܪ̈ܝܝܐ

Aramaic is the ancient language of the Semitic family and is full of rich and complex linguistics. The many branches of the language have created many diverse and unique accents that have been spoken by many tribes throughout the Middle East. The Babylonians, Chaldeans, Hebrews, Assyrians, Arameans, and Arabs all have a common language ancestor in Aramaic. A majority of both the Arabic and Hebrew languages is borrowed from Aramaic, including their Alphabets. The modern Hebrew (square) script is called "Ashuri or Ashurit", which is the Hebrew name for Assyrian. This was used to signify the ancestor of the Assyrians: Ashur the son of Shem, the son of Noah (Genesis 10:22).

The Aramaeans learned the art of writing from Phoenicians. They based the characteristics of their own language by adapting the language of Aramaic words such as "ܒ ܒܪ" (son of) and "ܒ ܒܝܬ" (family of. **Literal**: house of). They gradually moved on from the Canaanite-Phoenician language and moved towards their own unique language.

The oldest texts that we received in Aramaic go back up to 10th and 11th centuries B.C., where the evolution from Canaanite to Aramaic is clear and understandable.

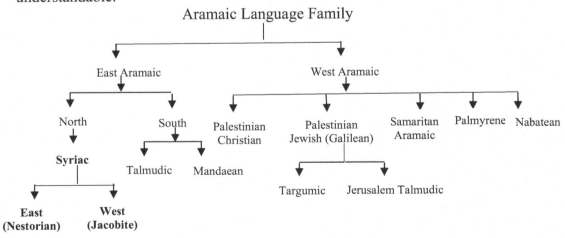

Figure 1-1 Aramaic Language Family

1

Aramaic language, as illustrated above, is known as the mother of many dialects. Syriac, the Aramaic dialect of Edessa (Urfa) in Turkey, was the native language of Jesus and the people known as Chaldeans, Assyrian, or Syriac. It has been in use since the 11th century B.C. and was quickly accepted as the literary language of all non-Greek eastern Christians. Syriac was the primary vehicle for the Christianization of large parts of central and south-central Asia.

The Arabic and Hebrew dialects adapted their own writing/spoken language styles from Eastern Syriac and Western Syriac (Serto). Both Eastern and Western Syriac styles can be identified from their established well-known Syriac scripts, or Estrangelo, which means "rounded". This constitutes a large portion of the commonalities between the Syriac and Arabic/Hebrew languages.

The Syriac dialect helped spread Christianity in a Semitic-speaking world. The traders, merchants, and businessmen who received the dialect as a technique to keep monetary records furthered the language without even being aware, they were doing so. Even after the split between the monotheistic Jacobite Church of Syria and the Nestorian Church of the East (which corresponded geologically with the Persian Empire) in the 5th century, Syriac remained the official language of these major institutions.

A large portion of the early Syriac writing in Mesopotamia from 1st to 4th centuries was composed of Christian, Jewish, Pagan, and Agnostic literature. Over sixty inscriptions are still accessible today, and it has been discovered that the dialect is a bridge between true Aramaic and Syriac languages and cultures. For the Old Testament to be translated into Syriac from Hebrew, Jews that spoke Syriac spent countless hours translating the documents. The "Persian Sage" writings, or the significant documents that have lasted the tests of time, were about faith, war, love, and food. Ephrem the Syriac was the most celebrated theologian-poet, and he produced literature with prose and artistic poetry.

The golden age of Syriac-speaking development was from the fifth to ninth centuries. More than 70 prominent authors emerged during this era, many of which are still heavily influential today. Both spiritual and mathematics experts make significant impacts on the Syriac culture. Ishodad of Merv, David of Dara, George of the Arabs, and the monk Sawira Sebokht (father of international numerals) were some of the experts of the time period.

During the fifth century, the Church split into different directions; however, it was the strong foundation of the Syriac tradition that enabled it to stay alive and relevant. Popular apologists, Philoxenos of Mabbug and Babi the Great, made significant impacts to keep culture strong. During the fifth century, there were also many well-known theologians from the Mesopotamian region whose lessons are still in taught today.

Philosophy, economics, medicine, and science first began to emerge in Syriac literature by way of a passed-down approach: the Mesopotamians and Egyptians transcended information down to the Greek and Romans, who in turn passed it down to the Arabs. From there, Western European countries received the translated information. During the 9th to the 13th centuries, Geek scientific knowledge translated into the Syriac language. Syriac was used as a main language to translate information from Greek to Persian, thus acting as a language barrier-breaker. We still see the Aramaic language in scientific terms used in chemistry, physics, medicine, and other similar topics.

The breadth of unique and influential authors during this period was astounding. Elijah of Nisibin authored a chronograph and an Arabic-Syriac guide. Bar Ebroyo wrote over 20 guides on numerous topics, and Bar Salibi created many encyclopedic publications.

Syriac literature was organized from top to bottom because of the decrease in perceptive actions in the Middle East after the 13th century. Authors still continuing to write in Syriac; however, when Patriarch Ignatius Ni'matallah left for Rome in the 16th century over fears of execution, a major vacuum of expertise was created. Patriarch Ni'matallah was involved in the calendar reform committee, which is where the Gregorian calendar was developed during Pope Gregory period.

Documentation of the Syriac language started in the 17th century using the Alqosh Neo-Aramaic language. During the 17th and the 18th centuries, many western spiritual documents were available in Syriac. The Syriac language was then introduced to the western world and Joseph Simon Assemani produced the Bibliotheca Orientals, which is the best encyclopedia of Syriac culture. The Syriac culture went through many hardships during the late 18th and 19th centuries.

The powerful Ottoman Empire in Turkey threatened the very existence of Syriac-speaking people. They committed mass oppression throughout their empire, causing Syriac people to refer to this period as "the year of the sword." The massacres against the Syriac people forced them to migrate to other countries in the region.

The 20th century was a time for revival for the Syriac culture and religious literature. With the end of the first World War, the Syriac culture saw a resurgence of traditions. It was during this time period that Toma Audo, a Chaldean author, created a Syriac dictionary. Star of the East, a Syriac periodical founded by Naoum Faiq, sparked a step forward for the culture as journalism began to take off in popularity.

It was during this time period that translations of Syriac books started becoming more widespread. Most literature was translated from Syriac to Malayalam, the language of St. Thomas's Christians. The writings were translated mostly for worshiping purposes. In a few Christian communities Syriac is the liturgical language. Some of these churches include: The Assyrian Church of the East, The Chaldean Catholic Church, and The Syriac Orthodox, etc.

Syriac is experiencing an expansion in the western academic society, thus providing students with the culture and language of the Syriac-speaking people. In the late 1980s, Oxford University offered a master's degree in Syriac studies. The University of Birmingham followed suit by offering a similar program. In most of the major universities, Syriac is taught either in Semitic departments, religious studies, or both. Mahatma Ghandi University in Kerala has recently started a Ph.D. program in Syriac. At the community level, Syriac is being taught to children in a few private community schools in the Middle East, and sometimes in the Diaspora. Magazines are being published in Syriac and Neo-Aramaic, and a few publishing houses have emerged with Syriac as a primary focus.

There are many positive things being done to keep the culture alive. Different, diverse groups, such as the North America-based Syriac Symposium, meet annually, and the International Symposium Syriacum, meets every four years. Talk of a Syriac center has come about to give the general public information on the culture. Even in individual communities, things are being done to keep the culture active, such as community schools teaching Syriac to children, and informational publications circulating.

Chapter 2

The Modern Syriac Language – Eastern Dialect

ܠܸܫܵܢܵܐ ܐܵܬܘܿܪܵܝܵܐ - ܠܸܠܵܐ ܡܲܕܢܚܵܝܵܐ

Learning Objectives

In this chapter, you will:

- learn the different types of the Syriac language dialects.
  - o The Eastern Dialect.
  - o The Western Dialect.
- the Syriac Translation.
- learn the different types of the Syriac language scripts:
  - o Estrangelo.
  - o Serto.
  - o Garshouni.
- introduce to the Eastern Syriac language alphabet and the corresponding English letter and sounds.
- learn the final forms of the three letters ܟ ، ܡ ، ܢ
- learn the special form of ܬ.
- learn the eight Un-joined letters.
- introduce to the Estrangelo letters.
- introduce to the Western Syriac letters and the five vowels.
- learn the Eastern Syriac seven vowels.
- learn the Eastern Syriac language alphabet ܐ to ܬ.
- learn the numerical values and names words from 1 - 499.

The animosity from the Greeks towards the Syriac people during the end of 5th century caused the Syriacs to escape to Persia. With the influx of Syriac people into Persia, a harsh division emerged amongst them. The Syriac language and culture developed distinct Western and Eastern differences. The two sides of the Syriac language still held a high level of comprehension at its foundation with the major differences residing in pronunciation, the writing system, and certain aspects of the vocabulary. The dividing line is the Euphrates River, which cause an Eastern and Western split.

Syriac Language Dialects

The Eastern Dialect is spoken by the Assyrians (Chaldean Catholics and Nestorians), which is more similar to the original Aramaic language. The Eastern dialect is found in the two great kingdoms, Babylon and Nineveh, Damascus, Aljazeera (Saudi Arabian Peninsula), Lebanon, the Syro-Malabar Church, amongst other nations in the region.

The Western Dialect is known as (Syriayo "Syr.ya.yo" – Serto), is the language of Maronite and Syriac Catholic and the Jacobins (Syriac Orthodox), and it is not found anywhere else except in the Aramaic Tur Abdin, and throughout the mountains near Mardin in southwestern Turkey.

The Syriac Translation it is a misconception that the Greek philosophic ideas spread throughout the world by the Arabic language when Muslims controlled Spain in 711 A.D. However, Greek philosophy, medicine, and science did not reach the Arab world directly, but instead by means of the Syriac-speaking people. Syriac translations of the of Aristotle's major works have been dated back to as far as the early 6th Century, although it was through the work of the Syriac Christians working in the Abbasid capital, Baghdad, in the 9th Century that these translations actually took place.
Hunyn Ibn Ishaq (died 873), one of the most famous translators, gave a detailed account of how he did the translations. Having collected the best Greek manuscripts he could find, he began to translate them from Greek into Syriac, and then from Syriac into Arabic. This is why it is essential that the study of Aristotelian philosophy among Arabs is started with a foundation of Syriac knowledge. Hunyn Ibn Ishaq was appointed by the Abbasid Caliph Al-Ma'mun to lead the Office of the Translation and the House of Wisdom.

Syriac Scripts

Estrangelo: The earliest Syriac inscriptions of the First and Second Centuries A.D, even early Fifth century A.D has taken on a more formalized character, known as "Estrangelo" (probably from Greek "Strongulos" which means "rounded", it is used by Chaldeans and Assyrians).

Serto: A new script is known as "Serto" (Literally, it means "scratch character", called by the European as "Jacobite"). It became the normal script employed by the Maronites and the Syriac Church Catholic and Orthodox.

Garshouni: Islam's numerous conflicts with the various languages; "Garshouni" emerged during the writing of the Koran. It is the Arabic language written with the Syriac alphabet or letters.

Syriac Language ܠܫܢܐ ܐܬܘܪܝܐ

Eastern Alphabet – ܐܠܦ ܒܝܬ ܡܕܢܚܝܐ

Unlike English language, the Syriac is written from right to left and has twenty-two consonants, or letters. Like studying any other language, one of the first things you must do while learning Syriac is memorizing the alphabet and vowels in order. While learning the order of the letter, you will learn the names and pronunciation of the letters. The Syriac alphabet is divided into six groups: ABGD, HWZ, HTY, KLMN, SAPS, and QRSHT:

ܐܒܓܕ، ܗܘܙ، ܚܛܝ، ܟܠܡܢ، ܣܥܦܨ، ܩܪܫܬ.

English Letter	Pronunciation	Name	Estrangela	Syriac Letter
A	Has the sound of the vowel. Silent if no vowel	Alap	ܐ	ܐ
B	B as in ball	Beth	ܒ	ܒ
G	G as in good	Gamal	ܓ	ܓ
D	D as in door	Dalath	ܕ	ܕ
H	H as in hello	Heh	ܗ	ܗ
W	W as in way	Wow	ܘ	ܘ
Z	Z as in zoo	Zain	ܙ	ܙ
No comparable	Heavily accented H	Heth	ܚ	ܚ
No comparable	Heavily accented T	Teth	ܛ	ܛ
Y	Y as in yes	Yod	ܝ	ܝ
K	K as in king	Kap & Kap	ܟ ܟ	ܟ ܟ
L	L as in lion	Lamath	ܠ	ܠ
M	M as in master	Meem & Meem	ܡ ܡ	ܡ ܡ
N	N as in now	Noon & Noon	ܢ ܢ	ܢ ܢ
S	S as in sit	Simkath	ܣ	ܣ
No comparable	Sliced E	Aeh	ܥ	ܥ
P	P as in please	Peh	ܦ	ܦ

8

No comparable	SS as in sun	Sade	ܨ	ܨ
No comparable		Qop	ܩ	ܩ
R	R as in run	Resh	ܪ	ܪ
Sh	Sh as in sheep	Sheen	ܫ	ܫ
T	T as in today	Taw	ܬ	ܬ

Figure 2-1: Syriac letters and the English equivalent.

There are two forms of letters used by Eastern Syriac writers: first column from right (above) and the earliest Syriac script is called Estrangela or Estrangelo (second column), whose name is derived from the Greek word *strongulos* meaning 'rounded'. Estrangela inscriptions date from as far back as the year 6 AD, and by the 3rd century, the Bible and Christian theological works had been translated into Syriac. As the city of Edessa became an important Christian center, Syriac spread throughout region as far as Palestine, and even travelled down the Silk Road and all the way to China.

The Estrangela set is mainly used for scriptures, titles, headings, and book and album titles. It usually has no vowels (dots), and it is used by both parts (Eastern and Western) Syriac dialects.

Only six (6) letters have different shape, the rest are the same.

ܟܬܒܐ، ܗܘܐ، ܣܒܕ، ܚܠܬ، ܗܕܩܝ، ܬܐܬܐ.

The six different letters are:

Estrangelo	Eastern Syriac
ܐ	ܐ
ܕ	ܕ
ܗ	ܗ
ܩ	ܩ
ܪ	ܪ
ܬ	ܬ

Figure 2-2: The six (6) different Estrangela Letters.

Final Form

Three of the Syriac letters have final forms, meaning that it appears differently when placed at the end of the word as opposed to the beginning or middle. The pronunciation remains the same. The three final forms are listed below. These final forms must be memorized in order to properly learn the language. The transliteration of the Syriac examples is written from left to right, and the Syriac examples are written from right to left.

Translation	Example	Final Form	Regular form
Your book	ܟܬܳܒܟ	ܟ	ܒ
Mariam	ܡܪܝܡ	ܡ	ܡ
Yohanan	ܝܘܚܢܢ	ܢ	ܢ

Figure 2-3: Final Form.

The Special Form of ܬ (Taw): ܬ (taw) has two forms too. It can be used anywhere in the word.

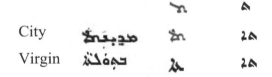

City	ܡܕܝܢܬܐ	ܬ	ܬܐ
Virgin	ܒܬܘܠܬܐ	ܬ	ܬܐ

Figure 2-4: Taw ܬ special from.

Un-Joined Letters

The Syriac alphabet is mostly a cursive script that means, most letters are joined one to another within a word. All letters connect from the right, and all but eight letters, connect forward to left. The eight letters that do not connect to their following letter (left) when they occurred in word are:

Figure 2-5: un-joined letters.

Vowels

The Eastern Syriac language has seven "no written system" of vowels, and although they do not exist in written form. While they do not exist in written form, they are still a part of the spoken language. They are added to the consonants by using dots. In Syriac, the letters represent consonant sounds, while vowels are indicated by dots that are written above or below the letters. However, the letters of the English alphabet represent both consonant sounds and vowels. For a full presentation of the Syriac Vowels, **see Chapter 3.**

Numerical Values

In the additional to the international numerical values, Syriac also use the letters to represent numbers. Each letter of the Syriac alphabet represents a numerical value. The consonants ܐ through ܛ represent numbers 1-9. Consonants ܝ through ܨ represent numbers 10 – 90. And ܩ through ܬ represent numbers 100 through 400. For a full presentation of the Syriac numerical system, **see Chapter 4.**

Western Letters: ܐܠܦ ܒܝܬ (ܡܥܪܒܐ)

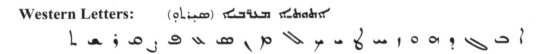

Figure 2-6: Syriac Western Syriac.

We will not cover the Western letters in this book. The common between the two dialects is that both use the same of the Estrangela letters form, but there are only five vowels used in Western dialect.

 Western Vowels: Western dialect has five vowels:

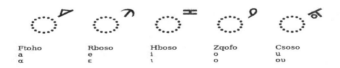

Ftoho	Rboso	Hboso	Zqofo	Csoso
a	e	i	o	u
α	ε	i	o	ou

Figure 2-7: Syriac Western five vowels.

11

The Eastern Syriac Seven Vowels — ܙܘܥܹ̈ܐ

In Syriac, the letters represent consonant sounds, while vowels are indicated by dots that are written above or below the letters. In this section, we introduce the seven vowels just to use them with the twenty-two letters. We will use the letter ܒ "B" as an example to apply the vowels. We will study the vowels and Syllabification in details in next chapter.

Sqapa ܙܩܵܦܵܐ

Sqapa is pronounced as an open **(long)** "A". It is indicated by placing two slanted points, one above other, directly over the letter. Sqapa is usually like "AH" as in "Father."

Example: ܒܵ

Pthaha ܦܬ݂ܵܚܵܐ

Pthaha is pronounced as a short "A". It is indicated by placing one point over the letter and another point under the letter. Pthaha is pronounced like "UH" as in "Hut" or "Utter."

Example: ܒܲ

Zlama Psheeqa ܙܠܵܡܵܐ ܦܫܝܼܩܵܐ

Zlama Psheeqa is pronounced as a very short "I". It is indicated by placing two even points, side by side, under the letter. Zlama Psheeqa is pronounced like "IH" as in "Sit" and "Hit."

Example: ܒܹ

Zlama Qishya ܙܠܵܡܵܐ ܩܸܫܝܵܐ

Zlama Qishya is pronounced as an open "E". It is indicated by placing two slanted points, one above the other, under the letter. Zlama Qishya is pronounced like "EH" as in "They" or "Net."

Example: ܒܸ

Rwahha   ܪܘܲܚܵܐ

Rwahha is pronounced as **"O"**. It is indicated by placing one point over the letter ܘ (Wow). It applies only to the letter ܘ (Wow). It is pronounced like "OH" as in "So" and "Row."

Example: ܒܿܘ

Rwassa   ܪܘܵܨܵܐ

Rwassa is pronounced as **"U"**. It is indicated by placing one point under the letter ܘ (Wow). It applies only to the letter ܘ (Wow). It is pronounced like "OO" or "UW" as in "Boo" and "Room."

Example: ܒܘܿ

Hwassa   ܚܒ݂ܵܨܵܐ

Hwassa is pronounced as a long **"E"**. It is indicated by placing one point under the letter ܝ (Yod). It applies only to the letter ܝ (Yod). It is pronounced like "EE" as in "Bee" and "Tree."

Example: ܒܝܼ

Characters Key

The following characters will be used for short to represent the words:

- **(c)**: classical Syriac language. (the word used for example to apply the vowels, verbs, or plural). It is barely used in the spoken languages).
- **(m)**: masculine form.
- **(f)**: feminine form.
- **(p)**: plural form (or g - group) same or mix of masculine or/and feminine.
- **(1ˢᵗ m/f/p)** – from first person male/female/plural.
- **(2ⁿᵈ m/f/p)** – to second person male/female/plural.
- **(3ʳᵈ m/f/p)** – third person male/female/plural.

The First Group — ܩܕܡܝܐ ܓܒܐ

ܐ

Alap   ܐܠܦ - ܐ

ܐ is the first letter of the Syriac alphabet and originally was shaped as the head of a ship, which is one of the gods from Mesopotamia.

- ܐ is comparable to the English letter A. Its sound is guttural.
- The numerical value of ܐ is (1): ܚܕ (m), ܚܕܐ (f).

Grammar 1: To make any letter silent, place a dash line above the letter to make it silent.
Examples: Mass, ܩܘܕܫܐ, Human ܒܪܢܫܐ, Bed ܬܫܘܝܬܐ. See **Appendix E** for more silent rules and examples.

- ܐ has NO sound without a vowel, making it silent by itself especially at the end of the word.
  o ܐ has the sound of the vowel applied on it.
- ܐ is the first of the three weakest letters.
- ܐ never appears in middle of the proper noun. It is either appears at the beginning or at the end of the proper noun.
  o If ܐ shows in the middle of the proper noun, this word is not originally a Syriac word. For example, to write "**Mark**" in Syriac, we write ܡܐܪܩܘܣ and it is silent.
- ܐ is one of the un-joined letters which never connects to any letter follows it.
  o It is joined on the right only when it is in the middle or end of the word.
  o Remember, letter always follow to the left.

Estrangela			Eastern Syriac		
Isolated	End	Begin & Mid	Isolated	End	Begin & Mid
ܐ	ܐ ܐ	ܐ ܐ	ܐ	ܐ ܐ	ܐ ܐ

14

How to Write Alap

Note: The step by step are only for Eastern Syriac fonts for all letters. See videos for how to write Estrangela.

1) Make a short horizontal line from right to left:
2) Place a small dot slightly above the left of the line.
3) Continue with a slightly slanted downward stroke from the dot to the left of the horizontal line.

ܐ	ܐ	ܐ	ܐ	ܐ	ܐ	ܐ	ܐ	ܐ

Read aloud and write ܐ with each vowel several times.

_____ _____ _____ _____ _____ _____ _____ ܐ

_____ _____ _____ _____ _____ _____ _____ ܐ

_____ _____ _____ _____ _____ _____ _____ ܐ

_____ _____ _____ _____ _____ _____ _____ ܐ

_____ _____ _____ _____ _____ _____ _____ ܐܘ

_____ _____ _____ _____ _____ _____ _____ ܐܘ

_____ _____ _____ _____ _____ _____ _____ ܐܝ

Pronunciation of ܐ (Alap) and vowels – ܩܪܝܬܐ ܕܐܠܦ ܥܡ ܙܘܥܐ

Transliteration[1]	Meaning	Example	Vowel sound	L & V
	August Doctor (m)	ܐܵܒ ܐܵܣܝܵܐ	long a	ܐܵ
	God Lion	ܐܲܠܵܗܵܐ ܐܲܪܝܵܐ	short a	ܐܲ
	Hundred	ܐܹܡܵܐ	short i	ܐܹ
	Where	ܐܲܝܟܵܐ	open e	ܐܸ
	Nation (f)	ܐܘܡܬܵܐ	oo	ܐܘ
	Old Testament (c, f)	ܐܘܪܵܝܬܵܐ	o	ܐܘ̇
	Tree (f)	ܐܝܠܵܢܵܐ	ee	ܐܝ

---

[1] Transliteration column will be left blank for reader to write the Syriac word using his/her native language. See chapters recordings at www.aramaicstudies.org for the words pronunciation.

ܒ

Beth ܒܝܬ – ܒ

ܒ is the second letter of the Syriac alphabet and originally was shaped like an ancient house.

- ܒ is comparable to the English letter B.
- It has a labial sound.

Grammar 2: When a single dot is placed above the letter, (ܒ݁) it has a hard "B" sound.

Grammar 3: When a single dot is placed beneath the letter, (ܒ݂) it becomes soft and it has a "W" sound. Like in: Neighbor ܫܒ݂ܒ݂ܐ.

- The numerical value of ܒ is (2) ܬܪܝܢ (m), ܬܪܬܝܢ (f).
- It is used as a preposition letter to indicate a certain relation to other words:
  - **With**: with peace you came (2nd m). ܒܫܠܡܐ ܐܬܝܬܘܢ.
  - **By**: by pen I wrote. ܒܩܢܝܐ ܟܬܒܬ.
  - **In** - as preposition of movement (where): In the temple. ܒܗܝܟܠܐ
  - **At** - as preposition of time (when): at night. ܒܠܠܝܐ

Note: night is ܠܠܝܐ and pronounced ܠܝܠܐ in spoken language.

  - Used to explain the reason: he died because of cancer.

    ܗܘ ܡܝܬ ܒܣܪܛܢܐ.

  - **To compare**:
    Mariam is better than you in mathematics.

    ܡܪܝܡ ܐܝܬܝܗ ܒܝܬ ܛܒܐ ܡܢܟ ܒܝܘܡ ܚܫܒܘܢܐ.

    (**Literal**: Mariam is stronger than you in mathematics).

  - **Present continuous**: when join a verb:
    "I am studying – 1st m". ܐܢܐ ܒܗܘܝ ܒܝܘܠܦܢܐ.

  - ܒ connects to any letter which follows it. When it is a medial letter, it is joined on both sides. Unless it follows one of the 8 un-joined letters.

Estrangela			Eastern Syriac		
Isolated	End	Begin & Mid	Isolated	End	Begin & Mid
ܒ	ܒ ܒ	ܒ ܒ	ܒ	ܒ ܒ	ܒ ܒ

How to Write Beth

1) Make a short vertical line downward starting from the top.
2) Make a short horizontal line from the top of the vertical line moving towards the left.
3) Continue a similar but longer horizontal line from the bottom of the vertical line moving towards the left.

Read aloud and write ܒ with each vowel several times.

ܒ݊ _____ _____ _____ _____ _____ _____ _____

ܒ݁ _____ _____ _____ _____ _____ _____ _____

ܒ݈ _____ _____ _____ _____ _____ _____ _____

ܒ _____ _____ _____ _____ _____ _____ _____

ܒܘ _____ _____ _____ _____ _____ _____ _____

ܒܘ _____ _____ _____ _____ _____ _____ _____

ܒ݈ _____ _____ _____ _____ _____ _____ _____

Read aloud and write each of the following words several times. These words are made from the letters you have learned. This will help you with reading and how to connect the Syriac letters together.

ܐܒ݂ August (m): ____ ____ ____ ____ ____ ____ ____

ܐܒ݂ܐ Father (m): ____ ____ ____ ____ ____ ____ ____

ܒܵܒ݂ܐ Dad : ____ ____ ____ ____ ____ ____ ____

18

Pronunciation of ܒ (Beth) and vowels – ܩܵܠܵܐ ܕܒܹܝܬ ܥܲܡ ܙܵܘܥܹ̈ܐ

Transliteration	Meaning	Example	Vowel sound	L & V
	Babylon (f)	ܒܵܒܸܠ	long a	ܒܵ
	Baghdad (f) House (m)	ܒܲܓܕܵܕ ܒܲܝܬܵܐ	short a	ܒܲ
	Bubble Onion (m)	ܒܲܒܘܼܟܹܐ ܒܨܸܠܵܐ	short i	ܒܸ
	Well (f)	ܒܹܐܪܵܐ	open e	ܒܹ
	Owl (f)	ܒܘܼܡܵܐ	oo	ܒܘܼ
	Unemployment	ܒܸܛܵܠܘܼܬܵܐ	o	ܒܘ
	Canal (m)	ܒܝܼܠܵܐ	ee	ܒܝܼ

ܒܵܒܸܠ ܬܲܪܥܵܐ ܕܐܲܠܵܗܹ̈ܐ!
Babylon – Gate of the gods.

ܒ – ܒܵܒܸܠ
ܒܘ – ܒܘܼܡܵܐ

ܓ

Gamal   ܓ – ܓܡܰܠ

ܓ is the third letter of the Syriac alphabet and originally was shaped to resemble a camel's saddle.

- ●   ܓ is comparable to the English letter G.
- ●   It has a palatal sound.

Grammar 4: When a single dot is placed beneath, (ܓ̣) it becomes soft and does not have comparable sound in English. Most the time, it gives " Gh" when transliterated in English. Like in ܦܓܪܐ (body).

- ●   The numerical value of ܓ is 3 ܬܠܳܬܳܐ (m), ܬܠܳܬ (f).
- ●   ܓ connects to any letter which follows it.
  - o   When it is a medial letter, it is joined on both sides.
  - o   Unless when it follows one of the 8 un-joined letters.

Estrangela			Eastern Syriac		
Isolated	End	Begin & Mid	Isolated	End	Begin & Mid
ܓ	ܓ ܓ	ܓ ܓ	ܓ	ܓ ܓ	ܓ ܓ

How to Write Gamal
1) Start with a long slanted downward stroke.
2) Continue with a short horizontal line at the center of the slanted line moving towards the left.

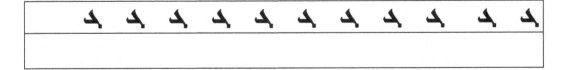

Read aloud and write ܠ with each vowel several times.

		ܠܲ
		ܠܵ
		ܠܸ
		ܠܹ
		ܠܘܿ
		ܠܘܼ
		ܠܝܼ

Read aloud and write each of the following words several times. These words are made from the letters you have learned. This will help you with reading and how to connect the Syriac letters together.

ܓܲܒ݂ܵܐ :Political Party (m) _____ _____ _____ _____ __ _____

ܒܠܵܛܵܐ : Marble (m) _____ _____ _____ _____ _____

ܓܲܒ݂ܵܐ – ܠ
ܓܲܒ݂ܵܐ ܕܝܼܡܘܿܩܪܵܛܵܝܵܐ. Democratic Party.
ܓܲܒ݂ܵܐ ܪܹܦܵܒ݂ܢܵܐ. Republican Party.

ܬܠܵܬ݂ܵܐ ܒܠܵܛܹ̈ܐ ܣܘܼܡܵܩܹ̈ܐ.
Three red marbles.

21

Pronunciation of ܓ (Gamal) and vowels – ܩܳܪܳܐ ܕܓܰܡܰܠ ܥܰܡ ܙܰܘܥܶܐ

Transliteration	Meaning	Example	Vowel sound	L & V
	Grinder (f)	ܓ̣ܳܪܘܿܣܬܐ	long a	ܓ̇
	Camel (m) Political Party (m)	ܓܰܡܠܐ ܓ̰ܰܬܐ	short a	ܓ̣
	Grass (m)	ܓܝܠܐ	short i	ܓ̣
	Raising/Ranching (c, f)	ܓ̣ܒܝܬܐ	open e	ܓ̣
	Wall (m) Island (m)	ܓܘܕܐ ܓ̣ܘܕܐ	oo	ܓܘ
	Color – class (m)	ܓܘܢܐ	o	ܓܘ
	Nile river (m)	ܓ̣ܝܣܢ	ee	ܓ̣

ܓܘܢܐ ܕܓܝܠܐ ܝܠܗ ܝܘܪܩܐ.
The grass's color is green.

ܓ̣ – ܓܝܠܐ
ܓܘ – ܓܘܢܐ

22

ܕ

Dalath ܕ ܕ — ܕܵܠܰܬ݂

ܕ is the fourth letter of the Syriac alphabet and is shaped to resemble the field at the mouth of a river.

- ܕ is comparable to the English letter D. It has a lingual sound.

Grammar 5: When a single dot is placed beneath the letter, (ܕ) it becomes soft and it has a "Th" sound, like in "the".

- The numerical value of ܕ is 4 ܐܲܪܒܿܥܵܐ (m), ܐܲܪܒܲܥ (f).
- It also functions as a preposition letter.
    - **Who, which, whose**: "The Lord who saved us." ܡܵܪܝܵܐ ܕܦܲܪܩܲܢ.
    - **Of**: The God's Book. ܟܬܵܒ݂ܵܐ ܕܐܲܠܵܗܵܐ. **Literal**: The Book of God.
    - **From**: Isaac from Nineveh. ܐܝܼܣܚܵܩ ܕܢܝܼܢܘܹܐ.
- ܕ is one of the un-joined letters which never connects to any letter follows it.
    - When it is a medial letter, it is joined on the right side only.

Estrangela				Eastern Syriac			
Isolated	End	Middle	Beginning	Isolated	End	Middle	Beginning
ܕ	ܕ ܕ	ܕ	ܕ	ܕ	ܕ ܕ	ܕ	ܕ

How to Write Dalath

1) Start at the right of the page, with a short horizontal line moving towards the left.
2) Continue with a line starting from the right of the horizontal line and curving upwards to finish perpendicular to the left of the original line.
3) Place a slash underneath the horizontal line to complete the letter.

ܕ	ܕ	ܕ	ܕ	ܕ	ܕ	ܕ	ܕ	ܕ	

Read aloud and write ܒ with each vowel several times.

ـــــــــ ـــــــــ ـــــــــ ـــــــــ ـــــــــ ـــــــــ ـــــــــ ـــــــــ ـــــــــ ܒܲ

ـــــــــ ـــــــــ ـــــــــ ـــــــــ ـــــــــ ـــــــــ ـــــــــ ـــــــــ ـــــــــ ܒܸ

ـــــــــ ـــــــــ ـــــــــ ـــــــــ ـــــــــ ـــــــــ ـــــــــ ـــــــــ ـــــــــ ܒܹ

ـــــــــ ـــــــــ ـــــــــ ـــــــــ ـــــــــ ـــــــــ ـــــــــ ـــــــــ ـــــــــ ܒܼ

ـــــــــ ـــــــــ ـــــــــ ـــــــــ ـــــــــ ـــــــــ ـــــــــ ـــــــــ ܒܘܿ

ـــــــــ ـــــــــ ـــــــــ ـــــــــ ـــــــــ ـــــــــ ـــــــــ ـــــــــ ܒܘ

ـــــــــ ـــــــــ ـــــــــ ـــــــــ ـــــــــ ـــــــــ ـــــــــ ـــــــــ ـــــــــ ܒܝܼ

Read aloud and write each of the following words several times. These words are made from the letters you have learned. This will help you with reading and how to connect the Syriac letters together.

ـــــــ ـــــــ ـــــــ ـــــــ ـــــــ : Baghdad(f) ܒܲܓܼܕܵܕ

ـــــــ ـــــــ ـــــــ ـــــــ ـــــــ : String(m) ܚܘܼܛܵܐ

ـــــــ ـــــــ ـــــــ ـــــــ : Bear(f) ܕܸܒܵܐ

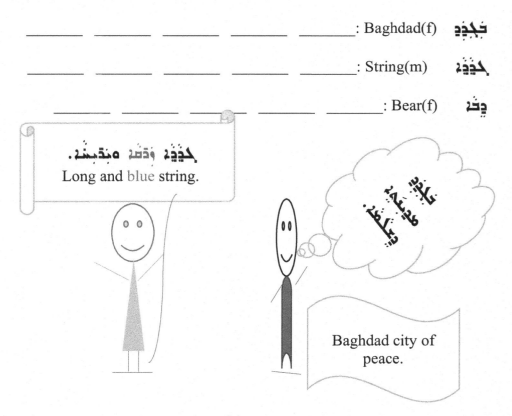

ܚܘܼܛܵܐ ܘܐܲܪܝܼܟ݂ܵܐ ܘܟܸܚܠܵܢܵܐ.
Long and blue string.

ܒܲܓܼܕܵܕ ܡܕܝܼܢ݇ܬܵܐ ܕܲܫܠܵܡܵܐ

Baghdad city of peace.

24

Pronunciation of ܕ (Dalath) and vowels – ܩܵܠܵܐ ܕܘܼܟ݂ܝܵܐ ܒܹܝܬ ܕܘܼܡܝܵܐ

Transliteration	Meaning	Example	Vowel sound	L & V
	Century	ܕܵܪܵܐ	long a	ܕܵ
	Judge (m)	ܕܲܝܵܢܵܐ	short a	ܕܲ
	Cradle (f)	ܕܲܪܓ݂ܘܿܫܬܵܐ		
	Bear (f)	ܕܸܒܵܐ	short i	ܕܸ
	House fly (m)	ܕܸܕܒܵܐ		
	The Tigris river	ܕܸܩܠܵܬ		
	Wolf (m)	ܕܹܐܒܵܐ	open e	ܕܹ
	Place (f)	ܕܘܼܟܵܐ	oo	ܕܘܼ
	Pillars of the well (f)	ܕܘܿܠܝܵܬܹ̈ܐ	o	ܕܘܿ
	Rooster (m)	ܕܝܼܟܵܐ	ee	ܕܝܼ

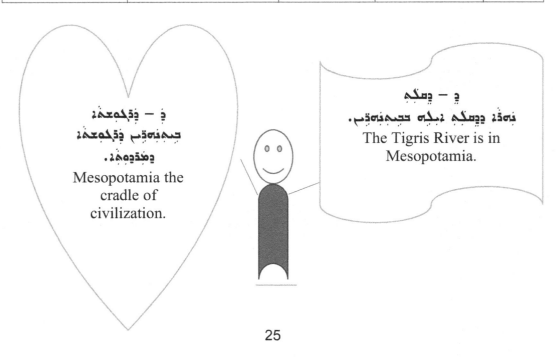

ܕܲ – ܕܲܪܓ݂ܘܿܫܬܵܐ
ܒܹܝܬܢܲܗܪܝܼܢ ܕܲܪܓ݂ܘܿܫܬܵܐ
ܕܡܲܪܕܘܼܬܵܐ.
Mesopotamia the
cradle of
civilization.

ܕܸ – ܕܸܩܠܵܬ
ܢܲܗܪܵܐ ܕܕܸܩܠܵܬ ܐܝܼܠܹܗ ܒܒܹܝܬܢܲܗܪܝܼܢ.
The Tigris River is in
Mesopotamia.

25

The Second Group — ܝܗ ܝܘܗ

Heh   ܗ ܗ – ܠܗ

ܗ is the fifth letter of the Syriac alphabet and is shaped to resemble the trap or pit.

- ܗ is comparable to the English letter H.
- It has a guttural sound. hvhm
- The numeric value is 5 ܚܡܫܐ (m), ܚܡܫ (f).
- ܗ is one of the un-joined letters which never connects to any letter follows it.
  - When it is a medial letter, it is joined on the right side only.

Estrangela			Eastern Syriac		
Isolated	End	Begin & Mid	Isolated	End	Begin & Mid
ܗ	ܗ ܗ	ܗ ܗ	ܗ	ܗ ܗ	ܗ ܗ

How to Write Heh

1) Start at the right of the page, make a short stroke in a downward position.
2) Make a short horizontal line from the top of the vertical line moving to the left.
3) Complete the letter with a small circle in the center of the vertical line.

ܗ	ܗ	ܗ	ܗ	ܗ	ܗ	ܗ	ܗ	ܗ	ܗ	ܗ	ܗ

Read aloud and write ܗ with each vowel several times.

ܗ	ܗ	ܗ	ܗ	ܗ	ܗ	ܗ	ܗ	*ha*
ܗ	ܗ	ܗ	ܗ	ܗ	ܗ	ܗ	ܗ	*hih*
							ܗ	*heh*
							ܗ	*hay*
							ܗܘ	*ho*
							ܗܘ	*who*
							ܗܘ	*he*

Read aloud and write each of the following words several times. These words are made from the letters you have learned. This will help you with reading and how to connect the Syriac letters together.

_____ _____ _____ _____ _____ : Rose(m)   ܘܪܕܐ

_____ _____ _____ _____ : Now   ܗܫܐ   *daha*

_____ _____ _____ _____ _____ : Attempt   ܟܘܫܐ   *gahe*

ܗ – ܘܪܕܐ

ܚܡܫܐ ܘܪܕܐ ܚܘܪܐ.

Five white roses.

white roses 5

27

Pronunciation of ܗ (Heh) and vowels – ܦܘܼܡܵܐ ܕܗܹܐ ܘܙܵܘܥܹ̈ܐ

Mah her

Transliteration	Meaning	Example	Vowel sound	L & V	
	Time/Attempt	ܗܵܐܹܬ	long a	ܗܵ	*haa*
	Temple (m) *ha scha*	ܗܲܝܟܠܵܐ	short a	ܗܲ	*heh*
	Hell (f) *geyhana*	ܓܹܗܲܢܵܐ			
	Excelled (m)	ܗܘ̣ܝܕܪ	short i	ܗ	*hin*
	Deacon (c, m)	ܗܘ ܩܵܘܢܬܵܐ	open e	ܗ	
	Manager, boss (c, m) *hoo parka*	ܗܘ ܦܵܩܕܵܐ	oo	ܗܘ	*hoo*
	Prophet name *hosha*	ܗܘܿܫܲܥ	o	ܗܘܿ	*hᵍ*
	Chemical element (c, m) *he yarta*	ܗܒ̣ܘܼܠܵܐ	ee	ܗܒ̣	*hec*

ܐܵܗܵܐ ܝܠܵܗܿ ܗܵܐܹܬ ܕܚܲܡܫܹܐ
ܚܲܕ݇ܠܲܒ ܠܠܸܒܢܲܢ.
This is the fifth time I
go to Lebanon.

28

ܩ

Wow   ܘ – ܘܰܘ

ܘ is the sixth letter of the Syriac alphabet and is shaped to resemble a flower opening.

ܘ is comparable to the English letter W.

The numerical value of ܘ is 6 ܐܸܫܬܵܐ (m), ܐܸܫܬ (f).

- ܘ is the second of the three weakest letters and it has a labial sound.
  - o It is silent when has no vowel at the end of the word.
- ܘ is one of the un-joined letters which never connects to any letter follows it.

Grammar 6: Two of the vowels are derived from the letter ܘ: See **Chapter 3** for more details:

- o When a single dot is placed above the letter, (ܘ̇) it becomes the vowel **Rwahha** and has an "OH" sound.
- o When a single dot is placed beneath the letter, (ܘ̣) it becomes the vowel **Rwassa** and has an "OO" or "UW" sound.
- It also functions as a preposition and other meanings:
  - o **And**: Paul and Peter came from homeland.

.ܦܵܘܠܘܿܣ ܘܦܸܛܪܘܿܣ ܡܸܢ ܐܲܬ݂ܪܵܐ

Estrangela			Eastern Syriac		
Isolated	End	Begin & Mid	Isolated	End	Begin & Mid
ܩ	ܩ ܩ	ܩ ܩ	ܘ	ܘ ܘ	ܘ ܘ

How to Write Wow
1) Start at the right of the page, make a short vertical line.
2) Start at the top of the line and make a half circle towards the left side connecting to the bottom of the initial line.

ܘ	ܘ	ܘ	ܘ	ܘ	ܘ	ܘ	ܘ	ܘ	ܘ
𝓞	𝓞	𝓞	𝓞	𝓞	𝓞	𝓞	𝓞	𝓞	𝓞

29

Read aloud and write ܘ with each vowel several times.

_____ _____ _____ _____ _____ _____ _____ _____ ܘ̇ *wah*

_____ _____ _____ _____ _____ _____ _____ _____ ܘ̈ *wawa*

_____ _____ _____ _____ _____ _____ _____ ܘ *weh*

_____ _____ _____ _____ _____ _____ _____ ܘ *way*

_____ _____ _____ _____ _____ _____ ܘܐ *woah*

_____ _____ _____ _____ _____ _____ ܘܐ *woo*

_____ _____ _____ _____ _____ _____ ܘܐ *wee*

Read aloud and write each of the following words several times. These words are made from the letters you have learned. This will help you with reading and how to connect the Syriac letters together.

_____ _____ _____ _____ : Barking (sound) (c) ܘܰܥܘܰܥ *wah wah*

_____ _____ _____ _____ _____ : Yard (c, m) ܕܳܪܬܐ *wah da*

ܟܰܠܒܐ ܕܝܠܗ ܡܢܒܚܢܐ.
The dog is barking.

Kelba

30

Pronunciation of ܘ (Wow) and vowels – ܩܵܠܵܐ ܕܝܼܵܬܹܐ ܥܲܡ ܘܵܘ ܡܸܬ

Transliteration	Meaning	Example	Vowel sound	L & V
	Duty (f)	ܘܵܠܝܼܬܵܐ	long a	ܘܵ
	Flower (m)	ܘܲܪܕܵܐ	short a	ܘܲ
	Added	ܙܘܼܕ	short i	ܘ
	Veil, cover (c, f)	ܘܲܠܵܐ	open e	ܘ
	Promise (m)	ܘܘܼܠܵܢܵܐ	oo	ܘܘ
	Companion (m)	ܟܘܿܦܵܐ	o	ܟܘ
	Friend (f)	ܠܝܼܡܬܵܐ	ee	ܘܝ

ܫܬܵܐ ܘܲܪܕܹܐ ܫܲܥܘܿܬܹܐ.
Six yellow flowers.

Zain   ܙ – ܙܝܢ

ܙ is the seventh letter of the Syriac alphabet and is shaped to resemble the head of a weapon or spear.

- ܙ is comparable to the English letter Z.
- It has a dental sound.
    - o Dentals are also called sibilants of their hissing sound.
    - o When a vocalized ܙ is followed by an un-vocalized Kap ܟ or ܩ Qop, the letter ܙ is pronounced as a "S" instead of "Z".
        - ▪ **Example**: Zechariah ܙܟܪܝܐ, Sqapa (the vowel) ܙܩܦܐ, and cross. ܙܩܝܦܐ.
- The numerical value of ܙ is 7 ܫܒܥܐ (m), ܫܒܥ (f).
- ܙ is one of the un-joined letters which never connects to any letter follows it.
    - o When it is a medial letter, it is joined on the right side only.

Estrangela				Eastern Syriac			
Isolated	End	Middle	Beginning	Isolated	End	Middle	Beginning
ܙ	ܙ �=ـܙ	ـܙ	ܙ	ܙ	ܙ ـܙ	ـܙ	ܙ

How to Write Zain
1) Start at the right of the page, make a short stroke in a downward position to the base line slightly curved to the left.
2) Beginning at the top of the line, make a slightly curved stroke towards the left, connecting the middle of the initial line.

ܙ	ܙ	ܙ	ܙ		ܙ	ܙ	ܙ	ܙ
ܙ	ܙ	ܙ	ܙ		ܙ	ܙ	ܙ	ܙ

Read aloud and write ܘ with each vowel several times.

								ܼܘ Zih
								ܹܘ Zebih
								ܸܘ Zeh
								ܼܘ Zih
								ܘܿ Zoo
								ܘܿ Zoh Zuyo
								ܘܼ Zee

Read aloud and write each of the following words several times. These words are made from the letters you have learned. This will help you with reading and how to connect the Syriac letters together.

					: River in Iraq (m) ܙܵܒ
					: Shield (m) ܙܵܒ Zebah
					: Butter (f) ܘܿܒܕܵܐ Wbedah
					: Money (m) ܙܘܼܙܵܐ Zuzah

33

Pronunciation of ܙ (Zain) and vowels – ܩܵܠܵܐ ܕܙܝܢ ܥܲܡ ܙܵܘܥܹ̈ܐ

Transliteration	Meaning	Example	Vowel sound	L & V
	Vowel (m)	Zawah ܙܵܘܵܐ	long a	ܙܵ
	Singer (m) Weapon (m)	Zamera ܙܲܡܵܪܵܐ Zaina ܙܲܝܢܵܐ	short a	ܙܲ
	Garbage (m)	Zibla ܙܸܒܠܵܐ	short i	ܙܸ
	Fraudster (c)	Zaypana ܙܹܐܦܵܢܵܐ	open e	ܙܹ
	Money (m)	Zoozah ܙܘܼܙܵܐ	oo	ܙܘܼ
	Cool weather (c)	Zopanah ܙܘܿܦܵܢܵܐ	o	ܙܘܿ
	Asceticism (c, f)	Zeerutha ܙܝܼܪܘܿܬܵܐ	ee	ܙܝܼ

Ziblah

ܐܵܢܵܐ ܒܝܼܡܟ̰ܒ ܫܒ݂ܥܵܐ ܕܘܿܠܵܪܹ̈ܐ.
I have $7.

ܙܘܼܙܹ̈ܐ – ܙܘܼ

34

The Third Group — ܣܗܕ

ܟܕ

Heth   ܚܝܬ - ܚ

ܚ is the eighth letter of the Syriac alphabet and is shaped to resemble a snake in motion.

- The numerical value of ܚ is 8 ܬܡܢܝܐ (m), ܬܡܢܐ (f).

- ܚ has no comparable English letter. It is pronounced as a heavily accented "H", almost doubling its pronunciation. Its sound is guttural; however, it comes from the chest near the trachea. ܚ connects to any letter which follows it. When it is a medial letter, it is joined on both sides.

- ܚ pronounced in two different sounds among the Syriac speakers:

    i.   **Mountain Dialect**   ܠܫܢܐ ܕܛܘܪܐ

    Regarding in classical or spoken language, ܚ _always_ has the sound like in "**Schumacher**" in German language. It does not have a comparable sound in English. Most the time, it gives "**Kh**" when transliterated in English.

    ii. **Nineveh Plain Dialect**   ܠܫܢܐ ܕܢܝܢܘܐ

    It has two sounds in Modern Syriac spoken accent. It sounds as heavily accented "**H**" if the word is a religion/spiritual word or barely used in spoken language like in:

Hymn (f)	ܙܡܝܪܬܐ	Glory (m)	ܫܘܒܚܐ
Grief (m)	ܚܫܐ	Spirt (m)	ܪܘܚܐ
Love (m)	ܚܘܒܐ	Christ (m)	ܡܫܝܚܐ
Eve	ܚܘܐ	Messenger (m)	ܡܠܐܟܐ

And it sounds "**Kh**" in any other words, and it is written like ܚ̇, (ܚ and a big single dot on the top of it. This is not grammar. We use this tyle to tell the

35

reader the sound of this ܚ letter is the sound of "kh" in this book). Examples, like in:

Salt (m):	ܡܸܠܚܵܐ
Oil (m):	ܡܸܫܚܵܐ
Donkey (m):	ܚܡܵܪܵܐ
Wine (m):	ܚܲܡܪܵܐ
Wedding (m):	ܚܠܘܼܠܵܐ

Milk (m): ܚܲܠܒ݂ܵܐ, (note here, ܚ has Pthaha vowel, so the big dot on top will replace the small dot of Pthaha vowel).

Note: In classical Syriac Language (ܠܸܫܵܢܵܐ ܟ݂ܵܬ݂ܘܿܒ݂ܵܝܵܐ), ܚ is <u>always</u> sounds as a heavily accented "H" in the Nineveh Plain Dialect ܠܸܫܵܢܵܐ ܕܘܿܥܹܐ.

Note: When the letter ܚ stands alone the short horizontal line ends with an upward stroke, however, when it joins another letter the horizontal line is written straight so that it may connect to the next letter.

Estrangela			Eastern Syriac		
Isolated	End	Begin & Mid	Isolated	End	Begin & Mid
ܚ	ܚ ܚ	ܚ ܚ	ܚ	ܚ ܚ	ܚ ܚ

How to Write Heth
1) Start at the right of the page, make a short-curved U.
2) Continue with a horizontal line from the bottom left side of the U.

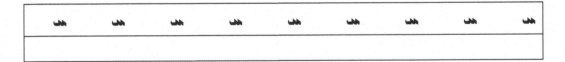

Read aloud and write ܣ with each vowel several times.

ܣܰ _____ _____ _____ _____ _____ _____ _____

ܣܶ _____ _____ _____ _____ _____ _____ _____

ܣܝ _____ _____ _____ _____ _____ _____ _____

ܣܷ _____ _____ _____ _____ _____ _____ _____

ܣܳܘ _____ _____ _____ _____ _____ _____

ܣܘ _____ _____ _____ _____ _____ _____

ܣܽ _____ _____ _____ _____ _____ _____

Read aloud and write each of the following words several times. These words are made from the letters you have learned. This will help you with reading and how to connect the Syriac letters together.

_____ _____ _____ _____ _____ ܣܢܘܿܪ : Helmet (f) *hoodha*

_____ _____ _____ _____ _____ ܚܕܐ : One (F) *hedha*

_____ _____ _____ _____ ܚܲܕ : One(m)

_____ _____ _____ _____ _____ ܚܘܿܒܐ : Love (m)

_____ _____ _____ _____ _____ ܚܘܐ : Eve *hawa*

Khooty h

37

Pronunciation of ܚ (Heth) and vowels – ܩ݇ܪܵܝܬܵܐ ܒܝܼܫ ܩܵܠܹܐ ܕܘܵܘܹܐ

Transliteration	Meaning	Example	Vowel sound	L & V
	Forbid (m) *hasha*	ܚܵܣܵܐ	long a	ܚܵ
	Wine (m) *chatha*	ܚܲܡܪܵܐ	short a	ܚܲ
	New (m)	ܚܲܕܬܵܐ		
	Friend (m)	ܚܲܒܪܵܐ	short i	ܚܷ
	Power (m)	ܚܲܝܠܵܐ	open e	ܚܹ
	Joy (f)	ܚܲܕܘܼܬܵܐ	oo	ܚܘܼ
	Health (m)	ܚܘܼܠܡܵܢܵܐ		
	Rounded box, Circle (c, m)	ܚܘܿܕܪܵܐ	o	ܚܘܿ
	Weak (m)	ܚܲܝܠܵܐ	e	ܚܝܼ

ܚܷ – ܚܲܕܬܵܐ

ܒܲܝܬܵܐ ܕܚܲܒܪܝܼ ܚܲܕܬܵܐ.

My friend's new house.

38

ܛ

Teth   ܛ – ܛܹܝܬ

ܛ is the ninth letter of the Syriac alphabet and is shaped to resemble a bird.

- ܛ has no comparable English letter.
- It is pronounced as a heavily accented "T" ("TD"), almost doubling its pronunciation.
- Its sound is guttural.
- The numerical value of ܛ is 9 ܛܸܫܥܵܐ (m), ܛܸܫܲܥ (f).
- ܛ connects to any letter which follows it.
  - When it is a medial letter, it is joined on both sides.

Estrangela			Eastern Syriac		
Isolated	End	Begin & Mid	Isolated	End	Begin & Mid
ܛ	ܛ ܛ	ܛ ܛ	ܛ	ܛ ܛ	ܛ ܛ

How to Write Teth

1) Start at the right of the page, make a medium horizontal line from right to left.
2) Continue at the right of the horizontal line and make a short downward diagonal left stroke to the center of the first line.
3) Begin at the base of the diagonal line and make an upward diagonal stroke to the left exceeding the base line.

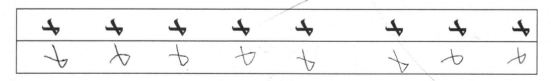

Read aloud and write ܛ **with each vowel several times.**

							ܛ tah
							ܛ ta
							ܛ tih
							ܛ tehh
							ܛܘ toe
							ܛܘ too
							ܛ tee

Read aloud and write each of the following words several times. These words are made from the letters you have learned. This will help you with reading and how to connect the Syriac letters together.

_____ _____ _____ _____ _____ : Good (m)   ܛܵܒ݂ܵܐ

_____ _____ _____ _____ _____ : News (m)   ܛܸܒ݂ܵܐ

_____ _____ _____ _____ _____ : Bless (m)   ܛܘܼܒ݂ܵܐ

40

Pronunciation of ܛ (Teth) and vowels – ܩܵܠܵܐ ܕܐܵܬܘܼܬ ܛܹܝܬ ܘܙܵܘܥܹ̈ܐ

Transliteration	Meaning	Example	Vowel sound	L & V
	Peacock (m) Twozin	ܛܵܘܣܵܐ		
	Flood (m)	ܛܵܘܦܵܢܵܐ	long a	ܛܵ
	Cat (m) Cahtah	ܩܛܵܐ		
	Bird (m) tah	ܛܲܝܪܵܐ	short a	ܛܲ
	Cup – bowl (f)	ܛܲܣܬܵܐ		
	Shadow, shade (f) tilenitha	ܛܸܠܵܢܝܼܬܵܐ	short i	ܛܸ
	The letter Teth	ܛܹܝܬ	open e	ܛܹ
	Cat (f) Catoatha	ܩܛܘܼܬܵܐ		
	Mountain (m) xoorah	ܛܘܼܪܵܐ	oo	ܛܘܼ
	Clan (m) tuhvmah	ܛܘܼܗܡܵܐ	o	ܛܘܿ
	Unemployed (m) bateelah	ܒܛܝܼܠܵܐ		
	Clay (m) teenah	ܛܝܼܢܵܐ	ee	ܛܝܼ

41

ܝ

Yod   ܝܘܿܕ – ܝ

ܝ is the tenth letter of the Syriac alphabet and is shaped to resemble a half open hand.

- ܝ is comparable to the English letter Y.
- Its sound is palatal sound.

Grammar 7: When a single dot is placed beneath the letter, (ܝ) it becomes the vowel Hwassa and has an "EE" sound. See Chapter 3.

- The numerical value of ܝ is 10 ܐܸܣܪܵܐ (m) ܥܣܲܪ (f).
  - **Note**: Beginning with ܝ, each succeeding letter is counted by tens until the letter ܩ (100). Thus, ܝܐ is 11 ܚܲܕܸܥܣܲܪ (**literal**: one ten), ܝܗ is 15 ܚܲܡܫܲܥܣܲܪ (**literal**: five ten), and ܝܛ is 19 ܛܫܲܥܣܲܪ (**literal**: nine ten).
    - Did you notice the first and the second (ending) parts of the name's numbers?
    - The second part (ten ܥܣܲܪ) is the feminine form.
    - The numbers from 11- 19 are the same for masculine and feminine.
- ܝ is the last of the three weakest letters. It is silent when has no vowel at the end of the word.
  - **Note**: that the letters ܐ , ܘ, and ܝ are known as the three weak consonants. They are pronounced together as "Oye" – ܐܘܝ.
- ܝ connects to any letter which follows it.
  - When it is a medial letter, it is joined on both sides.

Estrangela			Eastern Syriac		
Isolated	End	Begin & Mid	Isolated	End	Begin & Mid
ܝ	ܝ ܝ	ܝ ܝ	ܝ	ܝ ܝ	ܝ ܝ

How to Write Yod
1) Start at the right of the page, make a short-curved U.

ܝ	ܝ	ܝ	ܝ	ܝ	ܝ	ܝ	ܝ	ܝ

Read aloud and write ܝ with each vowel several times.

____ ____ ____ ____ ____ ____ ____ ____ ____ ܝ *yah*

____ ____ ____ ____ ____ ____ ____ ____ ____ ܝ *yeh*

____ ____ ____ ____ ____ ____ ____ ____ ____ ܝ *yih*

____ ____ ____ ____ ____ ____ ____ ____ ____ ܝ *yiih*

____ ____ ____ ____ ____ ____ ____ ____ ____ ܝ *yo*

____ ____ ____ ____ ____ ____ ____ ____ ____ ܝ *you*

____ ____ ____ ____ ____ ____ ____ ____ ____ ܝ *yee*

Read aloud and write each of the following words several times. These words are made from the letters you have learned. This will help you with reading and how to connect the Syriac letters together.

____ ____ ____ ____ ____ : Canal (m)   ܒܝܒܐ *beebah*

____ ____ ____ ____ ____ : Praise (c, m)   ܝܘܒܒܐ *youbahvah*

43

Pronunciation of ܝ (Yod) and vowels – ܩܵܠܵܐ ܕܝܘܿܕ ܥܲܡ ܙܵܘܥܹ̈ܐ

Transliteration	Meaning	Example	Vowel sound	L & V
yomah	Day (m)	ܝܵܘܡܵܐ	long a	ܝܵ
yel khah senker	Month (m)	ܝܲܪܚܵܐ	short a	ܝܲ
	Wrap (m)	ܟܝܼܟ	short i	ܝܼ
	Israel (country, f)	ܝܼܣܪܵܐܝܼܠ	open e	ܝܹ
	Education (m)	ܝܘܼܠܦܵܢܵܐ	oo	ܝܘܼ
yod	Letter Yod (f)	ܝܘܿܕ	o	ܝܘܿ
eeshuh	Jesus	ܝܼܫܘܿܥ	ee	ܝܼ

ܝ - ܝܵܘܡܵܐ

ܝܲܬܝܼܪ ܥܸܣܪܵܐ ܝܵܘܡܵܢܹ̈ܐ ܩܵܐ ܡܵܪܲܢ ܝܼܫܘܿܥ ܡܫܝܼܚܵܐ.

Ten more days to our Lord Jesus Christ birthday.

44

The Fourth Group — ܚܠܝܡ ܚܠܡ

ܟ

Kap and Kap[2]   ܟܦ ܘ ܟܦ ܟ ܟ

ܟ is the eleventh letter of the Syriac alphabet and is shaped to resemble a fist or closed hand.

- It is only one Kap. The reason we say Kap and Kap is to remember that this letter has two forms. First form ܟ when it is at the beginning/middle of the word, and the second form ܟ when it is at the end of the word.
- ܟ is comparable to the English letter K.
- It has a palatal sound.

Grammar 8: When a single dot is placed above the letter (ܟ̇) it becomes a hard "K".

Grammar 9: When a single dot is placed beneath the letter (ܟ̣) it becomes soft "KH".

- The numerical value of ܟ is 20 ܥܣܪܝܢ. Thus, ܟܓ is 23 ܥܣܪܝܢ ܘܬܠܬܐ (literal: twenty and three), and ܟܗ is 25 ܥܣܪܝܢ ܘܚܡܫܐ. (literal: twenty and five).

Estrangela			Eastern Syriac		
Isolated	End	Begin & Mid	Isolated	End	Begin & Mid
ܟ	ܟ ܟ	ܟ ܟ	ܟ	ܟ ܟ	ܟ ܟ

---

[2] There are no two Kaps (ܟ). It is only one Kap and the reason we say Kap and Kap is to remind the reader of the two forms this letter has. One when falls at the beginning or the middle of the word (ܟ) and the second when falls at the end of the word (ܟ). This applies to the other two letters have two forms (ܡ 'm', and ܢ 'n')

45

How to Write Kap

1) Start at the right of the page, make a curved line moving from the bottom right to the top left.
2) Make a medium horizontal line from the base of the line towards the left.

؟	؟	؟		ܒ	ܒ	ܒ	ܒ	ܒ

Read aloud and write ܟ **with each vowel several times.**

_____ _____ _____ _____ _____ _____ _____ ܟ݂ *Kah*

_____ _____ _____ _____ _____ _____ _____ ܟ݁ *Keh*

_____ _____ _____ _____ _____ _____ _____ ܟ *Kih*

_____ _____ _____ _____ _____ _____ _____ ܟ *Kay*

_____ _____ _____ _____ _____ _____ _____ ܟܘ *Koe*

_____ _____ _____ _____ _____ _____ _____ ܟܘ *Yoo*

_____ _____ _____ _____ _____ _____ _____ ܟ *Kee*

Read aloud and write each of the following words several times. These words are made from the letters you have learned. This will help you with reading and how to connect the Syriac letters together.

_____ _____ _____ _____ _____ : Depression (c, f) ܟܐܒ݂ܐ

_____ _____ _____ _____ _____ : Your dad (f) ܒܐܒܟ݂ *babech*
scratchy

_____ _____ _____ _____ : Your dad (m) ܒܐܒܘܟ݂ *babooche*
scratchy

Second
person

46

Pronunciation of ܟ (Kap) and vowels – ܒܘ̈ܢܹܐ ܒܝܬ ܟܬ̣ܒܼܐ ܟܵܦ

Transliteration	Meaning	Example	Vowel sound	L & V
	Writer (m) *Kathawa*	ܟܵܬ݂ܒ݂ܐ	long a	ܟܵ
	Dog (m) *Kelba*	ܟܲܠܒܐ	short a	ܟܲ
	Door Locker (m) *Kilya*	ܟܸܠܝܐ	short i	ܟܸ
	Harp (f) *Kaynera*	ܟܹܢܪܐ	open e	ܟܹ
	Chair (m) *Koolsia*	ܟܘܿܪܣܝܐ	oo	ܟܘ
	Notebook (m) *KashKole*	ܟܫܟܘ̈ܠ	o	ܟܘ
	Chemistry (f) *KeeKemia*	ܟܝܡܝܐ	ee	ܟܝ

ܝܣܪܝ ܟܵܬ݂ܒܹܐ ܘܝܣܪܝ ܘܚܕ ܟܘܿܪܣܝܐ.
20 writers and 21 chairs.

ܟܵ - ܟܵܬ݂ܒ݂ܐ
ܟܘ - ܟܘܿܪܣܝܐ

ܠ

Lamath   ܠ - ܠܵܡܲܕ

ܠ is the twelfth letter of the Syriac alphabet and is shaped to resemble a jaw bone.

- ܠ is comparable to the English letter L.
- It has a lingual sound.
- The numerical value of ܠ is 30 ܬܠܵܬ݂ܝܼܢ. Thus, ܠܗ is (35) ܬܠܵܬ݂ܝܼܢ ܘܚܲܡܫܵܐ (**literal**: thirty and five), and ܠܚ is (38) ܬܠܵܬ݂ܝܼܢ ܘܬܡܵܢܝܵܐ (**literal**: thirty and eight).
- It also functions as a preposition to indicate:
  o To: .ܠܡܲܕܪܲܫܬܵܐ ܟܹܐ ܘܵܠܹܐ [3] ܒܵܥܹܝܢ ܕܐܵܙܹܠܢ (I want to go to school) – 1st m.
- ܠ connects to any letter which follows it.
  o When it is a medial letter, it is joined on both sides.

Estrangela			Eastern Syriac		
Isolated	End	Begin & Mid	Isolated	End	Begin & Mid
ܠ	ܠ ܠ	ܠ ܠ	ܠ	ܠ ܠ	ܠ ܠ

How to Write Lamath
1) Start at the right of the page, begin above the base line, and make a slanted downward stroke from left to right to the base line.
2) Join a short horizontal line at the base of the slanted line from right to left.

ܠ	ܠ	ܠ	ܠ	ܠ	ܠ	ܠ
ܠ	ܠ	ܠ	ܠ	ܠ	ܠ	ܠ

---

[3] ܐܲܕ also means "to" and proceed the verb, and most the time pronounces "ܕ" (d). When pronounced "ܐܲܕ" this is to emphasize the verb.

Read aloud and write ܠ with each vowel several times.

ܠܲ *Lah* _____ _____ _____ _____ _____ _____ _____

ܠܵ *leh* _____ _____ _____ _____ _____ _____ _____

ܠܹ *bih* _____ _____ _____ _____ _____ _____ _____

ܠܝܼ *lin* _____ _____ _____ _____ _____ _____ _____

ܠܘܿ *loo* _____ _____ _____ _____ _____ _____ _____

ܠܘ *loo* _____ _____ _____ _____ _____ _____ _____

ܠܝ *lee* _____ _____ _____ _____ _____ _____ _____

Read aloud and write each of the following words several times. These words are made from the letters you have learned. This will help you with reading and how to connect the Syriac letters together.

ܟܲܠܒܵܐ Dog (m) : _____ _____ _____ _____ _____

ܠܸܒܵܐ *libbeh* Heart (m) : _____ _____ _____ _____ _____

ܠܘܼܚܵܐ Board (m) : _____ _____ _____ _____ _____

ܙܸܒܠܵܐ *zibleh* Garbage (m) : _____ _____ _____ _____ _____

49

Pronunciation of ܠ (Lamath) and vowels – ܩܪܵܝܬܵܐ ܕܠܵܡܲܕ ܥܲܡ ܙܵܘܥܹ̈ܐ

Transliteration	Meaning	Example	Vowel sound	L & V
	Strong (m) *heilana*	ܚܲܝܠܵܢܵܐ	long a	ܠܵ
	Stork (m) *Lahklaka*	ܠܲܩܠܲܩܵܐ	short a	ܠܲ
	Twisted (f) big dos absentminos 3rd person female	ܦܠܝܼܠܬܵܐ	short i	ܠܝܼ
	Twisted (m)	ܦܠܝܼܠܝܗ		
	Deacon (m)	ܠܸܦܵܐ	open e	ܠܸ
	Upper jaw (m) *Looah*	ܠܘܿܥܵܐ	oo	ܠܘ
	Almond nut (m) *lowez*	ܠܘܿܙܵܐ	o	ܠܘܿ
	Wrapped up (m) *Leebun*	ܠܒܝܼܟܵܐ	ee	ܠܒ

ܠܘܿ – ܠܘܿܙ
ܠܘ – ܠܘܿܥܵܐ

50

ܡ

Meem and Meem   ܡܝܡ ܘ ܡܝܡ — ܡـ ܡ

ܡـ is the thirteenth letter of the Syriac alphabet and is shaped to resemble a shape of a pond containing water.

- ܡـ is comparable to the English letter M.
- It has a labial sound.
- It has two forms. First form ܡـ when it is at the beginning/middle of the word, and the second form ܡ when it is at the end of the word.
- The numerical value of ܡـ is (40) ܐܪܒܥܝܢ. Thus, ܡܐ is (41) ܐܪܒܥܝܢ ܘܚܕ (**literal**: Forty and one), and ܡܛ is (49) ܐܪܒܥܝܢ ܘܬܫܥܐ (**literal**: Forty and nine).
- It connects to any letter which follows it.
  o When it is a medial letter, it is joined on both sides.

Estrangela			Eastern Syriac		
Isolated	End	Begin & Mid	Isolated	End	Begin & Mid
ܡ	ܡ ـܡ	ـܡـ ـܡ	ܡ	ܡ ـܡ	ـܡـ ܡـ

How to Write Meem
1) Start at the right of the page, Make a half circle from right to left.
2) Beginning at the left of the half circle make a very short slanted upward stroke to the left.
3) Make a medium horizontal stroke beginning at the right of the half circle exceeding beyond the short upward stroke.

Read aloud and write ـܡ with each vowel several times.

ܡܲ   _mah_ _____ _____ _____ _____ _____ _____ _____ _____

ܡܵ   _me_ _____ _____ _____ _____ _____ _____ _____ _____

ܡܹ   _mih_ _____ _____ _____ _____ _____ _____ _____ _____

ܡܸ   _meh_ _____ _____ _____ _____ _____ _____ _____ _____

ܡܿܘ   _moe_ _____ _____ _____ _____ _____ _____ _____ _____

ܡܘ   _moo_ _____ _____ _____ _____ _____ _____ _____ _____

ܡܝ   _mee_ _____ _____ _____ _____ _____ _____ _____ _____

Read aloud and write each of the following words several times. These words are made from the letters you have learned. This will help you with reading and how to connect the Syriac letters together.

ܦܘܿܡܵܐ : Mouth (m)   _____ _____ _____ _____ _____

ܡܲܠܵܠܵܐ : Speaker (m)   _____ _____ _____ _____ _____

ܟܘܿܡܵܐ _Koma_ : Black (m)   _____ _____ _____ _____ _____

ܚܲܟܝܼܡܵܐ : Wiseman   _____ _____ _____ _____ _____

Pronunciation of ـمـ (Meem) and vowels – ܒܘܵܥܹܐ ܥܲܡ ܡܝܼܡ ܕܡܲܦܠܲܚܬܵܐ

Transliteration	Meaning	Example	Vowel sound	L & V
	Village (f)	ܡܵܬ̣ܵܐ	long a	ܡܵـ
	Spoon (f) Mariam	ܡܲܠܲܩܸܒ̣ܵܐ ܡܲܪܝܲܡ	short a	ܡܲـ
	Salt (m)	ܡܝܼܠܚܵܐ	short i	ܡܝܼـ
	Grape juice (f)	ܡܸܨܕܝܵܐ	open e	ܡܸـ
	Brain (m)	ܡܘܿܚܵܐ	oo	ܡܘ
	Death (m)	ܡܵܘܬܵܐ	o	ܡܵܘ
	Mile (m)	ܡܝܼܠܵܐ	ee	ܡܝܼـ

ܡܵـ - ܡܵܬ̣ܵܐ
Small village - ܡܵܬ̣ܵܐ ܘܝܼܕܵܬ̣ܵܐ
ܡܝܼـ – ܡܝܼܠܵܐ
45 miles - ܡܝܼܠܵܐ ܚܲܡܫܝܼ ܘܐܲܪܒܥܵܐ

53

Noon and Noon   ܢ ܢ – ܢܘ ܘ ܢܘ

ܢ is the fourteenth letter of the Syriac alphabet and is shaped to resemble an axe.

- ܢ is comparable to the English letter N.
- It has a lingual sound.
- It has two forms. First form ܢ when it is at the beginning/middle of the word, and the second form ܢ when it is at the end of the word.
- The numerical value of ܢ is (50) ܢܡܣܝܢ. Thus, ܢܗ is (55) ܢܡܣܝܢ ܘܚܡܫܐ, and ܢܙ is (57) ܢܡܣܝܢ ܘܫܒܥܐ.
- ܢ connects to any letter which follows it.
    - When it is a medial letter, it is joined on both sides.

Estrangela			Eastern Syriac		
Isolated	End	Begin & Mid	Isolated	End	Begin & Mid
ܢ	ܢ	ܢ ܢ	ܢ	ܢ ܢ	ܢ ܢ

How to Write Noon
1) Start at the right of the page, make a very short vertical line in a downward position.
2) Make a horizontal line connecting at the bottom of the short vertical line to the left.

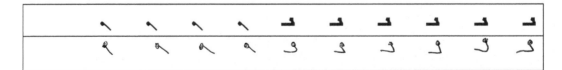

54

Read aloud and write ܢ **with each vowel several times.**

ــــ ــــ ــــ ــــ ــــ ــــ ــــ ــــ ܢܲ *neh*

ــــ ــــ ــــ ــــ ــــ ــــ ــــ ــــ ܢܸ *neh*

ــــ ــــ ــــ ــــ ــــ ــــ ــــ ــــ ܢܝ *nih*

ــــ ــــ ــــ ــــ ــــ ــــ ــــ ــــ ܢܹ *ne*

ــــ ــــ ــــ ــــ ــــ ــــ ــــ ܢܘ *no*

ــــ ــــ ــــ ── ── ──── ──── ── ܢܘ *new*

ــــ ــــ ــــ ── ── ──── ──── ── ܢܝ *nee*

Read aloud and write each of the following words several times. These words are made from the letters you have learned. This will help you with reading and how to connect the Syriac letters together.

ــــ ــــ ــــ ــــ ــــ : Nineveh (f)   ܢܝܢܘܹܐ *Nineway*

ــــ ــــ ── ── ── : Number (m)   ܡܸܢܝܵܢܵܐ *Manyana*

── ── ── ── ── : Right (m)   ܝܲܡܝܼܢܵܐ *yammeh*

── ── ── ── ── : Time (m)   ܘܲܕܵܐ *Zowuneh*

ܢܝܢܘܹܐ ܡܕܝܼܢ݇ܬܵܐ ܪܲܒܬܵܐ.
Nineveh the big city.

55

Pronunciation of ܢ (Noon) and vowels – ܩܵܠܵܐ ܕܢܘܢ ܥܲܡ ܙܵܘܥܹ̈ܐ

Transliteration	Meaning	Example	Vowel sound	L & V
	Salvation (m)	ܢܘܼܩܵܢܵܐ	long a	ܢܵ
	Carpenter (m)	ܢܲܓܵܪܵܐ	short a	ܢܲ
	Gift (m)	ܢܝܼܫܵܐ	short i	ܢܝܼ
	Lawyer claims (c, m)	ܡܒܲܢܢܹܐ	open e	ܢܹ
	Explanation, lecture (m)	ܢܘܼܗܵܪܵܐ		
	Fire (m) _Nenruh_	ܢܘܼܪܵܐ	oo	ܢܘ
	Noah _Noheh_	ܢܘܿܚ	o	ܢܘܿ
	Yoke (m) _neerah_	ܢܝܼܪܵܐ		
	Rest, Comfort (f)	ܢܝܵܚܘܼܬܵܐ	ee	ܢܝܼ

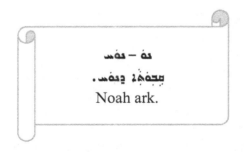

ܢܘܿ – ܢܘܿܚ

ܩܹܒܘܿܬܵܐ ܕܢܘܿܚ.

Noah ark.

56

The Fifth Group – ܗܲܕ݂ܟ݂ܝ ܗܲܕ݂ܟ݂ܝ

ܣ

Simkath   ܣܸܡܟܲܬ݂ – ܣ

ܣ is the fifteenth letter of the Syriac alphabet and is shaped to resemble a moon with a face. The moon was the goddess of all Mesopotamia.

- ܣ is comparable to the English letter S. It pronounces Z if it proceeds by letter with vowel as in: ܓܸܠܵܐ (grass) and pronounces ܝ as in "Sun" if it follows by ܟ like in: ܣܸܦܪܵܐ chapter(c), book. Also pronounces "ܝ" if it follows by "ܪ" like in: ܒܸܣܪܵܐ meat, ܣܲܪܛܵܢܵܐ cancer.
- It has a dental sound sibilant.
- The numerical value of ܣ is (60) ܐܸܫܬܝܼ. Thus, ܣܣ is (66) ܐܸܫܬܝܼ ܘܐܸܫܬܵܐ, and ܣܒ is (62) ܐܸܫܬܝܼ ܘܬܪܹܝܢ .
- ܣ connects to any letter which follows it.
  - When it is a medial letter, it is joined on both sides.

Estrangela			Eastern Syriac		
Isolated	End	Begin & Mid	Isolated	End	Begin & Mid
ܣ	ܣ ܣ	ܣ ܣ	ܣ	ܣ ܣ	ܣ ܣ

How to Write Simkath
1) Start at the right side of the page. Make a short-curved line upward from right to left.
2) Continuing from the bottom of the curved line, make a slanted upward stroke to the left.
3) Complete the upward stroke by adding a semi-circle from left to the middle of the initial curve.
4) Make short horizontal line from the top center of the letter moving to the left.

Read aloud and write ܣ **with each vowel several times.**

_____ _____ _____ _____ _____ _____ _____ _____ ܣܶ *sah*

_____ _____ _____ _____ _____ _____ _____ _____ ܣܰ *sah*

_____ _____ _____ _____ _____ _____ _____ _____ ܣܷ *seh*

_____ _____ _____ _____ _____ _____ _____ _____ ܣܹ *say*

_____ _____ _____ _____ _____ _____ _____ _____ ܣܘ *so*

_____ _____ _____ _____ _____ _____ _____ _____ ܣܘ *suw*

_____ _____ _____ _____ _____ _____ _____ _____ ܣܺ *see*

Read aloud and write each of the following words several times. These words
are made from the letters you have learned. This will help you with reading _ *Alep is silent*
and how to connect the Syriac letters together.

_____ _____ _____ _____ _____ : Satan   ܣܳܛܵܢܵܐ *Satanah*

_____ _____ _____ _____ _____ : Horse (m)   ܣܘܣܝܐ *Sooslah*

_____ _____ _____ _____ : Doctor (m)   ܐܵܣܝܵܐ

_____ _____ _____ _____ _____ : Delicious (m)   ܒܵܣܝܡܵܐ *Beemah*

_____ _____ _____ _____ _____ : Incent (m)   ܒܸܣܡܵܐ

"nice" → ~~weather~~ *weather* ܐܲܘܵܐ

58

Pronunciation of ܣ (Simkath) and vowels – ܩܵܠܵܐ ܕܐܵܬܘܿܬܵܐ

Transliteration	Meaning	Example	Vowel sound	L & V
	Oldman	ܣܵܒ݂ܵܐ	long a	ܣܵ
	Cancer (m)	ܣܲܪܛܵܢܵܐ	short a	ܣܲ
	Sword	ܣܲܝܦܵܐ		
	Ladder (f)	ܣܸܒܲܠܬܵܐ	short i	ܣܸ
	Silver (m)	ܣܹܐܡܵܐ	open e	ܣܹ
	Horse (f)	ܣܘܼܣܬܵܐ	oo	ܣܘܼ
	Syriac man	ܣܘܼܪܝܵܝܵܐ [4]		
	Spear (c, m)	ܣܘܿܓ݂ܢܵܐ	o	ܣܘܿ
	Association (f)	ܣܝܼܥܬܵܐ	ee	ܣܝܼ

(handwritten notes in right margin: Sahwah, Sembelta, Syma, Soostah, Sooryeh, Soewconuh)

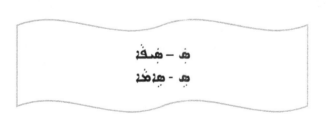

ܣܲ – ܣܲܝܦܵܐ

ܣܹ – ܣܹܐܡܵܐ

---

[4] ܣܘܼܪܝܵܝܵܐ or ܣܘܼܪܝܵܝܵܐ and sometime spelled ܣܘܿܪܵܝܵܐ also means Chaldean, Assyrian man. Do you know how to say Syriac woman?

Aeh   ܥ – ܥܹ   *Ehh*   ܥ

ܥ is the sixteenth letter of the Syriac alphabet and is shaped to resemble the side of a human eye.

- ܥ has no comparable English letter. It is pronounced as a sliced "EH", without the "Y" sound at the end.
- In the spoken dialect, sometimes the letter ܥ is pronounced ܐ and have the same sound of ܐ when has vowel or not. In this case, when ܥ has the sound ܐ, we will write it as ܥ (ܥ and a small line underneath it) to make the different between the two sounds. For example: Earth (f) ܐܲܪܥܵܐ, Festival (m) ܥܹܐܕܵܐ. This is not a grammar. We use this tyle to tell the reader the sound of the ܥ letter is an "ܐ" sound in this book.
- It has a guttural sound. It is a glottal stop.
- The numerical value of ܥ is (70) ܫܲܒ݂ܥܝܼܢ. Thus, ܥܓ is (73) ܫܲܒ݂ܥܝܼܢ ܘܲܬܠܵܬܵܐ, and ܥܚ is (78) ܫܲܒ݂ܥܝܼܢ ܘܲܬܡܵܢܝܵܐ.
- ܥ connects to any letter which follows it. When it is a medial letter, it is joined on both sides.

Estrangela			Eastern Syriac		
Isolated	End	Begin & Mid	Isolated	End	Begin & Mid
ܥ	ܥ ܥ	ܥ ܥ	ܥ	ܥ ܥ	ܥ ܥ

How to Write Aeh
1) Start at the right side of the page, make a short horizontal line.
2) Continuing from the left of the line, make an upward slanted stroke towards the left.
3) Complete the letter by making a short horizontal line beginning at the left of the initial stroke.

	ܥ	ܥ	ܥ	ܥ	ܥ	ܥ	ܥ	ܥ
	ܥ	ܥ	ܥ	ܥ	ܥ	ܥ	ܥ	ܥ

Read aloud and write ܬ with each vowel several times.

_____ _____ _____ _____ _____ _____ _____ _____ ܬܲ *ahh*

_____ _____ _____ _____ _____ _____ _____ _____ ܬܵ *ahaa*

_____ _____ _____ _____ _____ _____ _____ _____ ܬܸ *ih*

_____ _____ _____ _____ _____ _____ _____ _____ ܬܹ *ayy*

_____ _____ _____ _____ _____ _____ _____ ܬܿ *oh*

_____ _____ _____ _____ _____ _____ _____ ܬܘܿ *ooh*

_____ _____ _____ _____ _____ _____ _____ ܬܝ *Aey*

Read aloud and write each of the following words several times. These words are made from the letters you have learned. This will help you with reading and how to connect the Syriac letters together.

_____ _____ _____ _____ _____ : Eye(f) ܥܲܝܢܵܐ *einuh*

_____ _____ _____ _____ _____ : Feast(m) ܥܹܐܕܵܐ *ayuntha*

_____ _____ _____ _____ _____ : Grapes(m) ܥܸܢܒܹܐ

---

aynuh dimeh

ܕܸܡܥܵܐ ܕܥܲܝܢܵܐ.

Eye tears.

61

Pronunciation of ܥ (Aeh) and vowels – ܩܵܐܡܲܬ ܕܝܲܢ ܒܝܲܕ ܕܘܿܡܝܼܵܐ

Transliteration	Meaning	Example	Vowel sound	L & V	
	Door (m)	ܬܲܪܥܵܐ *tarrah*	long a	ܵ	*ahh*
	Deep (m)	ܥܲܡܘܿܩܵܐ *ahmuqah*	short a	ܲ	*ah*
	Wedding ring (f)	ܥܲܙܩܬܵܐ *soekthu*	short i	ܸ	
	Holiday (m)	ܥܹܕܵܐ *ehhtha*	open e	ܹ	
	Age (m)	ܥܘܿܡܪܵܐ *aohmiruh*	oo	ܘܿ	
	Yellow (m)	ܫܥܘܿܬܵܐ *shooftha*	o	ܘܿ	
	Toad (frog) (m)	ܥܙܵܙܵܐ *eezena*	ee	ܝܼ	

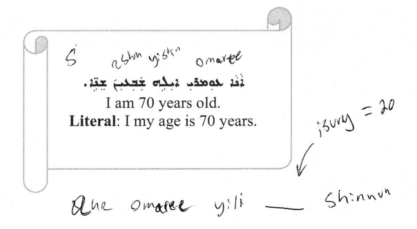

S   *ashn yishn   omaree*

ܐܢܵܐ ܥܘܿܡܪܝܼ ܝܼܠܹܗ ܫܲܒܥܝܼ ܫܸܢܹ݁ܐ.

I am 70 years old.
Literal: I my age is 70 years.

isvny = 20

ana omaree yili — shinnun

62

ܦ

Peh   ܦܹܐ – ܦ

ܦ is the seventeenth letter of the Syriac alphabet and is shaped to resemble the shape of a mouth.

- ܦ is equivalent to the English letter P.
- It has a labial sound.

Grammar 10: When a small semicircle is place beneath the letter, (ܦ̮), it becomes soft and has a "ܘ, W" sound. Like in, ܢܝ̣ܫܡܐ = Breath – breath of life, ܟܬܦܐ = Shoulder.

- The numerical value of ܦ is (80) ܬܡܢܝ̣ܢ. Thus, ܦܕ is (84) ܬܡܢܝ̣ܢ ܘܐܪܒܥܐ (**literal**: eighty and four), and ܦܘ is (86) ܬܡܢܝ̣ܢ ܘܐܫܬܐ (**literal**: eighty and six).
- ܦ connects to any letter which follows it.
  - When it is a medial letter, it is joined on both sides.

Estrangela			Eastern Syriac		
Isolated	End	Begin & Mid	Isolated	End	Begin & Mid
ܦ	ܦ ܦ	ܦ ܦ	ܦ	ܦ ܦ	ܦ ܦ

How to Write Peh
1) Start at the right side of the page, make a downward stroke slanted a bit towards the right.
2) Make a small half circle starting from the top of the line to about the middle of the slanted line.
3) Make a short horizontal line at the base of the slanted line from right to left.

ܦ	ܦ	ܦ	ܦ	ܦ	ܦ	ܦ	ܦ	ܦ	ܦ

Read aloud and write ܦ with each vowel several times.

							ܦَ pah
_____	_____	_____	_____	_____	_____	_____	ܦَ pa
_____	_____	_____	_____	_____	_____	_____	ܦܝ pen
_____	_____	_____	_____	_____	_____	_____	ܦܝ pay
_____	_____	_____	_____	_____	_____	_____	ܦܳܘ po
_____	_____	_____	_____	_____	_____	_____	ܦܘ poo
_____	_____	_____	_____	_____	_____	_____	ܦܝ pee

Read aloud and write each of the following words several times. These words are made from the letters you have learned. This will help you with reading and how to connect the Syriac letters together.

_____ _____ _____ _____ _____ : Mouth (m) ܦܘܡܐ poomah

_____ _____ _____ _____ _____ : Permission (m) ܦܣܣܐ psasa

_____ _____ _____ _____ _____ : Teacher (m) ܡܠܦܢܐ melpana

_____ _____ _____ _____ : Joseph ܝܘܣܦ

_____ _____ _____ _____ : Elephant (m) ܦܝܠܐ peela

_____ _____ _____ _____ _____ : Pope ܦܦܐ papa

Pronunciation of ܦ (Peh) and vowels – ܩܵܪܹܐ ܒܹܝܕ ܕ݂ܘܵܡܹܐ

Transliteration	Meaning	Example	Vowel sound	L & V
	Moment (f) *mappapa*	ܦ݂ܵܩ݂ܵܐ	long a	ܦ݁
	Watermelon (f) *wdela*	ܦ݁ܝܼܢܹܐ		ܦ݂
	Potato (f) *Pateta*	ܦ݁ܵܦ݁ܵܐ	short a	
	Wisdom (m) *Pihtnuh*	ܦ݁ܝܠܹܐ	short i	ܦ݁
	Censer (m) *Perma*	ܦ݁ܪܡܵܐ	open e	ܦ݁
	Work (m) *Poolhana*	ܦ݁ܘܠܚܵܢܵܐ	oo	ܦ݁ܘ
	Air, wind (m) *Poha*	ܦ݁ܘܚܵܐ	o	ܦ݁ܘ
	Stayed, Left over (m) *Peesha*	ܦ݁ܝܼܫܵܐ	ee	ܦ݁ܝ

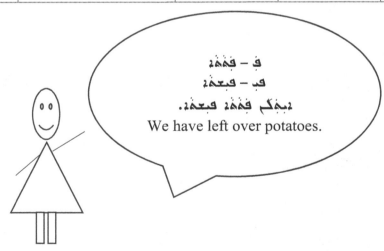

ܦ݁ – ܦ݁ܵܦ݁ܵܐ
ܦ݁ܝ – ܦ݁ܝܼܫܵܐ
ܐܝܼܬܠܲܢ ܦ݁ܵܦ݁ܵܐ ܦ݁ܝܼܫܹܐ.
We have left over potatoes.

65

ܨ

Sade   ܨܵܕܹܐ – ܨ

ܨ is the eighteenth letter of the Syriac alphabet and is shaped to resemble a statue.

- ܨ is not comparable to any English letter.
  - o It is similar to an accented "SS" sound as in "Son" and "Sun."
- It has a dental sound (sibilant).
- The numerical value of ܨ is (90) ܬܸܫܥܝܼܢ. Thus, ܨܐ is (91) ܬܸܫܥܝܼܢ ܘܚܲܕ (literal: Ninety and one), and ܨܛ is (99) ܬܸܫܥܝܼܢ ܘܬܸܫܥܵܐ (literal: Ninety and nine).
- ܨ is one of the un-joined letters which never connects to any letter follows it.
  - o It is joined on the right side only.

Estrangela			Eastern Syriac		
Isolated	End	Begin & Mid	Isolated	End	Begin & Mid
ܨ	ܨ ܨ	ܨ ܨ	ܨ	ܨ ܨ	ܨ ܨ

How to Write Sade
1) Start at the right side of the page, make a short U.
2) Beginning at the left side of the U make a downward slightly curved medium stroke to the right.
3) Beginning at the end of the curve make a medium horizontal stroke to the left.

ܨ	ܨ	ܨ	ܨ	ܨ	ܨ	ܨ	ܨ	ܨ	ܨ

Read aloud and write ܝ with each vowel several times.

_____ _____ _____ _____ _____ _____ _____ ܝܰ _Sah_

_____ _____ _____ _____ _____ _____ _____ ܝܶ _Suh_

_____ _____ _____ _____ _____ _____ _____ ܝܝ _Sih_

_____ _____ _____ _____ _____ _____ _____ ܝܺ _Say_

_____ _____ _____ _____ _____ _____ ܝܳ _So_

_____ _____ _____ _____ _____ _____ ܝܳܘ _Soo_

_____ _____ _____ _____ _____ ܝܽ _See_

Read aloud and write each of the following words several times. These words are made from the letters you have learned. This will help you with reading and how to connect the Syriac letters together.

_____ _____ _____ _____ _____ : Face (m) ܦܰܐܬ݂ܳܐ _Selma_

_____ _____ _____ _____ _____ : Fast (m) ܨܰܘܡܳܐ _Sawma_

_____ _____ _____ _____ _____ : Cymbal (m) ܨܺܨܠܳܐ _Svsla_

ܩܥܝܢ ܬܠܬܐ ܡܝ ܡܐܐ ܚܝܢܫܒܝ ܝܳܘܡܳܐ ܕܬܟܘܗܿܐ ܕܢܝܢܘܝܬܐ.
90% of people fast the Nineveh fast.

67

Pronunciation of ܨ (Sade) and vowels – ܩܵܠܵܐ ܕܢܘܩܙܵܐ ܥܲܡ ܨܘܡܵܟܹ

Transliteration	Meaning	Example	Vowel sound	L & V
	Tamarind (m) *Snbn* ܨܲܢܒܵܐ		long a	ܵܨ
	Echo (m) *Sudwa* ܨܲܕܘܵܐ		short a	ܲܨ
	Cockroach (m) *Sisrah* ܨܝܼܨܪܵܐ		short i	ܸܨ
	Bird (m) *Suprra* ܨܸܦܪܵܐ			
	Goat (c, m) *Suprya* ܨܸܦܪܵܝܵܐ		open e	ܹܨ
	Picture (f) *Soorta* ܨܘܿܪܬܵܐ		oo	ܘܨ
	Braids (f) *Sosita* ܨܘܿܨܝܼܬܵܐ		o	ܿܨ
	Fasting (m) *Seema* ܨܝܼܡܵܐ		ee	ܝܼܨ

68

e Sixth Group - ܫܬܝܬܝܐ ܣܕܪܐ

ܩ

Qop   ܩܘܦ – ܩ

ܩ is the nineteenth letter of the Syriac alphabet and is shaped to resemble an ancient basket made of reefs.

- ܩ is not comparable to any English letter.
  - It is often compared to as the English letter Q.

Grammar 11: Gives the sound ܟ if it follows by ܦ like in ܦܘܩܕܢܐ (commandment).

- It has palatal sound.
- The numerical value of ܩ is (100) ܡܐܐ. Thus, ܩܣܗ is (165) ܡܐܐ ܘܫܬܝܢ ܘܚܡܫܐ, (**literal**: hundred and ninety and five), and ܩܠܐ is (131) ܡܐܐ ܘܬܠܬܝܢ ܘܚܕ (**literal**: hundred and thirty and one).
  - Beginning with ܩ each succeeding letter is by hundreds until ܬ.
- ܩ connects to any letter which follows it. When it is a medial letter, it is joined on both sides.

Estrangela			Eastern Syriac		
Isolated	End	Begin & Mid	Isolated	End	Begin & Mid
ܩ	ܩ ܩ	ܩ ܩ	ܩ	ܩ ܩ	ܩ ܩ

How to Write Qop
1) Start at the right side of the page, make a downward vertical stroke.
2) Make a medium horizontal line from the top of the vertical stroke.
3) Beginning from the base of the vertical line make a horizontal line almost the length of the top horizontal line then slightly curve the stroke into a vertical line touching the top horizontal line.

ܩ	ܩ	ܩ	ܩ	ܩ	ܩ	ܩ	ܩ	ܩ

Read aloud and write ܦ **with each vowel several times.**

_____ _____ _____ _____ _____ _____ ܦ݂ *Cay*

_____ _____ _____ _____ _____ _____ ܦ݁ *Ca*

_____ _____ _____ _____ _____ _____ ܦܹ *Cy*

_____ _____ _____ _____ _____ _____ ܦܹ *Cay*

_____ _____ _____ _____ _____ _____ ܦܿ *Co*

_____ _____ _____ _____ _____ _____ ܦܘ *Coo*

_____ _____ _____ _____ _____ _____ ܦܼ *Kee*

Read aloud and write each of the following words several times. These words are made from the letters you have learned. This will help you with reading and how to connect the Syriac letters together.

_____ _____ _____ _____ _____ : Grasshopper (m) ܩܰܡܨܳܐ *Kamsah* *Kansah*

_____ _____ _____ _____ _____ : Wood (m) ܩܰܝܣܳܐ *Boopa*

_____ _____ _____ _____ _____ : Ascension (m) ܣܘܠܳܩܳܐ *Soola ca*

_____ _____ _____ _____ : Commandment (m) ܦܘܩܕܳܢܳܐ *Pogedanah*

_____ _____ _____ _____ _____ : Pencil (f) ܩܰܢܝܳܐ *Kehnin*

70

Pronunciation of ܩ (Qop) and vowels – ܩܳܦ ܥܡ ܩܳܠܶܐ ܕܙܵܘܥܶܐ

Transliteration	Meaning	Example	Vowel sound	L & V
	Cat (m) *Cata* Cat (f) *Cabutch*	ܩܵܛܘ ܩܵܛܘܿܬܐ	long a	ܩ
	Bald (m) *Carana* First (m) *Calma*	ܩܲܪܚܵܐ ܩܲܕܡܵܝܐ	short a	ܩ
	Ash, dust (m) *Cetma* Nest (f) *Ken*	ܩܸܛܡܵܐ ܩܸܢܐ	short i	ܩ
	Ship (c, f) *Kaywutha*	ܩܹܒܘܿܬܐ	open e	ܩ
	Holy (m) *Koodhisha*	ܩܘܿܕܫܐ	oo	ܩܘ
Coloma	Intestines, colon (m)	ܩܘܿܠܘܿܡܐ	o	ܩܘ
rakeyka	Soft (m)	ܪܩܝܩܐ	ee	ܩܝ

71

ܪ

Resh ܪܹܫ – ܪ ܪ

ܪ is the twentieth letter of the Syriac alphabet and is shaped to resemble a human head with a curl of hair on top.

- ܪ is comparable to the English letter R. It has a lingual sound.
- The numerical value of ܪ is (200) ܡܲܐܬܹܝܢ ܗܵܘܹܐ. Thus, ܪܨܒ is (292) ܗܵܘܹܐ ܡܲܐܬܹܝܢ ܘܬܸܫܥܝܼܢ ܘܬܪܹܝܢ (Literal: two hundreds and ninety and two), ܪܐ is (201) ܗܵܘܹܐ ܡܲܐܬܹܝܢ ܘܚܲܕ.
- ܪ is one of the un-joined letters which never connects to any letter follows it.
  - When it is a medial letter, it is joined on the right side only.

Estrangela			Eastern Syriac		
Isolated	End	Begin & Mid	Isolated	End	Begin & Mid
ܪ	ܪ ܪ	ܪ ܪ	ܪ	ܪ ܪ	ܪ ܪ

How to Write Resh
1) Start at the right side of the page, make a horizontal line from right to left.
2) Make a curved line moving from right to left over the short horizontal line.
3) Make a short horizontal line above the letter.

ܪ	ܪ	ܪ	ܪ	ܪ	ܪ	ܪ	ܪ	ܪ	ܪ	ܪ	ܪ	ܪ

Read aloud and write ܪ with each vowel several times.

_____ _____ _____ _____ _____ _____ _____ ܪܲ *rah*

_____ _____ _____ _____ _____ _____ _____ ܪ݂ *ra*

_____ _____ _____ _____ _____ _____ _____ ܪ *rih*

_____ _____ _____ _____ _____ _____ _____ ܪ݁ *ray*

_____ _____ _____ _____ _____ _____ _____ ܪܘ *ro*

_____ _____ _____ _____ _____ _____ _____ ܪܘ *roo*

_____ _____ _____ _____ _____ _____ _____ ܪܹ *ree*

Read aloud and write each of the following words several times. These words are made from the letters you have learned. This will help you with reading and how to connect the Syriac letters together.

_____ _____ _____ _____ : Syriac man ܣܘܪܝܝܐ *Surayeeb*

_____ _____ _____ _____ : Cherub (m) ܟܪܘܒ *grewan*

_____ _____ _____ _____ : Seraph (m) ܣܪܦ *Surapa*

_____ _____ _____ : Leg (f) ܪܓܠܐ *rugla*

_____ _____ _____ _____ : Moon (m) ܣܗܪܐ *Sahra*

_____ _____ _____ : Big (m) ܪܒܐ *raba*

_____ _____ _____ _____ _____ : Spirt (m) ܪܘܚܐ *rooha*

_____ _____ _____ _____ : High (m) ܪܡܐ *rama*

73

Pronunciation of ܪ (Resh) and vowels – ܩܵܠܵܐ ܕܪܝܼܫ ܥܲܡ ܙܵܘܥܹ̈ܐ

Transliteration	Meaning	Example	Vowel sound	L & V
yawirya	Drunkard (m)	ܪܵܘܵܢܵܐ	long a	ܪܵ
ramsha	Evening (m)	ܪܲܡܫܵܐ	short a	ܪܲ
ripna	Gain, win, profit (m)	ܪܝܼܚܢܵܐ	short i	ܪܝܼ
reeheh	Odor, scent (m)	ܪܹܝܚܵܐ	open e	ܪܹ
ruwsah	Rice (m)	ܪܘܼܙܵܐ		
rugza	Anger (m)	ܪܘܼܓܼܙܵܐ	oo	ܪܘܼ
rowda	Flower (f)	ܪܘܿܕܵܐ	o	ܪܘܿ
reeban	Countryside (m)	ܪܝܼܦܵܐ	ee	ܪܝܼ

74

ܫ

Sheen　　　　ܫܝܢ – ܫ

ܫ is the twenty-first letter of the Syriac alphabet and is shaped to resemble an ancient eastern lamp.

- ܫ is comparable to the English sound "sh". It has a dental sound (sibilant).
- The numerical value of ܫ is (300) ܬܠܬܡܐܐ. Thus, ܫܟ is (320) ܬܠܬܡܐܐ ܘܥܣܪܝܢ, and ܫܝܐ is (311) ܬܠܬܡܐܐ ܘܚܕܥܣܪ.
- ܫ connects to any letter which follows it.
   - When it is a medial letter, it is joined on both sides.

Estrangela			Eastern Syriac		
Isolated	End	L & V	Isolated	End	Begin & Mid
ܫ	ܫ　ܫ	ܫ　ܫ	ܫ	ܫ　ܫ	ܫ　ܫ

How to Write Sheen
1) Start at the right side of the page, make a short horizontal line with an upward vertical stroke.
2) Make a short horizontal line over the top of the vertical line starting from the right.
3) Retrace the vertical stroke downwards and make a short horizontal line to the left.

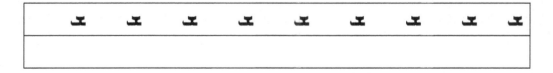

Read aloud and write ܫ with each vowel several times.

_____ _____ _____ _____ _____ _____ _____ ܫَ Shah

_____ _____ _____ _____ _____ _____ _____ ܫܰ sha

_____ _____ _____ _____ _____ _____ _____ ܫܻ shi

_____ _____ _____ _____ _____ _____ _____ ܫܶ shey

_____ _____ _____ _____ _____ _____ _____ ܫܿ sho

_____ _____ _____ _____ _____ _____ _____ ܫܘ shoo

_____ _____ _____ _____ _____ _____ _____ ܫܺ shee

Read aloud and write each of the following words several times. These words are made from the letters you have learned. This will help you with reading and how to connect the Syriac letters together.

_____ _____ _____ _____ _____ : Priest (m) ܟ݇ܗܢܐ

_____ _____ _____ _____ _____ : Head (m) ܪܝܫܐ

_____ _____ _____ _____ _____ : Evil (m) ܒܝܫܐ

_____ _____ _____ _____ _____ : Deacon (m) ܫܡܫܐ *Shamasha*

_____ _____ _____ _____ _____ : Sun (f) ܫܡܫܐ *Shimsha*

_____ _____ _____ _____ _____ : Evening (m) ܪܡܫܐ *Ramsha*

_____ _____ _____ _____ _____ : Human (m) ܒܪܢܫܐ *barnasha*

76

Pronunciation of ܫ (Sheen) and vowels – ܩܵܠܵܐ ܕܥܹܝܢ ܒܹܝܬ ܕܘܿܡܝܵܐ

Transliteration	Meaning	Example	Vowel sound	L & V
Shaka	Trunk(m)	ܫܵܩܵܐ	long a	ܫܵ
Shamasha	Deacon (m)	ܫܲܡܵܫܵܐ	short a	ܫܲ
Shebha	Glorifies, Praise	ܫܲܒܚ		
Shimshvh	Sun (f)	ܫܸܡܫܵܐ	short i	ܫܸ
Sheira	Saint's Day (m)	ܫܹܪܐ	open e	ܫܹ
Shoohah	Glory (m)	ܫܘܿܚܬܵܐ	oo	ܫܘܿ
Showka	Market (m)	ܫܘܼܩܵܐ	o	ܫܘܼ
Sheveh	Glue (m)	ܫܝܼܦܵܐ	ee	ܫܝܼ

ܬ

Taw   ܬ ܐ— ܘܬܼ

ܐ is the final letter of the Syriac alphabet and is shaped to resemble a jar.

- ܐ is comparable to the English letter T. It has a lingual sound.

Grammar 12: When a dot is placed beneath the ܐ it becomes soft "th" as in "Third".

     o ܐ also has another form ܐ and can be anywhere in the word.

         See page 8 for more examples of ܐ.

- The numerical value of ܐ is (400) ܐܪܒܥܡܐܐ. Thus, ܬܟ is (420) ܐܪܒܥܡܐܐ ܘܥܣܪܝܢ (literal: four hundred and twenty), and ܬܨܗ is (495) ܐܪܒܥܡܐܐ ܘܬܫܥܝܢ ܘܚܡܫܐ (literal: four hundreds and ninety and five).
- ܐ is one of the un-joined letters which never connects to any letter follows it.
  - o When it is a medial letter, it is joined on the right side only.

Estrangela			Eastern Syriac		
Isolated	End	Begin & Mid	Isolated	End	Begin & Mid
ܬ	ܬ ܬ	ܬ ܬ	ܐ	ܐ ܐ	ܐ ܐ

How to Write Taw

1) Start at the right side of the page, Make a long slanted downward stroke to the right.
2) Beginning at the top of the slanted line make a downward slanted stroke to the left forming a peak.
3) Make a short loop from the left slanted line to the right.

Read aloud and write ܕ with each vowel several times.

							ܕ dah
							ܕ da
							ܕ dih
							ܕ deh
							ܘܕ do
							ܘܕ doo
							ܝܕ dee

Read aloud and write each of the following words several times. These words are made from the letters you have learned. This will help you with reading and how to connect the Syriac letters together.

_____ _____ _____ _____ _____ : Holiness (f) ܩܘܕܫܘܬܐ *Ke*dishutha

_____ _____ _____ _____ : Drank (f) ܫܬܝܠܗ Shtayla

_____ _____ _____ _____ : Drank (m) ܫܬܝܠܗ Stayl:

_____ _____ _____ _____ _____ : Virgin ܒܬܘܠܬܐ dishbubtuh

_____ _____ _____ _____ : Glory- Hymn (f) ܫܘܒܚܐ dahamn

79

Pronunciation of ܬ (Taw) and vowels – ܩ̈ܠܐ ܕܐܬܐ ܥܡ ܙܘܥܐ

Transliteration	Meaning	Example	Vowel sound	L & V
dama	There	ܬܵܡܵܐ	long a	ܬ݁
dayla	Fox (m)	ܬܲܥܠܵܐ	short a	ܬܲ
tohra	Bull, Ox	ܬܵܘܪܵܐ		
dumura	Palm Date (m)	ܬܸܡܪܵܐ	short i	ܬ݂
dfeologyah	Theology (f)	ܬܹܐܘܠܘܓܝܹܐ	open e	ܬ݂
dooma	Garlic (m)	ܬܘܡܵܐ	oo	ܬܘ
tootha	Berry	ܬܘܬܵܐ		
tolaytha	Worm	ܬܘܠܲܥܬܵܐ	o	ܬܘ
teenih	Urine (f, p)	ܬܝܼܢܹܗ	ee	ܬܝ

Vocabulary

English	Syriac – ܣܘܪܝܬ
	thuwana baba
Merciful father.	ܒܒܐ ܡܪܚܡܢܐ.
Stupid man.	ܓܒܪܐ ܫܛܝܐ.
Teenager boy.	ܛܠܝܐ ܥܠܝܡܐ.
Good leather.	ܓܠܕܐ ܛܒܐ.
Virgen Mary.	ܡܪܝܡ ܒܬܘܠܬܐ.
Cold air.	ܐܐܪ ܩܪܝܪܐ.
Snow covers the grass.	ܬܠܓܐ ܚܦܝܐ ܠܥܠܐ.
Lunch.	ܟܘܢܐ.
Catholicism.	ܩܬܘܠܝܩܘܬܐ.
Bad dream.	ܚܠܡܐ ܒܝܫܐ.
Sleep.	ܫܢܬܐ.
Lord Jesus Christ king of the kings.	ܡܪܝ ܝܫܘܥ ܡܫܝܚܐ ܡܠܟܐ ܕܡܠܟܐ.

81

Chapter 2 Exercises

1. **Write out and pronounce the twenty-two letters of the Syriac alphabet several times. It is essential to learn how to recognize, write and pronounce each letter.**

-----	-----	-----	-----	-----	-----	-----	-----	ܐ
-----	-----	-----	-----	-----	-----	-----	-----	ܒ
-----	-----	-----	-----	-----	-----	-----	-----	ܓ
-----	-----	-----	-----	-----	-----	-----	-----	ܕ
-----	-----	-----	-----	-----	-----	-----	-----	ܗ
-----	-----	-----	-----	-----	-----	-----	-----	ܘ
-----	-----	-----	-----	-----	-----	-----	-----	ܙ
-----	-----	-----	-----	-----	-----	-----	-----	ܚ
-----	-----	-----	-----	-----	-----	-----	-----	ܛ
-----	-----	-----	-----	-----	-----	-----	-----	ܝ
-----	-----	-----	-----	-----	-----	-----	-----	ܟ
-----	-----	-----	-----	-----	-----	-----	-----	ܠ
-----	-----	-----	-----	-----	-----	-----	-----	ܡ
-----	-----	-----	-----	-----	-----	-----	-----	ܢ
-----	-----	-----	-----	-----	-----	-----	-----	ܣ
-----	-----	-----	-----	-----	-----	-----	-----	ܥ
-----	-----	-----	-----	-----	-----	-----	-----	ܦ

----- ----- ----- ----- ----- ----- ----- ----- ܓ

----- ----- ----- ----- ----- ----- ----- ----- ܦ

----- ----- ----- ----- ----- ----- ----- ----- ܕ

----- ----- ----- ----- ----- ----- ----- ----- ܒ

----- ----- ----- ----- ----- ----- ----- ----- ܬ

2. **Circle the letter ܐ, ܐ, and ܟ in the following Syriac words:**

Holy Bible.	ܟܬܵܒ݂ܵܐ ܩܲܕܝܼܫܵܐ.	ܟܬܒܐ ܩܕܝܫܐ.
Good News.	ܛܵܒ݂ܬܵܐ ܣܒ݂ܲܪܬܵܐ.	ܛܒܬܐ ܣܒܪܬܐ.
Greetings Joseph.	ܫܠܵܡܵܐ ܠܘܼܟ݂ ܝܵܘܣܸܦ.	ܫܠܡܐ ܠܘܟ ܝܘܣܦ.

3. **Match the correct sound with the following ܐ and vowels:**

_____ OO a. ܐܘܼ

_____ UH b. ܐܹ

_____ EE c. ܐܵ

_____ EH d. ܐܲ

_____ IH e. ܐܝܼ

_____ OH f. ܐܘܿ

_____ AH g. ܐܸ

4. **Circle the letters ܐ , ܒ, ܓ , and ܬ in the following Syriac words:**

The month of August is a hot month.	ܝܲܪܚܵܐ ܕܐܵܒ݂ ܝܲܪܚܵܐ ܚܲܡܝܼܡܵܐ.
Babylon is a big city.	ܒܵܒ݂ܸܠ ܡܕܝܼܢ݇ܬܵܐ ܪܒ݂ܬܵܐ.
Mariam's house is a big house.	ܒܲܝܬܵܐ ܕܡܲܪܝܲܡ ܒܲܝܬܵܐ ܪܲܒܵܐ.

Wild dog.   ܟܠܒܐ ܗܕܝܒܐ.

Lovely father.   ܐܒܐ ܪܚܝܡܐ.

5. **Write the letter ܐ, ܒ, ܠ and ܓ together ten times:**

ܐܒܠܓ

—   —   —   —   —   —   —   —   —

ܒܓܠܐ

—   —   —   —   —   —   —   —   —

ܠܓܐܒ

—   —   —   —   —   —   —   —   —

ܓܠܒ

—   —   —   —   —   —   —   —   —

6. **Read aloud the following letters:**

ܐ ܒ ܓ ܠ ܐ - ܓ ܒ ܐ ܠ - ܐ ܠ ܓ ܒ ܓ - ܒ ܓ ܠ ܐ

ܒ ܓ ܠ ܒ - ܠ ܒ ܟܢ ܓ - ܠ ܓ ܟܢ ܒ - ܒ ܟܢ ܓ ܒ

7. **Write the following words 7 times:**

ܠܩܐ

ܩܘܡܐ

ܡܩܬܘܣܐ

ܢܩܠܐ

ܡܩܘܒܐ

8. **Name and write the eight consonants which do not join to the letter which follows them.**

      _____   _____   _____   _____

      _____   _____   _____   _____

84

9. Write the letter ܗ, ܠ, ܐ, ܕ, ܟ and ܒ together ten times:

ܗܐܠܩ

— — — — — — — —

ܟܠܐܗ

— — — — — — — —

ܟܠܐܠܩ

— — — — — — — —

ܟܕܐܠ

— — — — — — — —

ܟܗܕܟ

— — — — — — — —

— — — — — — — —

10. Write the following numbers in Syriac.

453	___	342	___	231	___	121	___	321	___	457	___
300	___	499	___	410	___	390	___	287	___	388	___
331	___	444	___	333	___	222	___	111	___	101	___
28	___	56	___	66	___	21	___	59	___	50	___
89	___	327	___	86	___	90	___	313	___	248	___

11. Write the corresponding international numbers for the following Syriac numbers.

____ ܗܨܠ ____ ܗܘ ____ ܠܐ ܟܕ ____ ܩܕ ____ ܠܐ

12. Give the final form for the following Syriac consonants.

ܒ ܩ ܠ

13. Transliterate the following Syriac nouns and proper names for which only the consonants have been given.

God	ܐܠܗܐ
Lord	ܡܪܝܐ
Son	ܒܪܘܝܐ
dad	ܒܒܐ

85

Month	ܝܰܪܚܳܐ
Word	ܡܶܠܬܳܐ
Righteousness	ܙܰܕܺܝܩܘܬܳܐ
King	ܡܰܠܟܳܐ
Road, way	ܐܘܪܚܳܐ
Messenger	ܫܠܺܝܚܳܐ

Garshouni: With the problems created by the Islam about the Arabic language of the Koran, Arabic language was written with the Syriac alphabet or letters. This kind of script was called "Garshouni".

14. **Write the following English nouns and words in Garshouni. The answer to the first one is given as an example.**

↘ in syriac language

Door	ܒܳܒ	Son	
King		Daughters	
Yellow		Teacher	
Books		Chair	
Mom		Queens	
Father		Computer	

86

The Vowels　　　ܩ݇ܢܵܬ݂ܘ݇

Learning Objectives

In this chapter, you will:

- learn the syllabification and pronunciation – ܢܩܘ݇ܵ

- practice more on reading and vowels:
  - Sqapa ̇　　**ܘܩܵܦ.**
  - Pthaha ̇　　**ܦܬ݂ܵܚ.**
  - Zlama Psheeqa ̣　　**ܘܠܵܡܵ ܦܥܝܩܵ.**
  - Zlama Qishya ̣　　**ܘܠܵܡܵ ܩܥܢܵ.**
  - Vowels Derived From The Letter **ܘ** :
    - Rwahha ܘ̇　　**ܕܘ݇ܚܵ**
    - Rwassa ܘ　　**ܕܘܨܵ**
  - Vowel Derived From The Letter **ܝ**
    - Hwassa ܝ　　**ܚܘܨܵ**

- learn more vocabulary.

Syllabification and Pronunciation   ܐܳܘܕܳܟ

Your pronunciation and spelling of the Syriac language will improve as you gain an understanding of syllabification. These concepts are important because proper pronunciation will enhance your ability to memorize elements of the language. Syllabification in Syriac is the process of splitting words into syllables (Syr·i·ac cul·ture). Some words have only one syllable (monosyllabic) and have no syllable divider.

Because most of the readers are not native speakers of Syriac, they will not have the ability to correctly analyze Syriac words.

In order to divide Syriac words into syllables, you must begin with two simple rules:

1. A syllable cannot begin with a vowel except the vowel ܝ Hwassa. Every syllable must begin with a consonant. A consonant can only have one vowel (with few exception) or simply no vowel. For example, the Syriac word for "Singer" is ܙܰܡܳܪܐ and it syllables as ܪܐ . ܡܳ . ܙܰ (Za-ma-ra). This example has three syllables, each beginning with a consonant and each having only one vowel.

2. Syllables are two types, open and close syllables. Open syllables end with a vowel and closed syllables end with a consonant. In the previous example, ܙܰܡܳܪܐ, it has these two types of the syllables. The first and second syllables ܙܰ (za) and ܡܳ (ma) are open because they end in a vowel. The third syllable, ܪܐ (ra) is closed because it ends in a consonant.

Consonant (no vowel) is part of the syllable regardless of its location in the word. If the consonant is at the beginning of the word, it will be part of the very next open syllable. If it is between two open syllables, will be part of the first open syllable from right to left order. This rule will help with pronunciation and spelling of the word.

The Eastern Syriac language has seven "no written system" of vowels, and although they do not exist in written form. While they do not exist in written form, they are still a part of the spoken language. They are added to the consonants by using dots. In Syriac, the letters represent consonant sounds, while vowels are indicated by dots that are written above or below the letters. However, the letters of the English alphabet represent both consonant sounds and vowels.

Sqapa ܙܩܵܦܵܐ

ܙܩܵܦܵܐ Sqapa is pronounced as an open **(long) "A."** Sqapa is usually like "AH" as in "Father."

It is indicated by placing two slanted points, one above other, directly over the letter.

Example: ܐܵ.

Words Containing Sqapa:

Singer (m)	ܙܵܡܵܪܵܐ : ܙܵ . ܡܵ . ܪܵܐ	(she) sleeps	ܕܵܡܟܵܐ : ܕܵܡ . ܟܵܐ
(she) sings	ܙܵܡܪܵܐ : ܙܵܡ . ܪܵܐ	I – Personal Pronoun	ܐܵܢܵܐ : ܐܵ.ܢܵܐ
To sing	ܙܡܵܪܵܐ : ܙܡܵ . ܪܵܐ	Soul (f)	ܓܝܵܢܵܐ : ܓܝܵ.ܢܵܐ
To take	ܫܩܵܠܵܐ : ܫܩܵ . ܠܵܐ	dad	ܒܵܒܵܐ : ܒܵ.ܒܵܐ
(she) takes	ܫܵܩܠܵܐ : ܫܵܩ . ܠܵܐ	Ear (f)	ܢܵܬܵܐ : ܢܵ . ܬܵܐ
(he) sweeps	ܟܵܢܸܫ : ܟܵ . ܢܸܫ	Voice (m)	ܩܵܠܵܐ : ܩܵ.ܠܵܐ
To sweep	ܟܢܵܫܵܐ : ܟܢܵ . ܫܵܐ	Sister	ܚܵܬܵܐ : ܚܵ.ܬܵܐ
Hall (m)	ܐܵܘܵܢܵܐ : ܐܵ.ܘܵ.ܢܵܐ	Girl	ܒܪܵܬܵܐ : ܒܪܵ.ܬܵܐ
Reading	ܩܪܵܝܵܢܵܐ : ܩܪܵ.ܝܵ.ܢܵܐ	To see	ܚܙܵܝܵܐ : ܚܙܵ.ܝܵܐ
Dancer (m)	ܪܵܩܘܿܕܵܐ : ܪܵ.ܩܘܿ.ܕܵܐ	Vision	ܚܙܵܝܬܵܐ : ܚܙܵܝ.ܬܵܐ
(she) writes	ܟܵܬܒܵܐ : ܟܵܬ . ܒܵܐ	Wind (m)	ܦܘܼܚܵܐ : ܦܘܼ.ܚܵܐ

Pthaha ܦܬܵܚܵܐ

ܦܬܵܚܵܐ Pthaha is pronounced as a short **"A."** Pthaha is pronounced like "UH" as in "Hut" or "Utter". It is indicated by placing one point over the letter and another point under the letter.

Example: ܐܲ.

Words Containing Pthaha:

King	ܡܲܠܟܵܐ : ܡܲܠ.ܟܵܐ	Flower (m)	ܘܲܪܕܵܐ : ܘܲܪ.ܕܵܐ
Our king	ܡܲܠܟܲܢ : ܡܲܠ.ܟܲܢ	Month (m)	ܝܲܪܚܵܐ : ܝܲܪ.ܚܵܐ
Country (m)	ܐܲܬܪܵܐ : ܐܲܬ.ܪܵܐ	Snow (m)	ܬܲܠܓܵܐ : ܬܲܠ.ܓܵܐ
Our Country	ܐܲܬܪܲܢ : ܐܲܬ.ܪܲܢ	Wood (m)	ܩܲܝܣܵܐ : ܩܲܝ.ܣܵܐ
Flour (m)	ܩܲܡܚܵܐ : ܩܲܡ.ܚܵܐ	Saturday – a week	ܫܲܒܬܵܐ : ܫܲܒ.ܬܵܐ
Awrahem - Abraham	ܐܲܒܪܵܗܵܡ : ܐܲܒ. ܪܵ . ܗܵܡ	Five (m)	ܚܲܡܫܵܐ : ܚܲܡ.ܫܵܐ
Mariam - Mary	ܡܲܪܝܲܡ : ܡܲܪ. ܝܲܡ	Merciful (m)	ܡܪܲܚܡܵܢܵܐ : ܡܪܲܚ. ܡܵ .ܢܵܐ
Bread (m)	ܠܲܚܡܵܐ : ܠܲܚ.ܡܵܐ	Teacher (m)	ܡܲܠܦܵܢܵܐ : ܡܲܠ.ܦܵ.ܢܵܐ
Leg (f)	ܐܲܩܠܵܐ : ܐܲܩ.ܠܵܐ	Yaqoo	ܝܲܥܩܘܒ : ܝܲܥ.ܩܘܒ

Zlama Psheeqa   ܙܠܵܡܵܐ ܦܫܝܼܩܵܐ

ܙܠܵܡܵܐ ܦܫܝܼܩܵܐ Zlama Psheeqa is pronounced as a very short "I." Zlama Psheeqa is pronounced like "IH" as in "Sit" and "Hit." It is indicated by placing two even points, side by side, under the letter.

Example: ܒ̣.

Words Containing Zlama Psheeqa:

(He) writes	ܟ̣ܵܬ̣ܒ : ܟ̣ . ܬ̣ܒ	(He) sings	ܙܵܡܸܪ : ܙ . ܡܸܪ
(He) sleeps	ܕ̣ܵܡܸܟ : ܕ̣ . ܡܸܟ	(He) dances	ܪܵܩܸܕ : ܪ . ܩܸܕ
Dark (m)	ܚܸܫܟܵܐ : ܚܸܫ . ܟܵܐ	Blood (m)	ܕܸܡܵܐ : ܕ . ܡܵܐ
Rain (m)	ܡܸܛܪܵܐ : ܡܸܛ . ܪܵܐ	(He) asks	ܫܵܐܸܠ : ܫ . ܐܸܠ
Plain – an open or level land (f)	ܕܸܫܬܵܐ : ܕܸܫ . ܬܵܐ	(He) learns	ܝܵܠܸܦ : ܝ . ܠܸܦ
Dream (m)	ܚܸܠܡܵܐ : ܚܸܠ . ܡܵܐ	(He) heals	ܐܵܣܸܐ : ܐ . ܣܸܐ
Incense (m)	ܒܸܣܡܵܐ : ܒܸܣ . ܡܵܐ	(He) blesses	ܒܵܪܸܟ : ܒ . ܪܸܟ
Meat (m)	ܒܸܣܪܵܐ : ܒܸܣ . ܪܵܐ	Sun (f)	ܫܸܡܫܵܐ : ܫܸܡ . ܫܵܐ
Eagle (m)	ܢܸܫܪܵܐ : ܢܸܫ . ܪܵܐ	Tiger (m)	ܢܸܡܪܵܐ : ܢܸܡ . ܪܵܐ
Oil (m)	ܡܸܫܚܵܐ : ܡܸܫ . ܚܵܐ		

Zlama Qishya ܘܟ݂ܠܡܵܐ ܩܸܫܝܵܐ

ܘܟ݂ܠܡܵܐ ܩܸܫܝܵܐ Zlama Qishya is pronounced as an open "E." Zlama Qishya is pronounced like "EH" as in "They" or "Net." It is indicated by placing two slanted points, one above the other, under the letter.

Example: ܒ݂ܷ.

Words Containing Zlama Qishya:

His name	ܫܸܡܹܗ : ܫܸ . ܡܹܗ
Church (f)	ܥܹܕܬܵܐ : ܥܹܕ . ܬܵܐ
Feast – Festival (m)	ܥܹܐܕܵܐ : ܥܹܐ . ܕܵܐ
Doorbell (m)	ܙܲܓܵܐ : ܙ . ܓܵܐ
Head (m)	ܪܹܫܵܐ : ܪܹ . ܫܵܐ
(he) unties	ܫܲܪܹܐ : ܫ . ܪܹܐ
Arrow (m)	ܓܹܐܪܵܐ : ܓܹܐ . ܪܵܐ

Vowels Derived From The Letter ܘ

Rwahha ܪܘܵܚܵܐ ܘ

Rwahha is pronounced as "O." It is pronounced like "OH" as in "So" and "Row". It is indicated by placing one point over the letter ܘ (Wow).

Words Containing Rwahha:

Glory (f)	ܡܫܲܒܚܵܢܘܼܬܵܐ : ܫܘܿ . ܚܵܢ . ܘܼܬܵܐ
Person (m)	ܦܲܪܨܘܿܦܵܐ : ܦܲܪ . ܨܘܿ . ܦܵܐ
Guard (m)	ܢܵܛܘܿܪܵܐ : ܢܵ . ܛܘܿ . ܪܵܐ
Learner (m)	ܝܲܠܘܿܦܵܐ : ܝܲ . ܠܘܿ . ܦܵܐ
Boy – Son (m)	ܒܪܘܿܢܵܐ : ܒܪܘܿ . ܢܵܐ
Old testament (f)	ܕܝܲܬܩܹܐ : ܕܝܲ . ܬܩܹܐ
Creator (m)	ܒܵܪܘܿܝܵܐ : ܒܵ . ܪܘܿ . ܝܵܐ
Savior (m)	ܦܵܪܘܿܩܵܐ : ܦܵ . ܪܘܿ . ܩܵܐ

Rwassa   ܗ ܪ̈ܘܵܨܵܐ

ܪ̈ܘܵܨܵܐ Rwassa is pronounced as **"U."** It is indicated by placing one point under the letter ܗ (Wow). It is pronounced like "OO" or "UW" as in "Boo" and "Room".

Words Containing Rwassa:

Spirit (m)	ܪܘܼܚܵܐ : ܪ ܘ ܚܵܐ
Salty (m)	ܡܠܝܼܚܵܐ : ܡ ܠ ܝ ܘ ܚܵܐ
Knowledge (m)	ܝܘܼܠܦܵܢܵܐ : ܝ ܘ ܠ ܦ ܢܵܐ
Light – not heavy (m)	ܩܲܠܘܼܠܵܐ : ܩ ܠ ܘ ܠܵܐ
Fish (f)	ܢܘܼܢܬܵܐ : ܢ ܘ ܢ ܬܵܐ
Heavy (m)	ܝܲܩܘܼܪܵܐ : ܝ ܩ ܘ ܪܵܐ
Way – Road (f)	ܐܘܼܪܚܵܐ : ܐ ܘ ܪ ܚܵܐ
Nation (f)	ܐܘܼܡܬܵܐ : ܐ ܘ ܡ ܬܵܐ
Brain (m)	ܡܘܼܚܵܐ : ܡ ܘ ܚܵܐ

93

Vowel Derived From The Letter ܝ

Hwassa ܚܒܨܐ ܝ

ܚܒܨܐ Hwassa is pronounced as a long "E." It is pronounced like "EE" as in "Bee" and "Tree." It is indicated by placing one point under the letter ܝ (Yod).

Words Containing Hwassa:

Slow (m)	ܢܝܚܐ : ܢܝ.ܚܐ
Evil (m)	ܒܝܫܐ : ܒܝ.ܫܐ
Jesus Christ	ܝܫܘܥ ܡܫܝܚܐ : ܝ.ܫܘܥ ܡܫܝ.ܚܐ
History (f)	ܬܫܥܝܬܐ : ܬܫ.ܥܝ.ܬܐ
Honor – Respect - Dignity (m)	ܐܝܩܪܐ : ܐܝ.ܩ.ܪܐ
My dad	ܒܒܝ : ܒ.ܒܝ
My house	ܒܝܬܝ : ܒܝ.ܬܝ
Hand (f)	ܐܝܕܐ : ܐܝ.ܕܐ
Dead (m)	ܡܝܬܐ : ܡܝ.ܬܐ
Key (m)	ܩܠܝܕܐ : ܩܠܝ.ܕܐ
Hot (m)	ܫܚܝܢܐ : ܫ.ܚܝ.ܢܐ
Nineveh (f)	ܢܝܢܘܐ : ܢܝ.ܢܘܐ
I have	ܐܝܬ ܠܝ : ܐܝܬ.ܠܝ
My mom	ܝܡܝ : ܝ.ܡܝ

Note: There is another vowel called "ܐܣܩܐ - Assaqa" which is the vowel "ܙܠܡܐ ܩܫܝܐ" "Zlama Qishya" followed by the letter "ܝ" Yod . Like in: ܚܝܠ Power.

More Syllabification and Pronunciation

Silver (m)   ܣܹܐܡܵܐ = ܣܹܐ . ܡܵܐ

Light (f)   ܒܲܗܪܵܐ = ܒܲܗ . ܪܵܐ

Bird (m)   ܛܲܝܪܵܐ = ܛܲܝ . ܪܵܐ

Flute (m)   ܙܘܿܪܢܵܐ = ܙܘܿܪ.ܢܵܐ

Money (m)   ܙܘܼܙܹܐ = ܙܘܼ . ܙܹܐ

Teacher (m)   ܡܲܠܦܵܢܵܐ = ܡܲܠ . ܦܵ . ܢܵܐ

Stone (m)   ܟܹܐܦܵܐ = ܟܹܐ . ܦܵܐ

Faith (f)   ܗܲܝܡܵܢܘܼܬܵܐ = ܗܲܝ . ܡܵ . ܢܘܼ . ܬܵܐ

Picture (f)   ܨܘܼܪܬܵܐ = ܨܘܼܪ . ܬܵܐ

Near (m)   ܩܘܼܪܒܵܐ = ܩܘܼܪ . ܒܵܐ

Feast (m)   ܥܹܐܕܵܐ = ܥܹܐ . ܕܵܐ

Donkey (m)   ܚܡܵܪܵܐ = ܚܡܵ . ܪܵܐ

Big (m)   ܪܵܒܵܐ=ܪܵ . ܒܵܐ

Orchard (m)   ܟܲܪܡܵܐ = ܟܲܪ . ܡܵܐ

Son   ܒܪܘܿܢܵܐ = ܒܪܘܿ . ܢܵܐ

Fire (m)   ܢܘܼܪܵܐ = ܢܘܼ . ܪܵܐ

Cheese (f)   ܓܘܼܒܬܵܐ = ܓܘܼܒ . ܬܵܐ

Girl (f)   ܒܪܵܬܵܐ = ܒܪܵ . ܬܵܐ

Flower (m)   ܘܲܪܕܵܐ = ܘܲܪ . ܕܵܐ

Mountain (m)   ܛܘܼܪܵܐ = ܛܘܼ . ܪܵܐ

Dawn (m)   ܨܲܦܪܵܐ = ܨܲܦ . ܪܵܐ

Castle (m)   ܩܲܣܪܵܐ = ܩܲܣ . ܪܵܐ

Chapter 3 Exercises

1. Syllabify and transliterate the following Syriac nouns. The answer to the first one is given as an example.

Adam, man	ܐܳ . ܕܳܡ	ܐܳܕܳܡ
Gold (m)		ܕܰܗܒܳܐ
House (m)		ܒܰܝܬܳܐ
Word (f)		ܡܶܠܬܳܐ
Judge (m)		ܕܰܝܳܢܳܐ
People		ܥܰܠܡܳܐ
Temple (m)		ܗܰܝܟܠܳܐ

2. Syllabify the following Syriac words. The answer to the first one is given as an example.

Apple	ܚܰ.ܒܘܼ.ܫܳܐ	ܚܰܒܘܼܫܳܐ
Ant (m)		ܫܘܼܡܢܵܐ
Light (m)		ܒܰܗܪܳܐ
Student (m)		ܬܰܠܡܺܝܕܳܐ
Christ		ܡܫܺܝܚܳܐ
Teacher (m)		ܡܰܠܦܳܢܳܐ
Priest		ܩܰܫܺܝܫܳܐ
Deacon (m)		ܫܰܡܳܫܳܐ

3. For the following words, circle if the syllable is closed and draw a line under the open syllable.

Oil (m)	ܡܶܫܚܳܐ
Learner (m)	ܝܳܠܘܿܦܳܐ
Beautiful girl.	ܒܪܳܬܳܐ ܫܰܠܺܝܬܳܐ.
History's teacher.	ܡܰܠܦܳܢܳܐ ܕܡܰܫܥܺܝܬܳܐ.
Detroit is a big city.	ܕܶܝܬܪܘܿܝܬ ܐܺܝܠܶܗ ܡܕܺܝܢܬܳܐ ܪܰܒܬܳܐ.
Prayer (f)	ܨܠܘܿܬܳܐ

Chapter 4

Numbers and Time - ܚܘܫܒܢܐ ܘ ܥܕܢܐ

Learning Objectives

In this chapter, you will:
- learn about The Plural.   ܣܓܝܐܢ
- learn about The Feminine and Masculine Forms.

    ܕܟܪܢܝܐ : ܢܩܒܬܢܝܐ
- learn the names of number in Syriac.
- learn the Masculine and Feminine forms of the numbers.
- learn the original fact of The International Numerals.
- learn how to read the Compound Numbers: 20 - 90.
- learn how to read the Hundreds.   ܡܐܘܬܐ
- learn the numerical values and names of the numbers beyond 499.
- learn how to read the Thousands.   ܐܠܦܐ
- learn how read the Ordinal Numbers.
- learn how read the Fractions.
- learn how read the Percentages.
- learn how to read the sum of money.
- learn how to Pronounce the Measurements.
- learn how to Pronounce the Years.
- learn how to Pronounce Centuries.
- learn the Times:
  - o   Parts of the Day.
  - o   Hour/Watch.
- learn and pronounce the Time.
- practice on numbers and times.

Before learning the numbers in Syriac, let us introduce two simple gramma plural, and masculine/feminine forms and how we formed both in Syriac.

The Plural Form ܗܣܬܟܐ

Plural nouns are indicated by placing two big dots (ܣܝܳܡܶܐ – Sia.mie) above a letter and replace the Ȯ (Sqapa) vowel with Ọ (Zlama Qishya) vowel on second letter from last in most cases:

If the word contains one (ܪ) then the two dots are placed above the (ܪ) regardless of where it is in the word. For example: monastery: ܕܲܝܪܳܐ, monasteries: ܕܲܝܪ̈ܶܐ, man: ܓܲܒܪܳܐ, men: ܓܲܒܪ̈ܶܐ.

- If the word contains two (ܪ) the two dots will be on last one.
- If a word does not contain letter Resh ܪ, then the two dots placed on top of a letter as is discussed in **Appendix F**.

Irregular Plural Forms

Although most nouns form their plurals as described above, there are exceptions to regular formation of the following types:

a. Some words have a feminine form in the singular, and a masculine form in the plural.

Words: ܡܶܠ̈ܐ	Word: ܡܶܠܬܳܐ
Eggs: ܒܝܥ̈ܐ	Egg: ܒܝܥܬܳܐ

b. Some words have a masculine form in the singular, and a feminine form in the plural.

Souls: ܢܲܦܫ̈ܳܬܳܐ	Soul: ܢܲܦܫܳܐ
dads: ܒܲܒ̈ܳܬܳܐ	dad: ܒܲܒܳܐ

c. Some other examples of irregular nouns:

Villages: ܩܘܼܪ̈ܝܳܐ	Village: ܩܪܝܼܬܳܐ
Women: ܢܶܫ̈ܐ	Woman: ܐܲܢ̄ܬܬܳܐ
Houses: ܒ̈ܳܬܶܐ	House: ܒܲܝܬܳܐ
Mornings: ܨܲܦܪ̈ܘܳܬܳܐ	Morning: ܨܲܦܪܳܐ
Years: ܫܢ̈ܝܐ	Year: ܫܲܢܬܳܐ

The Feminine and Masculine Forms   ܕܟܪܢܝܐ : ܢܩܒܬܢܝܐ

The nouns and adjectives are masculine or feminine. There is no "neuter" in Syriac. Almost all feminine nouns are marked by the ending ܬܐ, whereas masculine nouns have no special ending other than the ܐ termination.

- All male names are male like in ܐܠܝܐ (Elijah), and ܐܝܣܚܩ (Isaac)
- All female names are females like in ܫܘܫܢ (Shooshan) and ܘܪܘܢܝܩܐ (Veronica), Name of the cities and villages (except few of them), cardinal directions, and all letters names.

Examples:

Noun	Plural F - M	Feminine	Masculine
King/queen	ܡܠܟܬܐ – ܡܠܟܬܢܐ	ܡܠܟܬܐ	ܡܠܟܐ
Man/woman	ܓܒܪܐ – ܐܢܬܬܐ	ܐܢܬܬܐ	ܓܒܪܐ
Teachers	ܡܠܦܢܐ – ܡܠܦܢܝܬܐ	ܡܠܦܢܝܬܐ	ܡܠܦܢܐ
Bull/cow	ܬܘܪܐ – ܬܘܪܬܐ	ܬܘܪܬܐ	ܬܘܪܐ
Self-conceited	ܙܥܝܪܐ – ܙܥܝܪܬܐ	ܙܥܝܪܬܐ	ܙܥܝܪܐ
Singer	ܙܡܪܐ – ܙܡܪܬܐ	ܙܡܪܬܐ	ܙܡܪܐ
	Zemaruh Zemergata	Zamarta	Zamara

The following are Common Nouns (places, things, and ideas) examples.

Mountain (m)	ܛܘܪܐ	ܛܘܪܐ
Book (m)	ܟܬܒܐ	ܟܬܒܐ
City (f)	ܡܕܝܢܬܐ	ܡܕܝܢܬܐ
Village (f)	ܩܪܝܬܐ	ܩܪܝܐ

Exceptions to the Rules: As with every set of rules or patterns, there are always, exceptions. Some of the most common exceptions are listed below:

- The only class of exceptions consists of nouns that are feminine in gender but do not have the ܬܐ ending, like:

Hand	ܐܝܕܬܐ	ܐܝܕܐ
Mom	ܝܡܬܐ – ܝܡܬܐ	ܝܡܐ

99

Earth	ܐܲܪܥܵܐ ‑ ܐܲܪܥܵܬ݂ܵܐ	ܐܲܪܥܵܐ
Sun	ܫܸܡܫܵܐ ‑ ܫܸܡܫܹ̈ܐ	ܫܸܡܫܵܐ
Tree	ܐܝܼܠܵܢܹ̈ܐ	ܐܝܼܠܵܢܵܐ
Belly	ܟܲܪܣܵܬ݂ܵܐ	ܟܲܪܣܵܐ
Eye	ܥܲܝ̈ܢܹܐ _Cynih_	ܥܲܝܢܵܐ _cynah_
Leg	ܐܲܩܠܵܬ݂ܵܐ	ܐܲܩܠܵܐ _aclah_
	aclaneh	

- The only class of exceptions consists of nouns that are masculine in gender but do have the ܬܐ ending, like:

He listened (c):	ܫܵܡܘܿܥܵܐ
Trap (c):	ܦܲܚܵܐ
Death:	ܡܵܘܬܵܐ
Rod of wood (c):	ܚܘܼܛܪܵܐ

Notes: _Those are feminine but do not have tav alap_

1. The pairing members of the human and animal body most of them are feminine in gender and do not end with ܬܐ, like, ܩܲܪܢܵܐ horn, ܥܲܝܢܵܐ eye, ܢܵܬ݂ܵܐ ear, ܟܲܬ݂ܦܵܐ shoulder (c), ܐܝܼܕܵܐ hand, ܐܲܩܠܵܐ leg.

Some nouns are masculine only, they do not have feminine noun, like, ܒܲܕܩܵܐ Hoopoe bird (c), ܚܲܡܵܐ mosquito, ܢܸܫܪܵܐ eagle, ܩܵܘܦܵܐ owl.

backam   _mghra_   _Oowtha_

100

Practicing Quizzes

Give the feminine and plural forms of the following masculine nouns.

Noun	Plural (f)	Feminine	Plural (m)	Masculine
Kid	yeltata	yelta	ܝܠܕܐ yaleh	ܝܠܕܐ Yalah
Horse	Soosiata	Soosta	ܣܘܣܐ Sooseh	ܣܘܣܐ Soosah
Donkey	Kmarta Kmarya	Kmarta	ܚܡܪܐ Kmareh	ܚܡܪܐ Kmarah
Youth	allaymatah	allaymtah	ܥܠܝܡܐ allaymeh	ܥܠܝܡܐ allaymah

Give the masculine and plural forms of the following feminine nouns.

Noun	Plural (m)	Masculine	Plural (f)	Feminine
Cow	towereh	towra	ܬܘܪܬܐ	ܬܘܪܬܐ towerta
Sheep	Pareh	Para	ܦܪܬܐ	ܦܪܬܐ Partah
Woman			ܒܬܐ	ܒܬܐ bechtah
Girl	gavreh	gavrah	ܒܪܬܐ	ܒܪܬܐ

101

The Names of Number in Syriac

Cardinal Numbers: 1 to 10

The names of number are either simple (single) or compound numbers. Single numbers like:

ܬ݂ܠܵܬ݂ܵܐ ،ܬܪܹܝܢ ،ܚܲܕ (one, two, three), and compound number like: ܬܪܸܥܣܲܪ (twelve), ܬܠܵܬ݂ܲܥܣܲܪ (thirteen).

These numbers can be masculine like:

ܚܲܕ ܓܲܒ݂ܪܵܐ (one man "a man"), ܬܪܹܝܢ ܬܲܠܡܝܼܕܹܐ (two students), ܚܲܕܲܥܣܲܪ ܟܬܵܒܹ̈ܐ (eleven books), or feminine like ܚܕ݂ܵܐ ܒܪܵܬ݂ܵܐ (one girl), ܬܲܪܬܹܝܢ ܡܲܠܦܵܢܝܵܬ݂ܵܐ (two teachers).

Note 1, the numbers from three to ten in the masculine form ends with Alap ܐ and Sqapa ◌ on proceeding letter and without Alap ܐ and Sqapa ◌ for feminine form except the number eight ends with Zlama Qishya ◌ and Alap ܐ. Just to remind our readers, the following names of number are in the spoken language. See **Appendix H** to know the fact of international numbers.

| | Examples | | No's Names | |
	F	M	F	M
1 boys/girls	ܚܕ݂ܵܐ ܒܪܵܬ݂ܵܐ	ܚܲܕ ܒܪܘܿܢܵܐ	ܚܕ݂ܵܐ	ܚܲܕ
2 Kings/queens	ܬܲܪܬܹܝܢ ܡܲܠܟܵܬ݂ܵܐ	ܬܪܹܝܢ ܡܲܠܟܹܐ	ܬܲܪܬܹܝܢ	ܬܪܹܝܢ
3 Books/teachers	ܬܠܵܬ݂ ܡܲܠܦܵܢܝܵܬ݂ܵܐ	ܬܠܵܬ݂ܵܐ ܟܬܵܒܹ̈ܐ	ܬܠܵܬ݂	ܬܠܵܬ݂ܵܐ
4 Priests/trees	ܐܲܪܒܲܥ ܐܝܼܠܵܢܹ̈ܐ	ܐܲܪܒܥܵܐ ܩܲܫܹ̈ܐ	ܐܲܪܒܲܥ	ܐܲܪܒܥܵܐ
5 Men/women	ܚܲܡܫܲܥ ܐܸܢܫܹ̈ܐ	ܚܲܡܫܵܐ ܓܲܒ݂ܪܹ̈ܐ	ܚܲܡܫܲܥ	ܚܲܡܫܵܐ
6 Apples/oranges	ܫܸܬ ܦܘܿܪܬܸܩܵܠܹ̈ܐ	ܫܸܬܵܐ ܚܲܙܘܿܪܹ̈ܐ	ܫܸܬ	ܫܸܬܵܐ
7 Bulls/cows	ܫܲܒ݂ܥܲܥ ܬܵܘܪܵܬ݂ܵܐ	ܫܲܒ݂ܥܵܐ ܬܵܘܪܹ̈ܐ	ܫܲܒ݂ܥܲܥ	ܫܲܒ݂ܥܵܐ
8 Students	ܬܡܵܢܹܐ ܬܲܠܡܝܼܕܵܬ݂ܵܐ	ܬܡܵܢܝܵܐ ܬܲܠܡܝܼܕܹ̈ܐ	ܬܡܵܢܹܐ	ܬܡܵܢܝܵܐ
9 Angels	ܬܸܫܥܲܥ ܡܲܠܲܐܟ݂ܵܬ݂ܵܐ	ܬܸܫܥܵܐ ܡܲܠܲܐܟܹ̈ܐ	ܬܸܫܥܲܥ	ܬܸܫܥܵܐ
10 Cucumbers /Peaches	ܥܣܲܪ ܚܲܒܘܼܫܹ̈ܐ	ܥܸܣܪܵܐ ܩܲܛܹ̈ܐ	ܥܣܲܪ	ܥܸܣܪܵܐ

Note 2: in the spoken Syriac language, which is the subject of this book, the names of number from 11 – 19 are the same for feminine and masculine and they come in masculine form:

Eleven	*hadeq* ܚܕܥܣܪܐ	Sixteen	ܐܫܬܥܣܪܐ
Twelve	ܬܪܥܣܪܐ	Seventeen	ܫܒܥܣܪܐ
Thirteen	*tilltasell* ܬܠܬܥܣܪܐ	Eighteen	ܬܡܢܥܣܪܐ
Fourteen	*arbasell* ܐܪܒܥܣܪܐ	Nineteen	ܬܫܥܣܪܐ
Fifteen	ܚܡܫܥܣܪܐ		

Counting By Tens (20 to 90)

Beginning with the letter ܟ, each following letter is counted by tens until the letter ܨ: 10-90 and ends with ܨ where ܢ is silent in spoken dialect and it is same for both masculine and feminine.

Sixty	ܫܬܝܢ	Twenty	ܥܣܪܝܢ
Seventy	ܫܒܥܝܢ	Thirty	ܬܠܬܝܢ
Eighty	ܬܡܢܝܢ	Forty	ܐܪܒܥܝܢ
Ninety	ܬܫܥܝܢ	Fifty	ܚܡܫܝܢ

Compound Numbers: 21 to 99

Reading compound numbers in Syriac is like reading the number in English. Therefore, the compound numbers (21 – 99) in Syriac are in the following order: the tenth proceed the ܘ letter proceed the singular number. For example:

21   ܥܣܪܝܢ ܘܚܕ. (**Literal**: Twenty and one).

33   ܬܠܬܝܢ ܘܬܠܬܐ. (**Literal**: Thirty and three).

There is another way the Syriac speakers read the compound numbers, which is in this order: the singular number proceed the tenth, for example:

21   ܚܕ ܘܥܣܪܝܢ. (**Literal**: one and Twenty).

We are going to use the first style (Tenth proceed the singular number) in this book.

Hundreds ܡܐܘܬܐ

Beginning with ܩ, each following letter is counted by hundreds until the letter ܬ: 100-400.

How to read hundreds?

To read hundreds, you say the number (1 - 9) proceed the word ܐܸܡܵܐ (singular), and ܐܸܡܵ̈ܐ (plural) proceed the noun in plural form if any. For example, to read 600, you say: ܐܸܫܬܵܐ ܐܸܡܵ̈ܐ (m) or ܐܸܫܬ ܐܸܡܵ̈ܐ (f).

One hundred	ܚܕ݂ܵܐ ܐܸܡܵܐ	Three hundred	ܬܠܵܬ݂ܵܐ ܐܸܡܵ̈ܐ
Two hundred	ܬܪܹܝܢ ܐܸܡܵ̈ܐ	Four hundred	ܐܲܪܒܥܵܐ ܐܸܡܵ̈ܐ

Note: in case of hundreds, thousands, millions (ܡܸܠܝܘܿܢܵܐ, ܡܸܠܝܘܿܢ̈ܐ), billions (ܡܸܠܝܵܪܕܵܐ, ܡܸܠܝܵܪ̈ܕܐ), etc., the numbers (1 – 9), you can use the masculine form for both masculine and feminine nouns. For example:

300 women
- m ܬܠܵܬ݂ܵܐ ܐܸܡܵ̈ܐ ܐܸܢܫܹ̈ܐ.
- f ܬܠܵܬ݂ ܐܸܡܵ̈ܐ ܐܸܢܫܹ̈ܐ.

Notice that the word ܐܸܢܫܹ̈ܐ is in the plural form. The big two dots over the letter "ܫ" in this example, "ܫ̈" means the noun is in plural form as was coved in previous section.

To read the three digits number, just like in English, you say the hundred(s) proceed tenth proceed the singular proceed the noun in plural form if any. For example:

325. ܬܠܵܬ݂ܵܐ ܐܸܡܵ̈ܐ ܘܥܸܣܪܝܼܢ ܘܚܲܡܫܵܐ.

(**Literal**: three hundred and twenty and five.)

The Numerical Values and Names Beyond 499

The numeric values for numbers 500, 600, 700, 800, and 900, are indicated by placing three dots as a triangle shape above letters ܗܒ through ܝ. You might not see all the three dots above the letter due to the computer font.

500	ܬ݊	ܚܡܫܡܐܐ ܙܪܩܐ
600	ܦ݊	ܫܬܡܐܐ ܙܪܩܐ
700	ܟ݊	ܫܒܥܡܐܐ ܙܪܩܐ
800	ܩ݊	ܬܡܢܡܐܐ ܙܪܩܐ
900	ܨ݊	ܬܫܥܡܐܐ ܙܪܩܐ

Example:

714 students: ܫܒܥܡܐܐ ܘܐܪܒܬܥܣܪ ܬܠܡܝܕ݁ܐ.

(**Literal**: seven hundreds and fourteen students.)

Thousands: ܐܠܦ݊ܐ

The numbers 1000 (ܐܠܦܐ) through 900,000 (ܬܫܥܡܐܐ ܙܪܩܐ ܐܠܦܐ) are indicated by placing a line above letters.

1000	ܐ̄	ܚܕ ܐܠܦܐ
2000	ܒ̄	ܬܪܝܢ ܐܠܦܐ
15000	ܝܗ̄	ܚܡܫܬܥܣܪ ܐܠܦܐ
90000	ܨ̄	ܬܫܥܝܢ ܐܠܦܐ
100000	ܩ̄	ܡܐܐ ܐܠܦܐ
300000	ܩ̄ܬ	ܬܠܬܡܐܐ ܐܠܦܐ
900000	ܨ̄	ܬܫܥܡܐܐ ܐܠܦܐ

Note: In Syriac, we do not say 23 hundred to read 2,300. Just read the number as is:

ܬܪܝܢ ܐܠܦܐ ܘܬܠܬܡܐܐ ܙܪܩܐ.

Literal: two thousands and three hundreds.

How to read thousands?

To read thousands, you say the number (1 – 900) proceed the word ܐܲܠܦܵܐ (singular) or ܐܲܠܦܹܐ (plural) proceed the noun in plural form if any. For example:

ܬܠܵܬ݂ܝܼܢ ܘܚܲܡܫܵܐ ܐܲܠܦܹܐ.   35,000

ܡܹܐܐ ܘܐܲܪܒܥܝܼ ܘܐܸܫܬܵܐ ܐܲܠܦܹܐ ܕܘܼܠܵܪܹܐ. $146,000

Literal: Hundred and forty and six thousand dollars.

To read the four digits number, you say the thousand(s) proceed hundred(s) proceed tenth proceed the singular proceed the noun in plural form if any. For example:

ܬܪܹܝܢ ܐܲܠܦܹܐ ܘܚܲܡܫܲܥܣܲܪ.   2015

Literal: Two thousands and fifteen.

ܐܲܪܒܥܵܐ ܐܲܠܦܹܐ ܘܬܪܹܝܢ ܡܹܐܐ ܘܬܠܵܬ݂ܲܥܣܲܪ ܒܵܬܹ̈ܐ.   4213 houses

Literal: Four thousands and two hundreds and thirteen houses.

Ordinal Numbers ܡܸܢ̈ܝܵܢܹܐ

	Plural	Feminine	Masculine
First	ܩܲܕܡܵܝܹ̈ܐ	ܩܲܕܡܵܝܬܵܐ	ܩܲܕܡܵܝܵܐ
Second	ܬܪܲܝܵܢܹ̈ܐ	ܬܪܲܝܵܢܬܵܐ	ܬܪܲܝܵܢܵܐ
Third	ܬܠܝܼܬ݂ܵܝܹ̈ܐ	ܬܠܝܼܬ݂ܵܝܬܵܐ	ܬܠܝܼܬ݂ܵܝܵܐ
Fourth	ܪܒ݂ܝܼܥܵܝܹ̈ܐ	ܪܒ݂ܝܼܥܵܝܬܵܐ	ܪܒ݂ܝܼܥܵܝܵܐ
Fifth	ܚܡܝܼܫܵܝܹ̈ܐ	ܚܡܝܼܫܵܝܬܵܐ	ܚܡܝܼܫܵܝܵܐ
Sixth	ܫܬ݂ܝܼܬ݂ܵܝܹ̈ܐ	ܫܬ݂ܝܼܬ݂ܵܝܬܵܐ	ܫܬ݂ܝܼܬ݂ܵܝܵܐ
Seventh	ܫܒ݂ܝܼܥܵܝܹ̈ܐ	ܫܒ݂ܝܼܥܵܝܬܵܐ	ܫܒ݂ܝܼܥܵܝܵܐ
Eighth	ܬܡܝܼܢܵܝܹ̈ܐ	ܬܡܝܼܢܵܝܬܵܐ	ܬܡܝܼܢܵܝܵܐ
Ninth	ܬܫܝܼܥܵܝܹ̈ܐ	ܬܫܝܼܥܵܝܬܵܐ	ܬܫܝܼܥܵܝܵܐ
Tenth	ܥܣܝܼܪܵܝܹ̈ܐ	ܥܣܝܼܪܵܝܬܵܐ	ܥܣܝܼܪܵܝܵܐ

Need to know these well

The first (ܩܕܡܝܐ 'm', ܩܕܡܝܬܐ 'f', ܩܕܡܝܐ̈ 'p') means "the beginning". The rest of ordinal numbers have a common with the corresponding root. For example, ܬܠܝܬܝܐ (third) and ܬܠܬܐ (three) have a common root.

Note: the last is (ܐܚܪܝܐ 'm", ܐܚܪܝܬܐ 'f', ܐܚܪܝܐ̈ 'p') in Syriac.

The masculine form of the ordinal number is different from the feminine form of the ordinal number by that the feminine form ends with ܬܐ, where ܬ is the symbol of the feminine form.

See **Appendix I** for mor Ordinal Numbers beyond tenth.

Using Regular Numbers For Ordinal Numbers

There is another way of reading ordinal numbers (except the first). It is by using the preposition letter "ܕ" proceed the regular number. For example: to read "third", say "ܕܬܠܬܐ" for masculine and "ܕܬܠܬ" for feminine – **Literal**: of the three.

Fractions ܡܢܘܬܐ

¼	ܪܘܒܥܐ pronounced ܪܘܒܥܐ	1/6	ܫܘܬܬܐ
1/3	ܬܘܠܬܐ	1/7	ܫܘܒܥܐ
½	ܦܠܓܐ pronounced ܦܠܓܐ	1/8	ܬܘܡܢܐ
3/4	ܬܠܬܐ ܪܘܒܥܐ pronounced ܬܠܬܐ ܪܘܒܥܐ	1/9	ܬܘܫܥܐ
1/5	ܚܘܡܫܐ	1/10	ܥܘܣܪܐ

Examples:

(**Literal**: half of the hour)	½ hour	ܦܠܓܐ ܕܫܥܬܐ.
(**Literal**: quarter of the dollar)	25¢	ܪܘܒܥܐ ܕܕܘܠܪܐ.
(**Literal**: three quarter of the hour)	45 minutes	ܬܠܬܐ ܪܘܒܥܐ ܕܫܥܬܐ.

Percentages

Percentages are easy to read aloud in Syriac. Just say the number and then add the word "ܒܡܐܐ - in hundred". Same rules for masculine and feminine for reading numbers 1 to 10 apply here too.

Literal		Feminine	Masculine
One in hundred	1%	ܚܕܐ ܒܡܐܐ	ܚܕ ܒܡܐܐ
Five in hundred	5%	ܚܡܫ ܒܡܐܐ	ܚܡܫܐ ܒܡܐܐ
Ten in hundred	10%	ܥܣܪ ܒܡܐܐ	ܥܣܪܐ ܒܡܐܐ

The following are the same for male and feminine

16%	ܫܬܬܥܣܪ ܒܡܐܐ	40%	ܐܪܒܥܝܢ ܒܡܐܐ
12%	ܬܪܬܥܣܪ ܒܡܐܐ	50%	ܚܡܫܝܢ ܒܡܐܐ
20%	ܥܣܪܝܢ ܒܡܐܐ	60%	ܫܬܝܢ ܒܡܐܐ
27%	ܥܣܪܝܢ ܘܫܒܥܐ ܒܡܐܐ	70%	ܫܒܥܝܢ ܒܡܐܐ
30%	ܬܠܬܝܢ ܒܡܐܐ	80%	ܬܡܢܝܢ ܒܡܐܐ

Reading Sums of Money

To read a sum of money in Syriac, first read the whole number, then add the currency name. If there is a decimal, follow with the decimal pronounced as a whole number, and if coinage has a name in the currency, add that word at the end. Note that normal decimals are not read in this way. We will use the dollar (ܕܘܠܪܐ) and cent (ܣܢܬ) as examples.

Note: Dollar (ܕܘܠܪܐ) and cent (ܣܢܬ) are in the masculine form, therefore, the masculine form of the number will be used with the money. ܣܢܬ also can replace with ܦܠܣܐ.

Written	Spoken
$10	ܥܣܪܐ ܕܘܠܪܐ.
$15.50	ܚܡܫܬܥܣܪ ܕܘܠܪܐ ܘܦܠܣܐ.

108

Written	Spoken
$25.99	ܥܣܪܝܢ ܘܚܡܫܐ ܕܘܠܪ̈ܐ ܘܬܫܥܝܢ ܘܬܫܥܐ ܦܠܣ̈ܐ.

Pronouncing Measurements

Just read out the number, followed by the unit of measurement, which will often be abbreviated in the written form.

30 meters	ܬܠܬܝܢ ܡܝܬܪ̈ܐ.	5ft	ܚܡܫܐ ܦܘܛ̈ܐ.
12 inches	ܬܪܬܥܣܪ ܐܝܢܟ̈ܐ.	4tbsp	ܐܪܒܥ ܡܟܠܝܬܢܝ̈ܬܐ ܕܐܝܟܠܐ.
40 Miles	ܐܪܒܥܝܢ ܡܝܠ̈ܐ.	1tsp	ܚܕܐ ܡܟܠܝܬܢܝܬܐ ܕܫܝܐ.
100km	ܡܐܐ ܟܝܠܘܡܝܬܪ̈ܐ.		

Pronouncing Years

Year "ܫܢܬܐ" is feminine in Syriac. So, the numbers from 1-10 should be in feminine form when used to represent the year.

Reading the year in Syriac is just like reading a number with adding "ܫܢܬܐ ܕ" (year of) at the beginning and "ܠܡܪܢ" for A.C and "ܩܕܡ ܡܪܢ" for B.C at the end.

For example, when the year is a four digits number, you say "ܫܢܬܐ ܕ" then read the first digit with adding the word (thousand(s) – ܐܠܦ̈ܐ / ܐܠܦܐ), then the "ܘ" and the next digit (if it is not a zero) with adding the word (hundred(s) - ܡܐܐ/ܡܐܐ̈), then the "ܘ" and then:

- the singular digit (1 – 9) in the feminine form if the tenth is zero or,
- the last two digits (10 – 99) with adding "ܠܡܪܢ" for A.C or "ܩܕܡ ܡܪܢ" for B.C at the end.

For example, to read the year:
2937 B.C, you will say.

ܫܢܬܐ ܕܬܪܝܢ ܐܠܦ̈ܐ ܘܬܫܥܐ ܡܐܐ ܘܬܠܬܝܢ ܘܫܒܥܐ ܩܕܡ ܡܪܢ.

(**Literal**: year of two thousands and night hundreds and thirty-seven before the Lord)
Note: most the time people do not say "ܠܡܪܢ" when the year is A.C.

Try to read the following year examples:

1614 AC. ܫܲܢ̱ܬܵܐ ܕܐܲܠܦܵܐ ܘܐܸܫܬܵܐ ܐܸܡܵܐ̈ ܘܐܲܪܒܲܥܬܲܥܣܲܪ ܠܡܫܝܼܚܵܐ.

Literal: year of a thousand and six hundreds and fourteen. We omit the word ܚܕܵܐ "one" from the "one thousand".

2017 AC. ܫܲܢ̱ܬܵܐ ܕܬܪܹܝܢ ܐܲܠܦܹ̈ܐ ܘܫܲܒܲܥܬܲܥܣܲܪ.

Example of three digits year number:

345 BC. ܫܲܢ̱ܬܵܐ ܕܬܠܵܬܵܐ ܐܸܡܵܐ̈ ܘܐܲܪܒܥܝܼܢ ܘܚܲܡܫܵܐ ܩܕܵܡ ܡܫܝܼܚܵܐ.

Example of feminine forms:

5 A.C. ܫܲܢ̱ܬܵܐ ܕܚܲܡܸܫ ܠܡܫܝܼܚܵܐ.

1810 ܫܲܢ̱ܬܵܐ ܕܐܲܠܦܵܐ ܘܬܡܵܢܝܵܐ ܐܸܡܵܐ̈ ܘܥܣܲܪ.

Note that the words "ܚܲܡܸܫ" (5) and "ܥܣܲܪ "(10) are in feminine form in last two examples.

If the third digit is zero value, and the number is made of four digits, read the first digit (thousand(s) – ܐܲܠܦܹ̈ܐ /ܐܲܠܦܵܐ), then "ܘ", then (hundred(s) - ܐܸܡܵܐ̈/ܐܸܡܵܐ), then "ܘ" and then the last digit (1-9) in feminine form. For example:

1903 ܫܲܢ̱ܬܵܐ ܕܐܲܠܦܵܐ ܘܬܸܫܥܵܐ ܐܸܡܵܐ̈ ܘܬܠܵܬ.

Literal: year of a thousand and nine hundreds and three.

Challenging quiz: read the following year examples in Syriac:

1400 ܫܲܢ̱ܬܵܐ ܕܐܲܠܦܵܐ ܘܐܲܪܒܥܵܐ ܐܸܡܵܐ̈.

2007 ܫܲܢ̱ܬܵܐ ܕܬܪܹܝܢ ܐܲܠܦܹ̈ܐ ܘܐܸܫܒܲܥ.

2000 ܫܲܢ̱ܬܵܐ ܕܬܪܹܝܢ ܐܲܠܦܹ̈ܐ.

2020 ܫܲܢ̱ܬܵܐ ܕܬܪܹܝܢ ܐܲܠܦܹ̈ܐ ܘܥܸܣܪܝܼܢ.

Note: reading a number in Syriac is always in masculine form, unless when needs to describe a feminine noun for numbers (1 to 10).

Pronouncing Centuries

Century "ܕܳܪܳܐ" is a masculine in Syriac. So, all numbers associate with it, should be in the masculine form.

There are two ways of pronouncing century:-

Using Regular Numbers:

To pronounce the century in Syriac, read "ܕܳܪܳܐ ܕ" (century of) proceed the number.

For example, to say the 4th century, you say ܕܳܪܳܐ ܕܐܲܪܒܥܵܐ (**Literal**: Century of the four).

Challenging quiz: read the following examples in Syriac:

21st Century.	ܕܳܪܳܐ ܕܥܸܣܪܝܼ ܘܚܲܕ.
13th Century.	ܕܳܪܳܐ ܕܬܠܵܬܲܥܣܲܪ.
7th Century.	ܕܳܪܳܐ ܕܫܲܒܥܵܐ.
10th Century.	ܕܳܪܳܐ ܕܥܸܣܪܵܐ.

Using Ordinal Numbers:

In this case, you do not need to say the preposition letter "ܕ" when reading the century. For example: ܕܳܪܳܐ ܩܲܕܡܵܝܵܐ (First Century).

In the next challenging quiz, say the following centuries example using Ordinal Numbers ܡܸܢܝܵܢܹܐ

3rd Century.	ܕܳܪܳܐ ܬܠܝܼܬܵܝܵܐ.
9th Century.	ܕܳܪܳܐ ܬܫܝܼܥܵܝܵܐ.
2nd Century.	ܕܳܪܳܐ ܬܪܲܝܵܢܵܐ.
5th Century.	ܕܳܪܳܐ ܚܡܝܼܫܵܝܵܐ.

Note: Decade is ܥܩܕܐ in Syriac and it is masculine.

111

The Times ܙܒܢ̈ܐ

Parts of the Day: ܡܢܘ̈ܬܐ ܕܝܘܡܐ

Midnight – **Literal**: middle of the night.	12:00am	ܦܠܓܗ ܕܠܠܝܐ
After midnight – **Literal**: after middle of the night.	12:01 to 2:59 am.	ܒܬܪ ܦܠܓܗ ܕܠܠܝܐ
Early morning.	3:01 to **5**:59am.	ܩܕܡܬܐ
Morning.	6:00 to 11:59 am.	ܨܦܪܐ
Noon – **Literal**: middle of the day.	12:00pm.	ܦܠܓܗ ܕܝܘܡܐ
After noon - **Literal**: after middle of the day.	12:01 to 2:59pm.	ܒܬܪ ܦܠܓܗ ܕܝܘܡܐ
Evening.	3:00 to 5:59pm.	ܪܡܫܐ - ܒܣܝܡܬܐ
Night.	6:01 to 11:59pm.	ܠܠܝܐ

Hour/Watch ܫܥܬܐ

ܒܟܡܐ ܝܠܗ ܫܥܬܐ؟ (What time is it?) "**Literal**: in how much is the hour?" is the way of asking for the time.

Hour/watch "ܫܥܬܐ" in Syriac is in the feminine form, therefore, all numbers in time/hour should be in feminine form.

There is no "AM/PM" in Syriac. The parts of the day ܝܘܡܐ is used to emphasize the time of the day. However, for most of the time, Syriac speaker use "ܒܝܘܡܐ' (at day – 6am to 6pm), and "ܒܠܠܝܐ" (at night – 6pm to 6am).

To say the time in Syriac, you say "ܫܥܬܐ ܒ" (**Literal**: the time at) proceed the numeric value of the hour, proceed the numeric value of the minutes if any and then the part of the day. For example:

9:30am ܫܥܬܐ ܒܬܫܥ ܘܦܠܓܗ ܒܝܘܡܐ.

Note: ܐܠܐ (except) is "to" after the half hour. For example, for 8:45, you can say: ܪܒܥܐ ܐܠܐ ܠܬܫܥ. (quarter to/except nine).

The following examples used the day's parts for how to say the time in Syriac:

Time	Literal	Time in Syriac
7:15 pm	Hour by seven and quarter at night	ܫܥܬܐ ܒܫܒܥܐ ܘܪܘܒܥܐ ܒܠܠܝܐ.
6:00 am	Hour by six in the morning	ܫܥܬܐ ܒܫܬ ܒܨܦܪܐ.
3:12pm		ܫܥܬܐ ܒܬܠܬ ܘܬܪܬܥܣܪܐ ܒܪܡܫܐ.
8:40pm	Hour by one third to/except nine at night	ܫܥܬܐ ܒܬܫܥ ܐܠܐ ܬܘܠܬܐ ܒܠܠܝܐ.
2:45pm		ܫܥܬܐ ܒܬܠܬ ܐܠܐ ܪܘܒܥܐ ܒܬܪ ܦܠܓܗ ܕܝܘܡܐ.
12:00pm	Hour by twelve at middle of the day (or at middle of the day)	ܫܥܬܐ ܒܬܪܬܥܣܪܐ ܒܦܠܓܗ ܕܝܘܡܐ (ܒܦܠܓܗ ܕܝܘܡܐ).
12:00am		ܫܥܬܐ ܒܬܪܬܥܣܪܐ ܒܠܠܝܐ (ܒܦܠܓܗ ܠܠܝܐ).
5:25pm	Hour by five and twenty and five at evening	ܫܥܬܐ ܒܚܡܫ ܘܥܣܪܝܢ ܘܚܡܫ ܒܪܡܫܐ.
3:55pm	Hour by quarter to/except five	ܫܥܬܐ ܒܪܘܒܥܐ ܐܠܐ ܚܡܫ ܒܪܡܫܐ.
1:50am		ܫܥܬܐ ܒܬܪܬܝܢ ܐܠܐ ܥܣܪܐ ܒܨܦܪܐ.

Numbers and Time Examples

1. How many brothers do you have? (**2ⁿᵈ m**)   ܟܡܐ ܐܚܘܢܘܬܐ ܐܝܬ ܠܘܟ؟

2. I have 5 brothers.   ܐܢܐ ܐܝܬ ܠܝ ܚܡܫܐ ܐܚܘܢܘܬܐ.

3. I have 7 sisters.   ܐܢܐ ܐܝܬ ܠܝ ܫܒܥܐ ܚܬܘܬܐ.

4. Two of my uncles are teachers.   ܬܪܝܢ ܡܢ ܚܠܘܢܝ ܐܝܠܗ ܡܠܦܢܐ.

5. Fifteen students failed the test.   ܚܡܫܥܣܪ ܬܠܡܝܕܐ ܢܦܠܠܗ ܒܒܘܚܪܢܐ.

6. Dial 586-342-7915 (**2ⁿᵈ m**).   ܡܚܝ ܡܢܝܢܐ 5863427915.

7. I want $78 (**1st m**).   ܐܢܐ ܒܥܝܢ ܫܒܥܝܢ ܘܬܡܢܝܐ ܕܘܠܪܐ.

8. Repeat # 7 but from female speaker.

9. The price of this shirt is $56.   ܛܝܡܐ ܕܗܕܐ ܩܡܝܨܐ ܐܝܠܗ ܚܡܫܝܢ ܘܐܫܬܐ ܕܘܠܪܐ.

10. Can you give me 32 books (**1st m to 2ⁿᵈ m**)?   ܡܨܝܬ ܗܐ ܝܗܒܠܬ ܠܝ ܬܠܬܝܢ ܘܬܪܝܢ ܟܬܒܐ؟

11. Can I take 7 pencils please (**1st m to 2ⁿᵈ f**)?   ܡܨܝܢ ܐܢܐ ܫܩܠܢ ܫܒܥܐ ܩܠܡܐ ܒܥܘܬܟ؟

12. Two of my aunts are coming next month.   ܬܪܝܢ ܡܢ ܚܠܘܢܝ ܐܝܠܝ ܒܐܬܝܐ ܝܪܚܐ ܕܐܬܐ.

13. The number of students is 123.   ܡܢܝܢܐ ܕܬܠܡܝܕܐ ܐܝܠܗ ܡܐ ܘܥܣܪܝܢ ܘܬܠܬܐ.

14. Time is: -
    a. 5:32pm: ܥܕܢܐ ܚܡܫ ܘܬܠܬܝܢ ܘܬܪܝܢ ܒܬܪܨܗܪܐ.
    b. 4:25am: ܥܕܢܐ ܐܪܒܥ ܘܥܣܪܝܢ ܘܚܡܫ ܒܨܦܪܐ.
    c. 7:58pm: ܥܕܢܐ ܫܒܥ ܘܚܡܫܝܢ ܘܬܡܢܝܐ ܒܠܝܠܐ.
    d. 12:30am: ܥܕܢܐ ܬܪܥܣܪ ܘܬܠܬܝܢ (ܦܠܓܐ) ܒܨܦܪܐ.
    e. 1:37pm: ܥܕܢܐ ܚܕܐ ܘܬܠܬܝܢ ܘܫܒܥ ܒܬܪܨܗܪܐ.
    f. 9:13pm: ܥܕܢܐ ܬܫܥ ܘܬܠܬܥܣܪ ܒܠܝܠܐ.

Vocabulary

End	ܫܘܠܡܐ، ܣܘܦܐ	Always	ܬܡܝܕ
Sometimes	ܓܗܐ ܓܗܐ	Every time	ܟܠ ܓܗܐ
		Start	ܫܘܪܝܐ

114

Chapter 4 Exercises

Q1. Read and write the following percentages in Syriac:

45%	29%	98%	14%
120%	33%	25%	19%
7%	200%	43%	2%
66%	74%	87%	88%

beta ohma

Multiple Choice:

Q2. Read the following statement and give the right answer to fill in the blank area.

ܐܝܬܠܗ - - - - - ܬܠܡܝܕ̈ܐ ܒܨܦܐ.

ܐ. ܚܡܫܝܢ ܒ. ܚܡܫܝܢܬܐ ܓ. ܚܡܫܝܢܐ ܕ. ܚܡܫܝܐ

Q3. Our house has three bedrooms.

ܐ. ܒܝܬܢ ܐܝܬܠܗ ܐܪܒܥ ܡܕܡܟ̈ܢܬܐ ܕܕܡܟܐ. ܓ. ܒܝܬܢ ܐܝܬܠܗ ܬܠܬ ܡܕܡܟ̈ܢܬܐ ܕܕܡܟܐ.

ܒ. ܢܘܗܪܐ ܕܫܡܫܐ ܐܝܬܠܗ ܫܚܢܐ. ܕ. ܒܝܬܢ ܐܝܬܠܗ ܬܠܬܝܢ ܡܕܡܟ̈ܢܬܐ ܕܕܡܟܐ.

Q4. I can count in Syriac.

ܐ. ܐܢܐ ܐܝܬܠܝ ܕܡܢܝܢ ܒܠܫܢܐ ܐܪܡܝܐ. ܓ. ܐܢܐ ܐܝܬܠܝ ܕܡܢܝܢ ܒܠܫܢܐ ܐܪܒܝܐ.

ܒ. ܐܢܐ ܐܝܬܠܝ ܕܡܢܝܢ ܒܠܫܢܐ ܐܪܡܢܝܐ. ܕ. ܐܢܐ ܐܝܬܠܝ ܕܡܢܝܢ ܒܠܫܢܐ ܗܘܕܝܐ.

Q5. Read the following math problem and circle the right answer:

ܡܢܝܢܐ ܕܬܠܡܝܕ̈ܐ ܕܨܦܐ ܩܕܡܝܐ ܫܪܫܝܐ ܒܡܕܪܫܬܢ (ܩܠܒ) ܬܠܡܝܕ̈ܐ، ܘܡܢܝܢܐ
ܕܬܠܡܝܕ̈ܐ ܕܨܦܐ ܬܪܝܢܐ (ܩܘ) ܬܠܡܝܕ̈ܐ ܕܨܦܐ ܬܠܝܬܝܐ (ܡܝܘ) ܬܠܡܝܕ̈ܐ،
ܘܡܢܝܢܐ ܕܬܠܡܝܕ̈ܐ ܕܨܦܐ ܪܒܝܥܝܐ(ܡܩܗ) ܬܠܡܝܕ̈ܐ. ܐܝܟܡܐ ܬܠܡܝܕ̈ܐ ܐܝܬ
ܒܨܦܐ ܬܠܝܬܝܐ ܘܪܒܝܥܝܐ؟

ܐ. ܫܦܓ ܒ. ܫܦܚ ܓ. ܫܦܒ ܕ. ܫܦܛ

Will be on 2nd exam

Vocabulary

Number	ܡܢܝܢܐ	School	ܡܕܪܫܬܐ	Class	ܨܦܐ
Students	ܬܠܡܝܕ̈ܐ	Elementary	ܫܪܫܝܐ		

Q6. Translate the following statements to English:

a. ܟܡܐ ܐܝܠܗ̇ ܛܝܡܐ ܕܒܝܬܐ ܕܐܠܦܐ ܘܡܐܬܐ ܐܪܒܥ ܘܡܐܬܝܢ ܘܐܪܒܥܐ.
b. ܬܪܥܐ ܐܝܠܗ̇ ܒܬܫܥܐ ܒܠܠܝܐ ܒܝܘܡܐ ܕܚܕ ܒܫܒܐ.
c. ܟܠܗ ܕܚܘܫܒܢܐ ܐܝܠܗ̇ ܒܪܘܒܥܐ ܕܡܐܐ.

Q7. Translate the following statements to Syriac:

a. The wedding party is on Sunday at 8pm.
b. This house has 4 bedrooms.
c. My house is 2400 fts.
d. The time is 2:37pm now.
e. 15% of my money are from my father.

Q8. Match the times in words in the first column, with the time in Syriac in the second column:

It is one o'clock.	ܫܥܬܐ ܐܝܠܗ̇ ܒܫܒܥܐ ܘܪܘܒܥܐ.
It is quarter past two.	ܫܥܬܐ ܐܝܠܗ̇ ܒܬܫܥܐ ܐܠܐ ܪܘܒܥܐ.
It is quarter past three.	ܫܥܬܐ ܐܝܠܗ̇ ܒܚܕܐ.
It is half past four.	ܫܥܬܐ ܐܝܠܗ̇ ܒܬܠܬ ܘܪܘܒܥܐ.
It is half past five.	ܫܥܬܐ ܐܝܠܗ̇ ܒܬܪܬܝܢ ܘܪܘܒܥܐ.
It is quarter to six.	ܫܥܬܐ ܐܝܠܗ̇ ܒܫܬܐ ܐܠܐ ܪܘܒܥܐ.
It is quarter to seven.	ܫܥܬܐ ܐܝܠܗ̇ ܒܬܡܢܐ.
It is quarter to eight.	ܫܥܬܐ ܐܝܠܗ̇ ܒܚܡܫ ܘܦܠܓܐ.
It is eight o'clock.	ܫܥܬܐ ܐܝܠܗ̇ ܒܬܡܢܐ ܐܠܐ ܪܘܒܥܐ.
It is quarter past nine.	ܫܥܬܐ ܐܝܠܗ̇ ܒܐܪܒܥ ܘܦܠܓܐ.
It is quarter to ten.	ܫܥܬܐ ܐܝܠܗ̇ ܒܥܣܪ ܐܠܐ ܪܘܒܥܐ.

Chapter 5

Learning Objectives

In this chapter, you will learn:

- the names of Horoscope.
- the seasons.
- the water and weather status.
- the colors.
- the directions.
- how to ask and answer for directions.
- the days of the week.
- how to pronounce the Days.
- the names of months in Syriac.
- the historical meaning of the names of the months.
- how to pronounce the Date.
- more vocabulary.

Horoscope ܛܠܥܬ̈ܐ or ܒܘܨܐ

ܡܠܘܫܐ or as is known by ܒܘܨܐ is masculine in Syriac. To say for example Leo, you say: ܒܘܨܐ ܕܐܪܝܐ.

Libra	ܡܣܬܐ	Aries	ܐܡܪܐ
Scorpio	ܥܩܪܒܐ	Taurus	ܬܘܪܐ *tora*
Sagittarius	ܩܫܬܐ	Gemini	ܬܐܡܐ
Capricorn	ܓܕܝܐ *gedya*	Cancer	ܣܪܛܢܐ
Aquarius	ܕܠܘܐ	Leo	ܐܪܝܐ *Liya*
Pisces	ܢܘܢܐ *nuna*	Virgo	ܒܬܘܠܬܐ

The Seasons ܩܘܛܣܐ

Winter	ܣܬܘܐ
Spring	ܪܒܝܥܐ (also, ܪܒܝܥܐ or ܕܢܚܐ) *rabiya*
Summer	ܩܝܛܐ
Fall	ܬܫܪܝܐ

Water Status Stage ܕܪܓܐ ܕܡܝ̈ܐ

Status	Plural	Feminine	Masculine
Ice	ܓܠܝܕܐ *gleethih / telgay*	ܓܠܝܕܬܐ *glitihta*	ܓܠܝܕܐ *gleetha / felga*
Snow	ܬܠܓܐ	------	ܬܠܓܐ *carrela / Caryeta*
Cold	ܩܪܝܪܐ *carrela*	ܩܪܝܪܬܐ *Caryeta*	ܩܪܝܪܐ *Carrela*
Warm	ܫܚܝܢܐ *Cashenih*	ܫܚܝܢܬܐ *Cashenthta*	ܫܚܝܢܐ *Cashenra*
Hot	ܚܡܝܡܐ *Shaheenih*	ܚܡܝܡܬܐ *Shehinta*	ܚܡܝܡܐ *Shahena*
Very Hot	ܚܡܝܡܐ[5] *hameemih*	ܚܡܝܡܬܐ *Hamenta*	ܚܡܝܡܐ *hameena*
Boil	ܪܬܚܐ *Mutheethih*	ܪܬܚܬܐ *Mathuchta*	ܪܬܚܐ *thuchah*

Temperature = ܫܚܝܢܘܬܐ *Shacknootha*

Note: most of the Syriac speakers use ܬܠܓܐ (snow) for both snow and ice.

---

[5] ܚܡܝܡܐ and ܫܚܝܢܐ used to describe the weather status too.

118

Weather Status

Hail — ܣܝܣܪܬܐ Seeserta

Thunder. Thunder's sound is: ܓܪܓܘܡܬܐ (f), ܓܪܓܘܡܝܬܐ (p) — ܓܪܓܘܡܬܐ - ܪܥܡܐ gargunta

Lightning — ܒܪܩܐ / ܒܪܩܐ berka

Frost — ܩܪܩܝܢܐ Carcena

Storm — ܥܠܥܠܐ alalay

Windy — ܦܘܚܢܐ pohana

Sunny — ܫܡܫܢܐ Shimshana

Rainy — ܡܛܪܢܐ matrona

Fog — ܢܝܓܒܘܬܐ negbootha

Snowy — ܬܠܓܢܐ telgana

Wet — ܬܠܝܠܐ: ܬܠܝܠܬܐ: ܬܠܝܠܐ feleeleh
ܪܛܒܐ: ܪܛܝܒܬܐ: ܪܛܝܒܐ

Humidity — ܪܛܝܒܘܬܐ ratayvootha

Examples:

Arizona's summer is very hot. — ܩܝܛܐ ܕܐܪܝܙܘܢܐ ܝܠܗ ܚܡܝܡܐ.

Winter in Michigan is cold and snowy. — ܣܬܘܐ ܕܡܝܫܝܓܢ ܩܪܝܪܐ ܝܠܗ ܘܬܠܓܢܐ.

Spring in Michigan is rainy and nice. — ܒܗܪ ܕܡܝܫܝܓܢ ܡܛܪܢܐ ܝܠܗ ܘܒܣܝܡܐ.

The Colors *gonch*

ܟܘܬܪ *Komyata*

Color	Plural	Feminine	Masculine
Black	ܟܘܡܹܐ : ܟܘܡܩܢܹܐ *Komeh*	ܟܘܡܬܐ *Komta*	ܟܘܡܐ *Koma*
White	*hwaryata* ܚܘܵܪܹܐ : ܚܘܵܪܩܢܹܐ *hwaren*	ܚܘܵܪܬܐ *hwarta*	ܚܘܵܪܐ *hwara*
Green	*yawaryata* ܝܪܘܩܹܐ : ܝܪܘܩܩܢܹܐ *Yarenkoh*	ܝܪܘܩܬܐ *yerenkta*	ܝܪܘܩܐ *yerenka*
Red	ܣܡܘܩܹܐ : ܣܡܘܩܩܢܹܐ	ܣܡܘܩܬܐ	ܣܡܘܩܐ *Smoka*
Yellow	ܫܥܘܬܹܐ : ܫܥܘܬܩܢܹܐ	ܫܥܘܬܐ	ܫܥܘܬܐ *Shaewtha*
Blue	ܙܪܩܹܐ : ܙܪܩܩܢܹܐ	ܙܪܩܐ	ܙܪܩܐ *Zarka*
Purple	ܒܢܘܫܹܐ : ܒܢܘܫܩܢܹܐ	ܒܢܘܫܐ	ܒܢܘܫܐ *benowsha*
Pink	ܘܪܕܹܐ : ܘܪܕܩܢܹܐ	ܘܪܕܐ	ܘܪܕܐ *Werdaya*

- Give me five red apples, please. (**2ⁿᵈ m**).

  ܗܒܠܝ ܚܡܫܐ ܚܒܘܫܐ ܣܡܘܩܐ ܒܒܥܘܬܘܟ.

- This is a white car.

  ܐܗܐ ܝܠܗ ܚܕܐ ܣܝܪܐ ܚܘܵܪܬܐ.

Adjectives must agree with nouns. In the first example above, the noun ܚܒܘܫܐ (apples) is a masculine and in the plural forms, therefore, the adjective ܣܡܘܩܐ (red, **Literal** – reds) must be in plural and masculine forms too. In the second example, the noun ܣܝܪܐ (car – a loaner word from Arabic – ܪܕܝܬܐ in Syriac) is a singular feminine form, therefore, the adjective ܚܘܵܪܬܐ (white) is a singular feminine form too.

The Directions ܟܘܬܐ

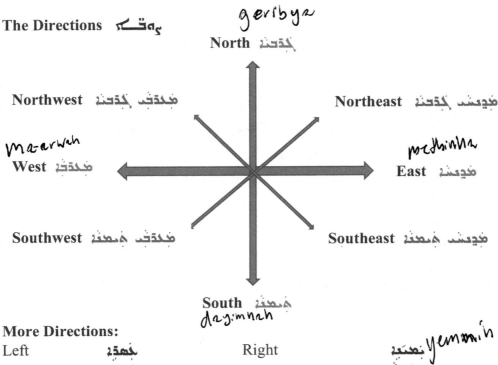

geribya
North ܓܪܒܝܐ

Northwest ܡܥܪܒܐ ܓܪܒܝܐ   Northeast ܡܕܢܚܐ ܓܪܒܝܐ

maarweh
West ܡܥܪܒܐ   *medhinha*
East ܡܕܢܚܐ

Southwest ܡܥܪܒܐ ܬܝܡܢܐ   Southeast ܡܕܢܚܐ ܬܝܡܢܐ

South ܬܝܡܢܐ
tayimnah

More Directions:

Left	ܣܡܠܐ	Right	ܝܡܢܐ *yemmnih*
Front/Before	ܩܘܕܡ	Back/Behind	ܚܕܪܐ
Near	ܩܘܪܒܐ — ܩܪܒܬܐ	Far	ܪܚܘܩܐ
Underneath	ܫܦܠܐ	Above	ܥܠܐ
Bottom	ܬܚܬܝܐ	Top	ܝܠܟܐ
Upstairs	ܝܠ	Downstairs	ܝܠܟܢܐ
Cross	ܩܘܡܣܠ	Beside	ܦܢܐ

Asking for Directions

Where is your house located? (2ⁿᵈ m, f, p)   ܒܝܬܐ ܕܝܠܗ ܟܡܘܗܘܐ؟

My house is cross the street from the church.   ܒܝܬܐ ܕܝܠܝ ܩܘܡܣܠ ܕܥܕܬܐ.

Can you tell me where is the hospital please? (2ⁿᵈ f)

ܡܨܝܬܝ ܕܐܡܪܡܟܒ ܒܝܬܐ ܕܝܠܗ ܒܝܬܚܝܠܘܬ ܒܝܢܝܕܚܐ؟

Go straight and make right. (2ⁿᵈ m)   (p ܗܦ ،f ܗܦ)   ܗܒ ܒܬܘܠ ܘܥܒܕܘܝ ܝܡܢܐ.

121

The Days ܩܘܼܕܗܝ̈ ܕܫܲܒܬܐ

The first day of the week is Sunday. Except Friday (ܥܪܘܼܒܬܐ) and Saturday (ܫܲܒܬܐ), days are formed with numbers and the phrase ܒܫܲܒܐ (in week) where ܒ is pronounced "ܒ' (w). For example, "one" is ܚܲܕ and Sunday is ܚܲܕܒܫܲܒܐ. "Two" is ܬܪܹܝܢ and Monday is ܬܪܹܝܢܒܫܲܒܐ.

"ܝܲܘܡܐ" (day), ܝܲܘܡܐ (or ܝܲܘܡܢܐ) (days) is a masculine noun in Syriac. The following are the days of the week:

Literal	Days	Plural	ܝܲܘܡܢܐ
One in week	Sunday(s)	ܚܲܕܒܫܲܒܐ ؛ ܚܲܕܒܫܲܒܬܐ	ܚܲܕܒܫܲܒܐ
Two in week	Monday(s)	ܬܪܹܝܢܒܫܲܒܐ	ܬܪܹܝܢܒܫܲܒܐ
Three in week	Tuesday(s)	ܬܠܵܬܒܫܲܒܐ	ܬܠܵܬܒܫܲܒܐ
Four in week	Wednesday(s)	ܐܲܪܒܲܥܒܫܲܒܐ	ܐܲܪܒܲܥܒܫܲܒܐ
Five in week	Thursday(s)	ܚܲܡܫܒܫܲܒܐ	ܚܲܡܫܒܫܲܒܐ
	Friday(s)	ܥܪܘܼܒܬܢܐ	ܥܪܘܼܒܬܐ
	Saturday(s), week(s)	ܫܲܒܬܐ	ܫܲܒܬܐ

Pronouncing Days

- to say **on Sunday**, you say ܝܲܘܡܐ proceed the preposition letter ܕ (of) proceed the name of the day:

  ܝܲܘܡܐ ܕܚܲܕܒܫܲܒܐ. (Literal: day of Sunday.)

- To say, **next Tuesday**, you add the preposition letter ܕ proceed the word ܐܵܬܝܐ (next, come) in masculine form:

  ܝܲܘܡܐ ܕܬܠܵܬܒܫܲܒܐ ܕܐܵܬܹܐ.

- To say, **this Friday**, you say ܐܵܗܐ (this "f") proceed the name of the day: ܐܵܗܐ ܥܪܘܼܒܬܐ.

Note: most the time the word ܐܵܗܐ (this) pronounced ܐܵ (silenced the last letter – no vowel ܗ).

122

Also, you can say: ܢܘܡܐ ܕܝܩܘܒܬܐ proceed ܕ (**which**, in this case), proceed ܐܝܠܗ (**is** – in masculine form), proceed ܒ (**ing**, in this case), proceed the verb ܕܐܬܐ (**come**):

ܢܘܡܐ ܕܝܩܘܒܬܐ ܕܐܝܠܗ ܒܐܬܐ.

(**Literal**: The day of Friday which is coming).

Note: The word ܐܝܠܗ (**is**) is in the masculine form because "ܢܘܡܐ" (day) is masculine.

- to say, **on Saturday**, you say it just like you say any day: ܢܘܡܐ ܕܫܒܬܐ.
- to say **next week**, you say, ܫܒܬܐ (**a week**) proceed the preposition letter ܕ (**which**, in this case) precedes the verb ܐܬܝܐ (**next, come**) in feminine form: ܫܒܬܐ ܕܐܬܝܐ (**Literal**: week which next).

Also, you can say, ܫܒܬܐ ܕܐܝܠܗ ܒܐܬܐ (**Literal**: the week which is coming). Here we use ܐܝܠܗ (**is** – in feminine form), because "ܫܒܬܐ" (**week**) is feminine.

More practicing examples:

Sunday is the Lord's day. (**Literal**: Sunday is day of the Lord.)	ܚܕܒܫܒܐ ܐܝܠܗ ܢܘܡܐ ܕܡܪܝܐ.
Last Tuesday I went to San Diego. (**Literal**: I went to San Diego the past day of Tuesday.)	ܘܠܝ ܠܣܢܕܝܢܟܘ ܢܘܡܐ ܕܐܬܠܬܒܫܐ ܕܥܒܪܗ.
Last Friday we had guests in our house.	ܝܩܘܒܬܐ ܕܥܒܪܬܐ ܐܝܬܘܠܢ ܐܪܚܐ ܒܒܝܬܢ.

123

The Months ܝܰܪ̈ܚܶܐ

NOTE: The Syriac year starts with April (ܢܝܣܢ) and ends with March (ܐܕܳܪ). Therefore, the Syriac New Year is April 1ˢᵗ.

April - Originally from ܢܝܣܢܘ in Babylonian and means to start and movement. In Syriac means grass.

ܢܝܣܢ

May - Means the luminance and light.

ܐܺܝܳܪ

June - Means the wheat. The month was named because of its connection with harvest.

ܚܙܺܝܪܳܢ

July - Sumerian word meaning "Son of the Life", were dedicated this month to the god of "Nunn Eb", which was to die and rise from the death again.

ܬܰܡܽܘܙ

August - Syriac word meaning "ripe fruit" and by the Babylonians means "hostility" because of extreme heat.

ܐܳܒ

September: - Originally from Babylonian and it means the screaming and wailing, because they were staying mourning the god "Nunn Eb".

ܐܺܝܠܽܘܠ

October - Means "first fall".

ܬܶܫܪܝ ܩܰܕܡܳܝܐ

November - Means "last fall".

ܬܶܫܪܝ ܐܚܪܳܝܐ

December: - Derived from the constancy and stability in the house because of no work during this month and month of January. First month of no work.

ܟܳܢܘܢ ܩܰܕܡܳܝܐ

January: - See December. Last month of no work.

ܟܳܢܘܢ ܐܚܪܳܝܐ

February: - Means "beating", so named because the severity of the cold and the wind.

ܫܒܳܛ

March: - It is ܐܕܳܪ in Babylonian and means a violent sound caused by storms.

ܐܕܳܪ

Pronouncing Date

ܟܡܘܬ؟ ܐܝܠܗ ܝܘܡܢܐ ܕܝܪܚܐ (What is today's date) "**Literal**: how many in the month is today" it uses to ask about the date.

ܝܪܚܐ (month), ܝܪ̈ܚܐ (months) and the names of all months are in the masculine form.

To read the date in Syriac, first you say the number (in masculine form) proceed by (ܒ "in", and the word ܝܪܚܐ "month") ܒܝܪܚܐ, proceed ܕ (of), then the name of the month.

For example, to say **June 05**, you say:

(**Literal**: five in month of June). ܚܡܫܐ ܒܝܪܚܐ ܕܝܘܢܝ

Also, you can say the date without saying the word month (ܝܪܚܐ) and moving/adding ܒ (in) at the beginning of the month's name. For example, to say September 11, you say ܚܕܥܣܪ ܒܐܝܠܘܠ (**Literal**: 11 in September).

Note: Also, Syriac speakers use the international months' numbers (1 -12) to represent the months. For example, to read 8/10 (August 10), you say: ܥܣܪܐ ܒܝܪܚܐ ܕܬܡܢܝܐ (**Literal**: ten in month of eight).

Pronouncing Full Date (Month, Day, Year)

To read the full date, say the date proceed ܒܫܢܬܐ ܕ "in year of - optional" proceed the year number.

Challenging quiz: read the following dates:

April 12, 1979. ܬܪܥܣܪ ܒܝܪܚܐ ܕܢܝܣܢ ܒܫܢܬܐ ܕܐܠܦܐ ܘܬܫܥܡܐ ܘܫܒܥܝܢ ܘܬܫܥ
(**Literal**: 12 in month of April in year of 1979).

Note, the number ܬܫܥ (9) is in feminine form because ܫܢܬܐ (year) is feminine.

In the following example, omit ܒܫܢܬܐ ܕ (in year of):

October 20, 2007. ܒܥܣܪܝܢ ܒܝܪܚܐ ܕܬܫܪܝܢ ܩܕܡܝܐ ܬܪܝܢ ܐܠܦܐ ܘܫܒܥ.

Did you notice? Even though, we omitted the word ܫܢܬܐ (year) still you need to say the number ܫܒܥ (7) in feminine form because it refers to the year.

Statements:

December is a cold month.	ܝܪܚܐ ܕܟܢܘܢ ܩܕܡܝܐ ܐܝܬܘ ܝܪܚܐ ܩܪܝܪܐ.
I was born in May.	ܐܢܐ ܗܘܝܠܕܝ ܒܝܪܚܐ ܕܐܝܪ.
In April, we celebrate religion and nation holidays.	ܒܚܘܒܐ ܕܝܪܚܐ ܕܢܝܣܢ ܒܢܥܒܕ ܥܐܕܐ ܕܗܝܡܢܘܬܢ ܘܐܘܡܬܢ.
April 1st is our nation new year.	ܚܕ ܒܢܝܣܢ ܐܝܬܘ ܥܐܕܐ ܕܪܝܫܐ ܕܫܢܬܢ.
Thanksgiving's holiday falls in last Thursday of November.	ܥܐܕܐ ܕܬܘܕܝܬܐ ܢܦܠ ܒܝܘܡܐ ܕܚܡܫܒܫܒܐ ܐܚܪܝܐ ܡܢ ܬܫܪܝܢ ܐܚܪܝܐ.
The first 3 Fridays of the next month, I have a job.	ܬܠܬ ܥܪܘܒܬܐ ܩܕܡܝܬܐ ܕܝܪܚܐ ܕܐܬܐ ܐܢܐ ܐܝܬܠܝ ܫܘܓܠܐ.

Vocabulary

Moment	ܪܦܦܐ	Tomorrow	ܨܦܪܐ
Soft	ܪܩܝܩܐ	Evening	ܪܡܫܐ
Minute	ܕܩܝܩܐ or ܩܛܝܢܬܐ	Noon	ܦܠܓܗ ܕܝܘܡܐ
Hour	ܫܥܬܐ	Good	ܛܒܐ
Day	ܝܘܡܐ	The best (good of the good)	ܛܒܐ ܕܛܒܐ
Night	ܠܠܝܐ	Slow down	ܢܝܚܐ ܢܝܚܐ
Week	ܫܒܬܐ	Today	ܐܕܝܘܡ
Month	ܝܪܚܐ	Little by little	ܩܠܝܠܐ ܩܠܝܠܐ
Leap Year	ܫܢܬܐ ܟܒܝܣܬܐ	Track, place	ܫܘܦܐ
Century	ܕܪܐ	Here	ܐܟܐ
Now	ܕܗܐ	Lord	ܡܪܝܐ
Yesterday	ܐܬܡܠܝ	Permission	ܦܣܣܐ

Chapter 5 Exercises

According to the following figure, answer the questions 1 and 2:

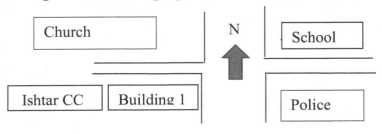

1. Building 1 is to/in the _____ of the Ishtar Cultural Center.

    a. ܢܲܥܡܲܝ   b. ܬܵܘܲܡܵܐ   c. ܠܚܵܕܲܝ   d. ܬܚܵܘܵܐ

2. The location of the school is on the _____ of the intersection.

    a. ܚܘܝܫ ܠܵܕܲܬܵܐ   b. ܚܘܝܫ ܗܲܡܥܵܐ   *east north*

    c. ܠܵܕܲܬܵܐ ܗܲܡܥܵܐ   d. ܠܵܕܲܬܵܐ ܗܲܡܥܵܐ

3. The location of Police is to the _____ of Building 1.

    a. ܠܚܵܕܲܝ   b. ܬܵܘܲܡܵܐ   c. ܢܲܥܡܲܝ   d. ܬܚܵܘܵܐ

4. The location of the Church is on the _____ of the intersection.

    a. ܚܘܝܫ ܠܵܕܲܬܵܐ   b. ܚܘܝܫ ܗܲܡܥܵܐ

    c. ܠܵܕܲܬܵܐ ܗܲܡܥܵܐ   d. ܠܵܕܲܬܵܐ ܗܲܡܥܵܐ

5. Translate the following statements to Syriac.
    a. My brother's house is far from here.
    b. Your socks are on top of the table.
    c. Go up and study!
    d. I need 3lbs of yellow apples.
    e. St. George church is after the school.

6. Translate the following statement to English.

a. ܬܒܝ ܪܒܝܠܗ ܬܘܿܡܗ ܘܦܘܿܕܿܥܡ؛.

b. ܘܕܒ ܗܿܒܬ ܠܠܿܓ̣ܗ ܘܢܘܿܕ؛.

c. ܗܒ ܠܓܿܒ ܡܥܘܿܗܗ ܘܡܗ؛ ܪܒܝܠܗ ܠܢܥܣܒܬ.

d. ܕܝ ܫܘܼܡܘܿܝ ܢܘܿܗܗ ܕܝܥܿܟܗܿ ܬܝܥܝܓܿܗ؛ ܬܢܥܝܥ ܬܘܿܡܥܢ؛.

e. ܬܒܩܣܗ ܘܗܿܟܿܗ؛ ܕܝ ܘܠܕ ܠܢܿܗܿܢ؛.

ܗܘܿܝܪܟ܀

ܐ: ܪܒܡܗ ܥܘܡܣܠܿܩ؛ ܚܒܬܝܓܿܗ ܒܝܟ ܚܿܬܒ؛ܪ؟

ܒ: ܬܪܒܡܗ ܥܘܡܣܠܿܩ؛ ܬܘܿܥܠܒ ܩܪܪܿ؟

ܠ: ܗܿܬܗ؛ ܪܒܝܠܗ ܪܒܓܘܡܿܪ؟

7. **Match the dates:** remember, January is the first month when represent the numerical values and the date format is **dd/mm/yyyy**.

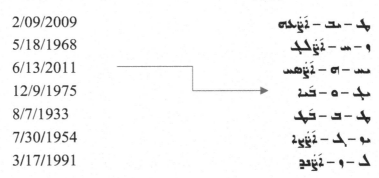

2/09/2009	ܠܬ – ܣܬ – ܬܢܿܝܢܟܗ
5/18/1968	ܘ – ܣ – ܬܢܿܘܠܟܒ
6/13/2011	ܣܒ – ܗ – ܬܢܿܘܗܣ
12/9/1975	ܒܠ – ܘ – ܬܒܬ
8/7/1933	ܠܬ – ܒ – ܬܿܒܠ
7/30/1954	ܒܘ – ܠ – ܬܢܿܝܒ؛
3/17/1991	ܠ – ܘ – ܬܢܿܝܒܕ

Chapter 6

The Basic Grammar ܬܘܪܨ ܡܡܠܠܐ

Learning Objectives

In this chapter, you will:

- learn the hard and soft letters.
- learn the prepositions in Syriac.
- learn the First Person ܦܪܨܘܦܐ ܩܕܡܝܐ , Second Person ܦܪܨܘܦܐ ܬܪܝܢܐ, and Third Person ܦܪܨܘܦܐ ܬܠܝܬܝܐ of:
    - The Subject Pronoun ܚܠܦܫܡܐ
    - Possessive Forms of Nouns
- learn the Syriac Nouns ܫܡܐ
    - Proper nouns ܫܡܐ ܩܢܘܡܝܐ
    - Common nouns ܫܡܐ ܓܘܢܝܐ
    - Collective Nouns ܫܡܐ ܟܢܘܫܝܐ
- Pronominal Prefixes and Suffixes
    - Possessive Forms of Nouns
    - Adjective Possessive
    - Absolute Possessive
- learn the Adjectives. ܫܘܡܗܐ
    - Common Adjective Suffixes in Syriac
    - Determiners in Syriac
        - Articles
        - Demonstratives
            - Adverb
                - **Quantifiers** ܡܢܝܢܐ
                    - Little ܩܠܝܠܐ
                    - Few ܒܨܝܪܐ
                    - Lot (lots, many, large) ܟܒܝܪܐ

- All of it ܟܠܗ (m) ܟܠܗ (f)
- All of them ܟܠܗܘܢ
- No one ܐܢܫ ܠܐ
  (m) ܐܢܫ ܠܐ (f)
- Big ܪܒܐ
- Medium (average, central)
  ܡܨܥܝܐ
- Small ܙܥܘܪܐ

- Time ܙܒܢܐ
- Demonstrative with singular/plural nouns
  o **This** ܗܢܐ (m) ܗܕܐ (f)
    These ܗܠܝܢ
  o **That** ܗܘ (m) ܗܝ (f)
    Those ܗܢܘܢ

- learn the Conjunction ܡܩܦܢܐ
  o And ܘ
  o Or ܐܘ
  o But ܐܠܐ - ܐܠܐ
  o Because ܡܛܠ
- learn the Comparative. ܡܢ
- learn the Every/Each. ܟܠ
- learn the Question Words in Syriac.

The Hard and Soft Letters ܟܬ̈ܐ ܐܬܘܬ̈ܐ ܘ ܩܫܝ̈ܬܐ ܐܬܘܬ̈ܐ

Six are the letters who have soft sound in addition of hard sounds. Hard sound means that the letter keeps its original sound. The letters are ܬ ܟ ܓ ܕ ܦ ܒ.

- To make the hard sound of the letter is by placing a **single dot above** the letter. If a dot is placed above the letter, the letter will have the original sound regardless of the rules below.
- To make the soft sound of the letter is by placing a **single dot below** the letter. Examples:

Book	ܟܬܒܐ	*byrvh*	ܒ
Body	ܦܓܪܐ	*bvgrvduh* Gh	ܓ
Dancer	ܪܩܘܕܐ	*Drkratha* Th	ܕ
Remembrance	ܕܘܟܪܢܐ	*Dv Khvrhanr*	
Wife - Woman	ܒܟܬܐ	*Bakhda* Kh	ܟ
Breath – breath of life	ܢܦܫܐ	*naphsha*	ܦ
Shoulder	ܪܘܫܐ	*rvesha*	
Catholic	ܩܬܘܠܝܩܐ	*Catholitha* Th	ܬ

See **Appendix C** for the hard and soft letters rules and more examples.

Prepositions in Syriac
The prepositions are used to establish a relationship among words (nouns). Examples of this type of relationship:

The Dependent Prepositions
Four Syriac letters also establish this type of the relationship. They are added directly at the beginning of their objects (names) and do not occur independently, and they called *inseparable*. These four letters are ܕܘܟܒ :

At, in, on, by means of.	ܒ
Of, like, as, according to.	ܕ
And.	ܘ
To, for.	ܠ

For example:

By the king	ܒܡܠܟܐ	*beh melka*
Of the king	ܕܡܠܟܐ	*ooh melka*
And the king	ܘܡܠܟܐ	*uh melka*
To the king	ܠܡܠܟܐ	*el melka*

Note: the two prepositions letters, ܒ and ܘ can be added to verb too, ܕܥܒܕ and ܘܥܒܕ. For examples:

What he did was a good job.	ܡܐ ܕܥܒܕܠܗ ܘܗܘܐ ܥܡܠܐ ܛܒܐ.
And she did a nice job.	ܘܥܒܕܠܗ ܥܡܠܐ ܛܒܐ.

See **Appendix D** for more information.

The Independent Prepositions

The majority of Syriac prepositions are words, they stands alone, and can be used with the suffix possessive of the first, second, and third person. See Adjective Possessive section in this chapter for how to use these prepositions in detail with more examples. The word following the preposition is called the object of the prepositions.

By/In	ܒܓܘܗ	*gahweh*	After	ܒܬܪ	*bether*
With	ܥܡ	*em*	Back/Behind	ܒܬܪܗ	*buthruh*
To the Top	ܠܥܠܬܐ	*elyech*	Before	ܩܕܡ	*kam*
Above	ܪܥܠ	*raysha*	Under	ܬܚܬ	*kotha*
From	ܡܢ	*min*	Between	ܒܝܢ	*behleth*

Examples:

Literal: After of the here   After the tree.   *eelana bather*
ܒܬܪ ܕܐܝܠܢܐ.

Back/Behind of the house.   *baytha buthruh*
ܒܬܪܗ ܕܒܝܬܐ.

Before of the house.   *baytha kamit*
ܩܕܡ ܕܒܝܬܐ.

(**Literal**: Under of the rain.)   Under the rain.   *Hmotduir kotha*
ܬܚܬ ܕܡܛܪܐ.

Between the animals.   *hywana beyneth*
ܒܝܢ ܚܝܘܬܐ.

Notice the big dot underneath ܡܢ preposition, this replaces the Zlama Psheeqa vowel (ܡܶܢ). If the big dot is on top of the letter ܡܢ this means *who*, which replaces the Pthaha vowel (ܡܰܢ)

From homeland Beth Nahrain (Iraq).   ܡܢ ܐܬܪܐ ܝܡܐ ܕܒܝܬܢܗܪܝܢ.

Who sent the letter?   ܡܢ ܡܫܘܕܪܗ ܐܓܪܬܐ؟

Note: ܒܝܬܢܗܪܝܢ (Mesopotamia – the land between the two <u>rivers</u>) is the original name of what is known "Iraq" in the present days.

Note: for short, the preposition ܡܢ (from) is pronounced ܡ only and attached at the beginning of the noun. For example, ܡܢ ܒܝܬܐ you can say ܡܒܝܬܐ (from home).

For / To: ܐܠ

The preposition ܐܠ has two meanings depends on its subject. If it follows by noun, it means "**for**". And it means "**to**" if it follows by verb. For example:

tabuli ela suikh li

This shirt is for my dad.   ܐܘܝܐ ܣܩܡܐ ܝܠܗ ܐܠ ܒܒܝ.

I want to sleep (m).   ܐܢܐ ܒܥܝܐ ܐܠ ܕܡܟܝ.

dunhem te kechu li

Notice that ܐܠ sound is like the sound of ܠ letter where is used with verb.

The Subject Pronoun ܫܲܠܝܼܛܵܢܵܐ

First Person ܦܲܪܨܘܿܦܵܐ ܩܲܕ݇ܡܵܝܵܐ

I ܐܵܢܵܐ *[handwritten: anna]*

used for <u>both masculine and feminine</u> first-person speaker.

Example: *[handwritten: Colin eyling shimmi ... anna]*

ܐܵܢܵܐ ܫܹܡܝܼ ܒܝܼܠܹܗ ܡܲܪܘܿܓܹܐ.

(My name is Marougee – **Literal:** I my name is Marougee.)

Note: Most the time the pronoun "ܐܵܢܵܐ" is omitted and only used first person possessive with the noun. For example, we can say: ܫܹܡܝܼ ܒܝܼܠܹܗ ܝܲܩܘܿܒ (My name is Yaqoo "Jacob"), without saying "ܐܵܢܵܐ". "ܐܵܢܵܐ" is used for emphasizing.

I am   m: ܐܵܢܵܐ ܝܘܸܢ. *[handwritten: eewin anna]*
       f: ܐܵܢܵܐ ܝܘܲܢ. *[handwritten: eewon anna]*

Example: I am Syriac.   m: ܐܵܢܵܐ ܝܘܸܢ ܣܘܼܪܵܝܵܐ. or ܝܘܸܢ ܣܘܼܪܵܝܵܐ. *[handwritten: Soorya / Sooryaya]*
       f: ܐܵܢܵܐ ܝܘܲܢ ܣܘܼܪܲܝܬܵܐ. ܝܘܲܢ ܣܘܼܪܲܝܬܵܐ.

Note: ܣܘܼܪܵܝܵܐ (m) and ܣܘܼܪܲܝܬܵܐ (f), means (Chaldean, Assyrian, Syriac.

Am I?   m: ܝܘܸܢ ܐܵܢܵܐ؟
        f: ܝܘܲܢ ܐܵܢܵܐ؟

[handwritten: drywena]

Example: Am I crazy?   m: ܝܘܸܢ ܐܵܢܵܐ ܕܝܼܘܵܢܵܐ؟ *[handwritten: drywena]*
        f: ܝܘܲܢ ܐܵܢܵܐ ܕܝܼܘܲܢܬܵܐ؟ *[handwritten: drywenta]*

I am not: it is by adding ܠܵܐ before "am". *[handwritten: anna laywen]*

   m: ܐܵܢܵܐ ܠܵܐ ܝܘܸܢ ܒܣܝܼܡܵܐ (m), for short, ܐܵܢܵܐ ܠܲܝܘܸܢ.
   f: ܐܵܢܵܐ ܠܵܐ ܝܘܲܢ ܒܣܝܼܡܬܵܐ (f), for short, ܐܵܢܵܐ ܠܲܝܘܲܢ.

Example: I am not doing good *[handwritten: anna laywen towa]*

   m: ܠܲܝܘܸܢ ܛܵܘܵܐ. or ܐܵܢܵܐ ܠܲܝܘܸܢ ܛܵܘܵܐ. *[handwritten: anna laywen]*
   f: ܠܲܝܘܲܢ ܛܵܘܬܵܐ. ܐܵܢܵܐ ܠܲܝܘܲܢ ܛܵܘܬܵܐ. *[handwritten: towta]*

Literal: I am not good.

[handwritten right margin: only use anna to emphasize, point, etc.]

[handwritten bottom: do not need anna]

134

I was
- m: *winwahanna* / *whenwah anna* [Syriac]
- f: [Syriac]

beyth *winwah anna*

Example: I was at home at this time.
- m: [Syriac]
- f: [Syriac]

anna winwah **Literal**: I was in home in this time.

Was I?
- m: *anna winwah* [Syriac]
- f: [Syriac]

Example: Was I there?
- m: *toma* [Syriac]
- f: *toma* [Syriac]

I was not - It is by adding [Syriac] before "was".
- m: *lah* [Syriac]
- f: *lah* [Syriac]

We — *achne* [Syriac]
We are. — *eewooch achne* [Syriac]
Are we? — *achne eewooch* [Syriac]
We are not. — [Syriac], for short [Syriac]. *achne laywooch* / *lah*

They are the same for both masculine and feminine.

Example:
We are from Michigan. *in Michigan min eewooch achne* [Syriac]
Are we from Iraq? *nahren min bith achne eewooch* [Syriac]
We are not from Iraq. *nahren min bith laywooch achne* [Syriac]

We were — *wah wuch achne* [Syriac]
It is the same for both masculine and feminine.

Example:
We were in Canada last month. *la hish bit yun canada wah wuch achne* [Syriac]
achne wah wuch **Literal**: we were in Canada the pass month.

Were we? [Syriac]

Example: Were we at his wedding? *wlihnveleh* [Syriac]

135

We were not ܠܲܝܬ *lah* ܟ݂ܘܐ ܗܘܵܐ ܗܘܵܐ

It is by adding ܠܵܐ before "were".

Note: in the plural form, pronouns are the same for both masculine and feminine in the first, second and the third person forms.

Second Person ܦܲܪܨܘܿܦܵܐ ܕ ܬܲܪ̈ܝܵܢܵܐ

You
- m: ܐܲܚܝܸܬ *ahyit* / ܐܲܢ݇ܬ *atyet*
- f: ܐܲܢ݇ܬܝ

You are.
- m: ܐܝܼܘܸܬ *eewit* ܐܲܢ݇ܬ
- f: ܐܝܼܘܲܬ *eewet* ܐܲܢ݇ܬܝ

Example: You are from Michigan.
- m: ܐܲܢ݇ܬ ܗܘܸܬ ܡܸܢ ܡܝܼܫܝܼܟܲܢ *michigan* *min*
- f: ܐܲܢ݇ܬܝ ܗܘܵܬ ܡܸܢ ܡܝܼܫܝܼܟܲܢ *michigan*

Are you?
- m: ܗܘܸܬ ܐܲܢ݇ܬ؟ *ryet* *eewit*
- f: ܗܘܵܬ ܐܲܢ݇ܬܝ؟ *ryet* *eewet*

You are not
- m: ܐܲܢ݇ܬ ܠܵܐ ܗܘܸܬ. *lah* or ܐܲܢ݇ܬ ܠܲܝܬ. *leynit*
- f: ܐܲܢ݇ܬܝ ܠܵܐ ܗܘܵܬ. *lah* or ܐܲܢ݇ܬܝ ܠܲܝܬ. *leynet*

Example: You are not Arab.
- m: ܐܲܢ݇ܬ ܠܵܐ ܗܘܸܬ ܥܲܪܒܵܝܵܐ. *arabaya*
- f: ܐܲܢ݇ܬܝ ܠܵܐ ܗܘܵܬ ܥܲܪܒܵܝܬܵܐ.

You were.
- m: ܐܲܢ݇ܬ ܗܘܵܐ ܗܘܹܝܬ. *witwah* *wet*
- f: ܐܲܢ݇ܬܝ ܗܘܵܐ ܗܘܹܝܬ. *wetwahwah*

Example: you were there playing cards (2nd f).
ܐܲܢ݇ܬܝ ܗܘܵܐ ܗܘܹܝܬ ܬܵܡܵܐ ܡܫܲܚܠܘܿܦܹܐ ܘܲܪ̈ܩܹܐ.
eyit *wah* *wet* *wahint* *enlawèh* / *lbsyah*

Were you?
- m: ܗܘܵܐ ܗܘܹܝܬ ܐܲܢ݇ܬ؟ *ayt* *Wah* *wit* *wit*
- f: ܗܘܵܐ ܗܘܹܝܬ ܐܲܢ݇ܬܝ؟

You were not.
- m: ܐܲܢ݇ܬ ܠܵܐ ܗܘܵܐ ܗܘܹܝܬ.
- f: ܐܲܢ݇ܬܝ ܠܵܐ ܗܘܵܐ ܗܘܹܝܬ.

136 *lah*

(handwritten at top) lebalgweynn lwatann lwrt lwab lah ay:t

Example: You were not there last night (**2nd m**).

(Syriac) ܐܢ̄ܬ ܠܵܐ ܝܘܼܬ ܬܵܡܵܐ ܒܠܲܝܠܹܐ *(handwritten)* achtoon achtoo

You (p)	ܐܢ̄ܬܘܿܢ also ܐܚܬܘܿܢ ← more used
You are (p).	ܝ̄ܬܘܿܢ ܐܢ̄ܬܘܿܢ *(handwritten)* eewrtoon achdoon
Are you? (p)	ܝ̄ܬܘܿܢ ܐܢ̄ܬܘܿܢ? *(handwritten)* achtoon eewrtoon
You are not (p).	ܐܢ̄ܬܘܿܢ ܠܹܐ ܝ̄ܬܘܿܢ *(handwritten)* lrywatoon achdoon
You were (p).	ܐܢ̄ܬܘܿܢ ܗ̄ܘܵܘ *(handwritten)* wah woóten achteen
Were you?	ܗ̄ܘܵܘ ܝ̄ܬܘܿܢ? *(handwritten)* toon ech witenweb
You were not (p).	ܐܢ̄ܬܘܿܢ ܠܵܐ ܗ̄ܘܵܘ. *(handwritten)* lah

They are the same for masculine and feminine.

Example:

(handwritten) surgee lrywootan achtoon

You are Syriac (2nd p). ܐܢ̄ܬܘܿܢ ܝܘܿܬܘܿܢ ܣܘܼܪ̈ܝܵܝܹܐ.

You are not from Michigan (2nd p). ܐܢ̄ܬܘܿܢ ܠܹܐ ܝܘܿܬܘܿܢ ܡܸܢ ܡܸܫܸܟ.

(handwritten) mrchgun mn lrywrloon

Kheethya Persopa

Third Person

ܩܢܘܡܐ ܕܬܠܬܐ

He — *ahwoo* — ܗܘ

He is. — ܗܘ ܝܠܗ — *Gawoo eelih*

Is He? — ܗܘ ܝܠܗ? — *awoo eelih*

He is not. — ܗܘ ܠܐ ܝܠܗ or ܗܘ ܠܝܬܠܗ — *laylih*

He was. — ܗܘ ܗܘܐ ܗܘܐ, also ܗܘ ܗܘܐ ܗܘܐ — *awoo way wah* or

Was he? — ܗܘܐ ܗܘܐ ܗܘ? — *awoo wah way*

He was not. — ܗܘ ܠܐ ܗܘܐ ܗܘܐ.

She — ܗܝ — *ahyee* / *ih*

She is. — ܗܝ ܝܠܗ. — *eeleh ahyee*

Is she? — ܗܝ ܝܠܗ?

She is not. — ܗܝ ܠܐ ܝܠܗ or ܗܝ ܠܝܬܠܗ — *laylah* / *ih*

She was. — ܗܝ ܗܘܐ ܗܘܐ. — *wah wah*

Was she? — ܗܘܐ ܗܘܐ ܗܝ?

She was not. — ܗܝ ܠܐ ܗܘܐ ܗܘܐ. — *lah*

Example:

He is a teacher. — ܗܘ ܝܠܗ ܡܠܦܢܐ. — *melpana eelih awoo*

She is a teacher. — ܗܝ ܝܠܗ ܡܠܦܢܬܐ. — *Mrpaneta eeleh ahyee*

They — ܐܢܝ — *any*

They are. — ܐܢܝ ܝܠܗ. — *eelah any*

Are they? — ܐܢܝ ܝܠܗ?

They are not — ܐܢܝ ܠܐ ܝܠܗ or ܐܢܝ ܠܝܬܠܗ. — *layla*

They were. — ܐܢܝ ܗܘܐ ܗܘܐ. — *wah wah any*

Were they? — ܐܢܝ ܗܘܐ ܗܘܐ?

They were not. — ܐܢܝ ܠܐ ܗܘܐ ܗܘܐ. — *lah*

Example: They are Telkeypners. — ܐܢܝ ܝܠܗ ܬܠܟܦܢܝܐ. — *telkepnyeh eelah any*

138

Note: To denote a person to which city or area originally is from, you take the name of the city or area and add ـنـَيـَا for male, ـيـَـثـَا for female, and ـنـَيـَا (plural). For example, from ܐܲܠܩܘܿܫ (City of Alqosh) you form: Alqoshiner.

p: ܐܲܠܩܘܿܫܢܵܝܹܐ   f: ܐܲܠܩܘܿܫܢܵܝܬܵܐ *nzytha*   m: ܐܲܠܩܘܿܫܢܵܝܵܐ *naya*

Note: the sound of these two words is very similar: ܐܵܢܝܼ (they) and ܐܵܢܝ (these).

Examples:

I am Telkeypner but I am from America (1st m)

ܐܵܢܵܐ ܐܝܼܘܸܢ ܬܸܠܟܹܦܢܵܝܵܐ ܒܲܣ ܐܵܢܵܐ ܐܝܼܘܸܢ ܡܸܢ ܐܲܡܹܪܝܼܟܵܐ.

You are Alqoshiners.   ܐܲܚܬܘܿܢ ܐܝܼܬܘܿܢܘܿܢ ܐܲܠܩܘܿܫܢܵܝܹܐ.

They are not studying.   ܐܵܢܝܼ ܠܹܐ ܒܵܠܸܕ ܩܵܪܹܝܢ.

I am a student.   ܐܵܢܵܐ ܐܝܼܘܸܢ ܝܵܠܘܿܦܵܐ.

She is my friend, and she is from Canada.   ܐܵܗܵ ܐܝܼܠܵܗ ܚܲܒܪܬܝܼ ܘܐܝܼܠܵܗ ܡܸܢ ܟܲܢܲܕܵܐ.

I am Syriac and Christian.   ܐܵܢܵܐ ܐܝܼܘܸܢ ܣܘܼܪܝܵܝܵܐ ܘܡܫܝܼܚܵܝܵܐ.

Wenshehiyth   *soorytha*   *eewrumna*

The Syriac Nouns ܫܡܗܐ

Syriac noun always has a gender. In other word, there is no "no-gender" in Syriac. Syriac nouns can be a singular or plural in number. Unlike English language, Syriac nouns do not need to capitalize the first letter of the noun, because there are no capital letters in Syriac.

Proper Noun ܫܡܐ ܡܫܘܕܥܐ

The proper nouns are the names of specific individuals. The proper name indicates only ONE person or thing and it does not need to be linked to another name. For Example:

Persons: person proper noun is masculine if the name is for a male, and it is feminine if the name is for a female:

Jesus	ܝܫܘܥ
Mary	ܡܪܝܡ
Yaqoo	ܝܥܩܘܒ

Places: Most cities names are in feminine form:

Michigan (f):	ܡܝܫܟ	*michigan mmwch*
Nineveh (f):	ܢܝܢܘܐ	
Babylon(f):	ܒܒܝܠ	*babel*
Mountain (m):	ܛܘܪܐ	*toorah*

For example: Nohadra's mountain: ܛܘܪܐ ܕܢܘܗܕܪܐ.

"**Literal**" Mountain *of Nohadra*[6].

Things:

Radio (m): ܩܠܐ ܢܩܠܐ

For example: Chaldeans Voice: ܩܠܐ ܢܩܠܐ ܕܟܠܕܝܐ.

"**Literal**" *Radio of Chaldeans.*

TV (m): ܩܠܐ ܣܝܘܦܐ

For example: Ashur TV ܩܠܐ ܣܝܘܦܐ ܕܐܫܘܪ.

The plural forms of proper nouns are uncommon, not because there is any grammatical restriction on them, but because we rarely need to use them. For example: **We have three Mariams.** ܐܝܬܠܢ ܬܠܬ ܡܪܝܡܐ.

---

[6] Nohadra is "Duhok, Iraq"

Common Noun ܫܡܐ ܟܘܢܝܐ

The common nouns are names of categories. The common noun in Syriac ends with ܐ (Alap) proceed with ܳ (Sqapa). For example:

		Plural	**Singular**
Persons:			
	Girl:	ܒ݂ܢܵܬ݂ܹܐ burnatha	ܒ݂ܪܵܬ݂ܐ bvata
	Mom:	ܝܸܡܵܬ݂ܹܐ yimatha	ܝܸܡܵܐ yima
	Teacher (m):	ܡܲܠܦܵܢܹܐ melpaneh	ܡܲܠܦܵܢܵܐ melpana
	Teacher (f):	ܡܲܠܦܵܢܝܵܬ݂ܹܐ melpanyatha	ܡܲܠܦܵܢܝܼܬ݂ܐ melpaneetha
	Angel (m):	ܡܲܠܲܐܟ݂ܹܐ melakheh	ܡܲܠܲܐܟ݂ܵܐ melakha
Places:			
	House (m):	ܒܵܬ݂ܹܐ behteh	ܒܲܝܬ݂ܐ baytha
	Mountain (m):	ܛܘܼܪܹܐ tooreh	ܛܘܼܪܵܐ tooran
	City (f):	ܡܕ݂ܝܼܢܵܬ݂ܹܐ Veenatha	ܡܕ݂ܝܼܢ݂ܬ݂ܐ Veetan
Things:			
	Lion:	ܐܲܪܝܵܘܵܬ݂ܹܐ Qryewatha	ܐܲܪܝܵܐ arya
	Wine (m):	ܚܲܡܪܵܢܹܐ Kchranvieh	ܚܲܡܪܵܐ Kchamra
	Pencil (m):	ܩܲܢܝܹܐ Kenyeh	ܩܲܢܝܐ Kanya
	Fire (m):	ܢܘܼܪܹܐ newrih	ܢܘܼܪܵܐ newrah

Ideas: Physically you cannot see, touch, taste, smell, or hear (abstract). Most have no plural form.

		Plural	**Singular**
	Respect (m):	ܐܝܼܩܵܪܹܐ eekarih	ܐܝܼܩܵܪܵܐ eekara
	Love (m):	ܚܘܼܒܹܐ hobeh	ܚܘܼܒܵܐ hoba
	Motherhood (f):	------	ܝܸܡܘܼܬ݂ܐ yemootha
	Fatherhood (f):	------	ܒܲܒܘܼܬ݂ܐ babootha
	Brotherhood (f):	------	ܐܲܚܘܼܬ݂ܐ hawootha
	Humanity (f):	------	ܢܵܫܘܼܬ݂ܐ nashootha

141

Collective Noun ܫܡܐ ܟܢܘܫܝܐ

Collective nouns refer to groups of people. It can be either singular or plural, but usually used in the singular.

Audience (m): ܟܢܫܐ

Class (m): ܨܦܐ Shipa

The class is outside. ܨܦܐ ܐܝܠܗ ܒܪܝܐ.

library: ee shipa

People (m): ܥܡܡܐ amma

The Syriac people has a rich culture. ܥܡܡܐ ܣܘܪܝܝܐ ܐܝܬܠܗ ܡܪܕܘܬܐ ܥܬܝܪܬܐ.

Note: there is no definite article "**the**" or indefinite article "**a/an**" in Syriac.

Pronominal Prefixes and Suffixes

In the last section, we studied the subjective (we, he, she, they) independent personal pronouns. In this section will study pronouns that can be either possessive (our, his, her, their), or objective (us, him, her, them). In Syriac, these possessive and objective pronouns appear as suffixes on nouns, prepositions, and the definite direct object marker and they called pronominal prefixes and suffixes.

Possessive Forms of Nouns

In Syriac, unlike English, does not have the "inflectional possessive" or the "of possessive" as two different types of possessive. In fact, both of these types are in one form in Syriac, which is by using the prefix (preposition) letter ܕ, by simply adding ܕ before the second noun. For example:

Mariam's house. ܒܝܬܐ ܕܡܪܝܡ.

"**Literal**" House of Mariam.

The Bible is the Lord's book. ܐܘܢܓܠܝܘܢ ܐܝܠܗ ܟܬܒܐ ܕܡܪܝܐ.

"**Literal**" The Bible is book of the Lord.

Shooshan is Yosip's wife. ܫܘܫܢ ܐܝܠܗ ܒܟܬܐ ܕܝܘܣܦ.

"**Literal**" Shooshan is wife of Yosip.

Adjective Possessive

The possessive for first, second, and third person is by using suffix endings to the noun. Suffixes are not words. They are groups of letters added to the end of the nouns.

First Person ܦܪܨܘܦܐ ܩܕܡܝܐ

Possessive is the same for masculine and feminine for first person with the following suffix for individual and group.

Individual: Simply drop the last letter ܐ and change the vowel ܵ (Sqapa) from the preceding letter to suffix ܝ (Hwassa) vowel.

Example:

My name	ܫܡܝ	ܫܡܐ
My dad	ܒܒܝ	ܒܒܐ
My mom	ܝܡܝ	ܝܡܐ
My "female" teacher	ܡܠܦܢܝܬܝ	ܡܠܦܢܝܬܐ
In me/by me	ܒܓܘܝ	ܒܓܘܐ

Also study the following examples:

My names	ܫܡܗܝ
My fathers	ܒܒܘܗܬܝ
My mothers	ܝܡܘܗܬܝ
My teachers	ܡܠܦܢܢܐܝ

Group: Simply replace the last letter ܐ with the suffix ܢ (**noon** - final form) letter and change the ܵ (Sqapa) vowel on preceding letter to ܲ (**Pthaha**) vowel.

Example:

Our house:	ܒܝܬܢ	ܒܝܬܐ
Our grandfather:	ܣܒܢ	ܣܒܐ
Our mom:	ܝܡܢ	ܝܡܐ
Our teacher:	ܡܠܦܢܢ	ܡܠܦܢܐ
with us	ܥܡܢ	ܥܡ

Study the following example:

Our houses	ܒ̈ܬܢ
Our grandfathers	ܣܒ̈ܬܢ
Our mothers	ܝܡ̈ܬܢ
Our teachers	ܡܠ̈ܦܢܬܢ

Note: ܒܝܬܐ also means "family". For example: Ilya's family:

"**Literal**: house of Ilya". ܒܝܬܐ ܕܐܠܝܐ .

Second Person   ܦܪܨܘܦܐ ܬܪܝܢܐ

INDIVIDUAL

a. **For male speaker**: replace the last letter ܐ with the ܟ (kh sound) letter and change the vowel ܵ (Sqapa) to ܘ (Rwassa) vowel on the preceding letter.

b.   **For feminine speaker**, replace the last letter ܐ with the suffix ܟܝ (kh sound, ܝ silent) letters.

Example:		2ⁿᵈ m: Your sister	ܚܬܘܟ
Sister	ܚܬܐ	2ⁿᵈ f: Your sister	ܚܬܟܝ
Brother	ܐܚܘܢܐ	2ⁿᵈ m: Your brother	ܐܚܘܢܘܟ
		2ⁿᵈ f: Your brother	ܐܚܘܢܟܝ
		2ⁿᵈ m: Your daughter	ܒܪܬܘܟ
Daughter, girl	ܒܪܬܐ	2ⁿᵈ f: Your daughter	ܒܪܬܟܝ
		2ⁿᵈ m:	ܡܕܪܫܬܘܟ
School	ܡܕܪܫܬܐ	2ⁿᵈ f:	ܡܕܪܫܬܟܝ

Study the following examples:

	2ⁿᵈ F	2ⁿᵈ M
Your sisters	ܚܬ̈ܘܬܟܝ	ܚܬ̈ܘܬܘܟ
Your brothers	ܐܚ̈ܘܢܘܬܟܝ	ܐܚ̈ܘܢܘܬܘܟ
Your daughters	ܒܢ̈ܬܟܝ	ܒܢ̈ܬܘܟ

144

Group

It is the same for masculine and feminine. Simply, replace the last letter ܐ with the suffix ܟ݂ܘܢ (khoon) letters and change the vowel Ọ (Sqapa) to ọ̇ (Rwahha) vowel on the preceding letter.

Examples:

Country: ܐܬܪܐ   Your country ܐܬܪܘܟ݂ܘܢ

Village: ܡܬܐ   Your village ܡܬܘܟ݂ܘܢ

Study the following the examples:

Your countries   ܐܬܪܘܬ݂ܘܟ݂ܘܢ

Your villages   ܡܬܘܬ݂ܘܟ݂ܘܢ

Third Person   ܦܪܨܘܦܐ ܬܠܝܬܝܐ

Individual

a. **For masculine**: replace the last letter ܐ with the suffix ܗ and change the vowel Ọ (Sqapa) to Ọ (Zlama Qishya) vowel on the preceding letter.

b. **For feminine**: replace the last letter ܐ with the suffix ܗ̇ (ܗ and dot above it) letter.

Note: ܗ̇ (ܗ and dot above it), this means possessive for feminine in Singular form.

Examples:

Book   ܟܬܒܐ

    His book: ܟܬܒܗ

    Her book: ܟܬܒܗ̇

Son, boy   ܒܪܘܢܐ

    His son: ܒܪܘܢܗ

    Her son: ܒܪܘܢܗ̇

Study the following examples:

His books: ܟܬܒܬܗ   Her books: ܟܬܒܬܗ̇

His sons: ܒܢܘܢܗ   Her sons: ܒܢܘܢܗ̇

Group

It is the same for masculine and feminine. Simply, replace the last letter ܐ with the suffix ܗܘܢ (where ܗ is silent in the most Syriac dialects).

Examples:

Grandmother, old woman:	Their grandmother	ܢܲܢܬܗܘܢ	ܢܲܢܬܐ
Uncle – mother's side:	Their uncle	ܚܵܠܗܘܢ	ܚܵܠܐ
Aunt – mother's side:	Their aunt	ܚܵܠܬܗܘܢ	ܚܵܠܬܐ
Uncle – father's side:	Their uncle	ܥܲܡܗܘܢ	ܥܲܡܐ
Aunt – father's side:	Their aunt	ܥܲܡܬܗܘܢ	ܥܲܡܬܐ

Study the following examples:

Their grandmothers	ܢܲܢܬܵܬ̈ܗܘܢ	Their uncles	ܚܵܠܵܘܵܬ̈ܗܘܢ
Their aunts	ܚܵܠܵܬ̈ܗܘܢ	Their uncles	ܥܲܡܵܘܵܬ̈ܗܘܢ
Their aunts	ܥܲܡܵܬ̈ܗܘܢ		

Note: In Syriac, there are terms which distinguish a maternal uncle from a paternal uncle. On the father's side, we say ܥܲܡܐ for "uncle." And we say ܚܵܠܐ on mother's side.

Absolute Possessive

This type of possessive is a word, which can used to give the meaning of the possessive just like in English.

First Person   ܩܲܕܡܵܝܐ ܕܝ ܢܘܼܩܙܐ

Mine (M & F):	ܕܝܼܝܼ
Ours:	ܕܝܼܢ

Examples:

This book is mine.   ܐܵܗܐ ܟܬܵܒ݂ܐ ܐܝܼܠܹܗ ܕܝܼܝܼ.

Your house is big, but not as big as ours.

ܒܲܝܬܵܘܟ݂ܘܢ ܐܝܼܠܹܗ ܪܲܒܵܐ، ܐܝܼܢܵܐ ܠܹܐܝܠܹܗ ܗܲܕ ܪܲܒܵܐ ܡܼܢ ܕܝܼܢ.

Second Person ܩܪ̈ܝܘܦ ܗܕ ܗܒ̈ܢܐ

	m:		ܕܝܠܘܟ
Yours	f:		ܕܝܠܢܟ
	p:		ܕܝܠܘܟܘܢ

Examples:

My car is not working, can I take yours? (1st m to 2nd f)

ܗܢܕܟܒ ܠܝܠܗ ܚܩܠܢܐ، ܐܝܠܢܐ ܕܥܡܠܝ ܕܝܠܢܟ؟

There was a big number of people in your wedding. (2nd p).

ܐܝܗܘܐܐ ܚܕ ܡܢܝܢܐ ܪܒܐ ܕܐܢܫܐ ܓܢܠܘܐܟ ܕܝܠܘܟܘܢ.

Third Person ܩܪ̈ܝܘܦ ܗܠܝܟܐ

His	ܕܝܠܗ
Hers	ܕܝܠܗ
Thiers	ܕܝܠܗܝ

Example:

I did not have my textbook for Syriac class, so Ashur lent me his.

ܐܢܐ ܠܐ ܐܝܬܗܘܐܠܝ ܟܬܒܐ ܕܐܗܘܕܝ، ܘܐܘܕܝ ܐܥܒܕ ܚܡܢܘܠܝ ܚܕܐ ܕܝܠܗ.

147

Challenging Quiz: fill in the blank with the proper noun possessive using the words between the parentheses. The answer to the first is given as example.

He is your nephew (sister's side – **2nd m**). ܗܘ ܐܝܠܗ ܒܪܐ ܕܚܬܘܟ (ܚܬܐ).

She is your niece (brother's side – **2nd f**). ܗܝ ܐܝܠܗ ܒܪܬܐ ܕ--------(ܐܚܘܢܐ).

Shamiran is your daughter in law (**2nd f**). ܫܡܝܪܢ ܐܝܠܗ--------(ܟܠܬܐ).

He is your son in law (**2nd m**). ܗܘ ܐܝܠܗ---------------(ܚܬܢܐ).

Yaqoo is your son in law (2nd p). ܝܥܩܘܒ ܐܝܠܗ----------(ܚܬܢܐ).

Ashur is their son in law. ܐܫܘܪ ܐܝܠܗ----(ܚܬܢܐ).

Peter is your sister in law's husband (**2nd m**) ܦܛܪܘܣ ܐܝܠܗ----(ܝܒܡܐ).

Sargon, your grandson (**2nd f**). ܣܪܓܘܢ،------------(ܢܘܟܕܐ).

Matthew, your friend (**2nd m**). ܡܬܝ،---------------(ܚܒܪܐ).

Murdoch , her boyfriend. ܡܪܕܘܟ،----------------(ܚܒܪܐ).

Mariam, his girlfriend. ܡܪܝܡ،----------------(ܚܒܪܬܐ).

Your teacher, Thomas (**2nd f**). ------------، (ܡܠܦܢܐ) ܬܐܘܡܐ.

Absolute Possessive

It is hers. ܐܝܠܗ ----------------.

Is this yours? (2nd p) ܐܝܠܗ ܗܕܐ ----------------؟

My pen will not work, can I borrow yours? (1st f to 2nd m)

ܦܫܝ ܠܝܬܠܗ ܥܒܕܐ، ܐܡܪܬ ܕܫܩܠܢ ---------؟

This cross is beautiful, is this mine? ܗܕܐ ܨܠܝܒܐ ܐܝܠܗ ܫܦܝܪܐ، ܐܝܠܗ ܗܕܐ ----؟

The Adjectives ܫܘܡ̈ܗܐ

The adjective indicates the type and status of the noun and needs to link with it, for example:

Adjective	Plural	Feminine	Masculine
Sweet	ܚܠܝ̈ܐ	ܚܠܝܬܐ	ܚܠܝܐ
Bitter	ܡܪܝܪ̈ܐ	ܡܪܝܪܬܐ	ܡܪܝܪܐ
Big	ܪ̈ܒܐ	ܪܒܬܐ	ܪܒܐ
Small	ܙܥܘܪ̈ܐ	ܙܥܘܪܬܐ	ܙܥܘܪܐ

Adjectives must agree with nouns in gender and number. For example, ܒܝܬܐ is a masculine, to say "big house", we say ܒܝܬܐ ܪܒܐ, but when we want to say, "big hand", ܐܝܕܐ (hand) is feminine, we say: ܐܝܕܐ ܪܒܬܐ, and "big houses" we say: ܒ̈ܬܐ ܪ̈ܒܐ.

Sometimes we use two or more adjectives together:

Sargon has a nice new house. ܣܪܓܘܢ ܐܝܬܠܗ ܚܕ ܒܝܬܐ ܚܠܝܐ ܘܚܕܬܐ.

In the sitting room there is a beautiful large heavy wooden table.
ܒܓܘܐ ܕܡܘܬܒܐ ܕܐܝܬܒܬܐ ܐܝܬܝ ܚܕ ܦܬܘܪܐ ܘܝܩܘܪܐ ܘܩܝܣܢܐ.

- **Adjectives like:**

	Plural	Feminine	Masculine
New	ܚܕ̈ܬܐ	ܚܕܬܬܐ	ܚܕܬܐ
Heavy	ܝܩܘܪ̈ܐ	ܝܩܘܪܬܐ	ܝܩܘܪܐ
Wooden	ܩܝܣܢ̈ܐ	ܩܝܣܝܢܝܬܐ	ܩܝܣܢܐ

they are fact adjectives. They give us objective information about something (age ܥܘܡܪܐ, color ܓܘܢܐ, etc.).

- **Adjectives like:**

Beautiful	ܫܲܦܝܼܪܵܐ	ܫܲܦܝܼܪܹܐ	ܫܲܦܝܼܪܬܵܐ
Cute	ܚܠܝܼܨܵܐ	ܚܠܝܼܨܹܐ	ܚܠܝܼܨܬܵܐ

they are opinion adjectives. They tell us what someone thinks of something. Also, we sue adjectives after:

Feel ܕܵܐܹܫ (m), ܕܵܝܫܵܐ (f) , Do you feel tired? ܩܵܕܝܼܫܹܐ ܕܝܼܡܣܘܼܦܹܐ ܝܠܘܼܟ݂?

Smell ܪܵܝܚܵܐ for m and f, Food smells good. ܪܹܝܚܹܗ ܕܝܼܢܹܗ ܛܵܒ݂ܵܐ.

Taste ܛܵܥܡܵܐ for m and f, This tea tastes strong.

ܛܲܥܡܵܐ ܕܝܼܘܵܝܹܐ ܗܵܘ ܒܝܼܠܹܗ ܫܲܦܝܼܪܵܐ.

Literal: The taste of this tea is strong.

Common Adjective Suffixes in Syriac

In previous section, we learned the pronominal prefixes and suffixes. There are other suffixes added to the noun to converted to an adjective. In this section we will learn these suffixes.

- Suffix ܝܵܐ - is by adding ܝܵܐ at the end:

Examples:	**Also you may say**: every (ܟܘܿܕ)		
ܟܘܿܕ ܝܵܘܡܵܐ	Daily	ܝܵܘܡܵܝܹܐ
ܟܘܿܕ ܫܵܒ݂ܬ݂ܵܐ	Weekly	ܫܵܒ݂ܬ݂ܵܝܹܐ
ܟܘܿܕ ܝܲܪܚܵܐ	Monthly	ܝܲܪܚܵܝܹܐ
ܟܘܿܕ ܫܹܢܬ݂ܵܐ	Yearly	ܫܹܢܬ݂ܵܝܹܐ

- Suffix ܢܵ / ܝܬܵܐ – is by replacing the final letter ܐ with ܢܵ for masculine, and ܝܬܵܐ for feminine:

	Feminine	Masculine		
Rainy	ܡܸܛܪ̈ܵܢܝܬܵܐ	ܡܸܛܪ̈ܵܢܵܐ	Rain	ܡܸܛܪܵܐ
Snowy	ܬܲܠܓܵܢܝܬܵܐ	ܬܲܠܓܵܢܵܐ	Snow	ܬܲܠܓܵܐ
Sunny	ܫܸܡܫܵܢܝܬܵܐ	ܫܸܡܫܵܢܵܐ	Sun	ܫܸܡܫܵܐ
Oily	ܡܸܫܚܵܢܝܬܵܐ	ܡܸܫܚܵܢܵܐ	Oil	ܡܸܫܚܵܐ
Salty	ܡܸܠܚܵܢܵܐ/ܡܸܠܚܵܢܝܬܵܐ	ܡܸܠܚܵܢܵܐ/ܡܸܠܚܵܢܵܐ	Salt	ܡܸܠܚܵܐ
Watery	ܡܵܝܵܢܵܐ/ܡܵܝܵܢܝܬܵܐ	ܡܵܝܵܢܵܐ	Water	ܡܲܝܵܐ

- Suffix ܐܘܬܵܐ – is by replacing the final ܐ letter by ܐܘܬܵܐ and removing the vowel Sqapa on the preceding letter. It is the same for masculine and feminine. For examples:

Christianity	ܡܫܝܼܚܵܝܘܼܬܵܐ	Christian	ܡܫܝܼܚܵܝܵܐ
Syriac Nation	ܣܘܼܪ̈ܝܵܝܘܼܬܵܐ	Syriac	ܣܘܼܪ̈ܝܵܝܵܐ
Islamic	ܡܲܫܠܡܵܢܘܼܬܵܐ	Muslim	ܡܲܫܠܡܵܢܵܐ
Judaism	ܝܗܘܼܕܵܝܘܼܬܵܐ	Jewish	ܝܗܘܼܕܵܝܵܐ

Exception:

Catholic	ܩܵܬܘܿܠܝܼܩܵܐ	Catholicism	ܩܵܬܘܿܠܝܼܩܘܼܬܵܐ

Determiners in Syriac

A determiner is a word that presents a noun. In English for example, we say "a car", "the car", "this house", etc.

Articles

In the classical Syriac, the noun ܡܰܠܦܳܢܳܐ means "**a teacher**", to say "**the teacher**", we add the letter ܗ at the beginning of the noun, for example:

ܘܡܰܠܦܳܢܳܐ.

In the Eastern Modern Syriac dialect, it is a little bit different. In the following examples we will explain 'a/an' and "the" determiners:

  The dog is barking (in this case you know which dog is barking), we say:

ܟܰܠܒܳܐ ܝܼܠܹܗ ܢܒܹܐܚܳܐ.

  A dog is barking (in this case you do not know which dog is barking), we say:

ܚܲܕ ܟܰܠܒܳܐ ܝܼܠܹܗ ܢܒܹܐܚܳܐ.

            "**Literal**": (one) dog is barking.

Demonstratives

Demonstratives show where an object, event, or person is in relation to the speaker. They can refer to a physical or a psychological closeness or distance. When talking about events, the near demonstratives are often used to refer to the present while the far demonstratives often refer to the past.

Adverb   ܡܲܠܘܲܫܬܳܐ

* **Place**   ܕܘܼܟܬܳܐ or ܕܘܼܟܳܐ

  Here: ܐܳܟ݂ܳܐ

      Your book is here (2nd m).   ܟܬܵܒ݂ܘܼܟ݂ ܝܼܠܹܗ ܐܳܟ݂ܳܐ.

 There: ܗܳܡܳܐ

  Go to church and your dad is there (2nd f).   ܣܝܼ ܠܥܹܕܬܳܐ ܘܒܵܒ݂ܘܿܟ݂ ܝܼܠܹܗ ܗܳܡܳܐ.

More about places:

Left	ܣܸܡܵܠܵܐ	Right	ܝܲܡܝܼܢܵܐ
Front/Before	ܩܸܕܡܵܐ	Back/Behind	ܒܵܬܪܵܐ
Near	ܩܲܪܝܼܒܵܐ - ܩܲܪܝܼܒܬܵܐ - ܩܲܪܝܼܒܹܐ	Far	ܪܵܚܘܿܩܵܐ - ܪܵܚܘܿܩܬܵܐ - ܪܵܚܘܿܩܹܐ
Underneath	ܬܲܚܬ	Above	ܪܹܫ
Bottom	ܬܲܚܬܵܝܵܐ	Top	ܥܸܠܵܝܵܐ
Upstairs	ܥܸܠ	Downstairs	ܠܬܲܚܬ
Cross	ܪܒܘܼܥܠ	Beside	ܓܸܢܒܵܐ

Quantifiers ܟܡܝܘܬܐ

Quantifiers are an important part of Syriac grammar. Quantifiers tell us something about the amount, size, or quantity of something (a noun). The one you choose depends on what type of noun you are describing. Most of them they come in the two forms singular (male and female) and plural. We can use:

Little ܩܸܢܵܐ

We use ܩܸܢܵܐ with uncountable nouns. For example:

We have a little rice left if you would like some.

ܐܸܢ ܒܥܹܝܬ ܕܐܵܟܠܲܬ، ܐܝܼܬܠܲܢ ܩܸܢܵܐ ܪܘܼܙܵܐ ܦܝܼܫܵܐ.

Literal: If you want to eat, there is a little rice left.

Few ܚܲܕܟܡܵܐ

We use ܚܲܕܟܡܵܐ with plural, countable nouns. For example:

A few students went to school yesterday.

ܚܲܕܟܡܵܐ ܬܲܠܡܝܼܕܹܐ ܐܸܙܠܝ ܠܡܲܕܪܲܫܬܵܐ ܬܸܡܵܠ.

There were few men outside the church. ܐܝܼܬܘܵܐ ܚܲܕܟܡܵܐ ܓܲܒܪܹܐ ܒܵܪ ܕܥܹܕܬܵܐ.

Lot (lots, many, large)   ܣܘܓܐܐ / ܣܘܓܐܐ / ܣܘܓܐܐ

Unlike English, ܣܘܓܐܐ / ܣܘܓܐܐ / ܣܘܓܐܐ uses for countable and uncountable
plural nouns. For example:

Lots of students showed up today.   ܣܘܓܐܐ ܡܠܦܝܕܐ ܐܬܝܠܗ ܐܕܝܘܡ.

Literal: Many students came today.

We have a lot of rice left.   ܐܝܬܠܢ ܣܘܓܐܐ ܕܘܙܐ ܦܝܫܐ.

There is a large quantity of women in this wedding.

ܐܝܬ ܡܢܝܢܐ ܣܘܓܐܐ ܕܢܫܐ ܒܗܕܐ ܫܠܡܟܐ.

All of it   ܟܠܗ (m)   ܟܠܗ (f)

I ate all of it. (f)   ܐܢܐ ܟܕܫܢܟܢܗ ܟܠܗ.

All of them   ܟܠܝܗܝ

All of them are sleeping.   ܟܠܝܗܝ ܐܝܠܗ ܕܡܝܟܐ.

No one   ܘܠܐ ܚܕ (m)   ܘܠܐ ܚܕܐ (f)

No one was there. (m)   ܘܠܐ ܚܕ ܠܐ ܐܝܗܘܐ ܬܡܐ.

The following quantifiers use to talk about the general size of something.

Big   ܓܘܪܐ / ܓܘܪܬܐ / ܓܘܪܐ

Elephant is big.   ܦܝܠܐ ܐܝܠܗ ܓܘܪܐ.

They are too big.   ܐܢܝ ܐܝܠܗ ܪܒܐ ܓܘܪܐ.

Huge   ܥܙܘܡܐ / ܥܙܘܡܬܐ / ܥܙܘܡܐ

He has a huge hand.   ܐܝܬܠܗ ܐܝܕܐ ܥܙܘܡܬܐ.

Medium (average, central)   ܦܠܓܝܐ / ܦܠܓܝܬܐ / ܦܠܓܝܐ

Medium coffee cup.   ܟܣܐ ܕܩܗܘܐ ܦܠܓܝܐ.

Medium size houses.   ܒܬܐ ܦܠܓܝܐ.

154

Small ܙܥܘܪܐ/ ܙܥܘܪܬܐ/ ܙܥܘܪ̈ܐ

Mouse is small. ܥܩܘܒܪܐ ܝܠܗ ܙܥܘܪܐ.

Small donkeys. ܚܡܪ̈ܐ ܙܥܘܪ̈ܐ.

Tiny ܕܩܝܩܐ / ܕܩܝܩܬܐ / ܕܩܝܩ̈ܐ

Give me 3 lbs. of tiny, cracked wheat. ܗܒܠܝ ܬܠܬܐ ܦܘܢ̈ܕܐ ܠܒܘܪܓܠܐ ܕܩܝܩܐ.

• **Time** ܙܒܢܐ / ܙܒܢ̈ܐ

Today ܐܕܝܘܡ

Another time ܓܗܐ ܐܚܪܬܐ

Tomorrow ܩܘܕܐ

Yesterday ܬܡܠ

Every day ܟܠ ܝܘܡܐ

Sometime ܒܥܕܢܐ ܓܗܐ

Example: Sometime I cannot work (1st m).

ܒܥܕܢܐ ܓܗ̈ܐ ܐܢܐ ܠܐ ܡܨܝܢ ܕܦܠܚܢ.

Demonstrative with singular/plural nouns

This ܐܗܐ (m) ܐܕܝ (f) **These**: ܐܢܝ

This is my mom. ܐܕܝ ܝܠܗ ܝܡܝ.

These are my money. ܐܢܝ ܝܠܗܘܢ ܙܘܙ̈ܝ.

That ܐܗܘ (m) ܐܗܝ (f) **Those**: ܐܗ̈ܢܐ

That is my house. ܐܗܘ ܝܠܗ ܒܝܬܝ.

Those are Syriacs. ܐܗ̈ܢܐ ܝܠܗܘܢ ܣܘܪ̈ܝܝܐ.

Examples:

This is a watch.	ܐܵܗܵܐ ܙܸܒܠܵܐ ܥܸܝܵܬܵܐ.
That is a watch.	ܐܵܗܵܐ ܙܸܒܠܵܐ ܥܸܝܵܬܵܐ.
Those are watches.	ܐܵܗܵܐ ܙܸܒܠܵܐ ܥܸܝܵܢܵܬܵܐ.
This is a ring.	ܐܵܗܵܐ ܙܸܒܠܵܐ ܟܵܘܣܵܐ.
That is a ring.	ܐܵܗܵܐ ܙܸܒܠܵܐ ܟܵܘܣܵܐ.
Those are rings.	ܐܵܗܵܐ ܙܸܒܠܵܐ ܟܵܘܣܵܬܵܐ.
This is a necklace.	ܐܵܗܵܐ ܙܸܒܠܵܐ ܓܠܵܟܕܵܐ.
That is a necklace.	ܐܵܗܵܐ ܙܸܒܠܵܐ ܓܠܵܟܕܵܐ.
Those are necklaces.	ܐܵܗܵܐ ܙܸܒܠܵܐ ܓܠܵܟܕܵܐ.
This is a bracelet.	ܐܵܗܵܐ ܙܸܒܠܵܐ ܥܸܙܕܵܗܵܐ.
That is a bracelet.	ܐܵܗܵܐ ܙܸܒܠܵܐ ܥܸܙܕܵܗܵܐ.
Those are bracelets.	ܐܵܗܵܐ ܙܸܒܠܵܐ ܥܸܙܕܵܢܵܐ.
This is a glove.	ܐܵܗܵܐ ܙܸܒܠܵܐ ܚܵܦܵܐ.
That is a glove.	ܐܵܗܵܐ ܙܸܒܠܵܐ ܚܵܦܵܐ.
Those are gloves.	ܐܵܗܵܐ ܙܸܒܠܵܐ ܚܵܦܵܬܵܐ.
This is a belt.	ܐܵܗܵܐ ܙܸܒܠܵܐ ܗܵܣܵܬܵܐ.
That is a belt.	ܐܵܗܵܐ ܙܸܒܠܵܐ ܗܵܣܵܬܵܐ.
Those are belts.	ܐܵܗܵܐ ܙܸܒܠܵܐ ܗܵܣܵܬܵܐ.

Conjunctions ܟܘܿܢܵܫܹ̈ܐ

And ܘ

The letter ܘ also functions as a conjunction.

My dad and I and my brother too. ܐܸܢܵܐ ܘܒܵܒ݂ܝ ܘܗܵܡ ܐܵܚܘܿܢܝ.

(**Literal**: I and my dad and also my brother.)

Note: ܗܵܡ means too/also.

Or ܝܲܢ

Take water or bread with you (2nd m). ܫܩܘܿܠ ܡܲܝ̈ܐ ܝܲܢ ܠܲܚܡܵܐ ܥܲܡܘܿܟ݂.

But ܐܸܠܵܝ- ܚܵܐ

It is cold, but it is nice today. ܐܝܼܠܵܗ ܩܲܪܬܵܐ ܚܵܐ ܚܡܝܼܨܬܵܐ ܐܝܼܠܵܗ ܐܸܕܝܘܿܡ.

The food is salty but delicious. ܒܘܿܫܵܠܵܐ ܐܝܼܠܹܗ ܡܸܠܚܵܢܵܐ ܐܸܠܵܝ ܚܡܝܼܨܵܐ ܐܝܼܠܹܗ.

Literal: Cooked food is salty, but it is delicious.

Note:

- when to describe a weather, use the feminine form of "is" (ܐܝܼܠܵܗ) which
  refers to ܕܘܿܢܝܹ (environment, life, weather) which is feminine in Syriac.

- The word (ܚܡܝܼܨܬܵܐ – ܚܡܝܼܨܵܐ) has more than one meaning in Syriac
  depends on the use of the word. For example:

  o it means "**delicious**" when describes the taste of the food. And

  o it means "**nice**" when describes a weather status, movie. But cannot used
    when describe a person, like to say: (s)he is a nice lady/guy. In this case
    use: ܡܝܼܗܓܢܵܐ for example:

He is a nice man. ܐܵܘܵܐ ܐܝܼܠܹܗ ܐܵܢܫܵܐ ܡܝܼܗܓܢܵܐ.

Also, ܡܝܼܗܓܢܵܐ – ܡܝܼܗܓܝܼܢܵܐ - ܡܝܼܗܓܢܵܐ in some dialects uses to describe the
wealthy status of a person which means "poor" in this case.

o It means "**blessed**":

Thank you (2nd m). ܒܪܝܼܟ݂ܵܐ ܢܲܦ̮ܫܘܿܟ݂.

Literal: Your soul be blessed.

Also, ܚܡܝܼܨܵܐ ܗܘܝܼ "be healthy" means "thank you" - 2nd m.

Because ܡܛܠܕ

I did not go to school because I was sick.

ܐܢܐ ܠܐ ܙܸܠܝ ܠܡܕܪܸܫܬܵܐ ܡܛܠܕ ܗܘܹܝܢ ܗܲܕ ܡܪܝܼܥܵܐ.

Literal: I not went to school because (I) was hurt.

Note: ܠܐ means no/not.

Comparative ܒܘܫ

There is no "er" in Syriac, to say "bigger", we say ܒܘܫ ܪܵܒܵܐ. It is by adding ܒܘܫ before the adjective. For example:

My house is bigger than yours.   ܒܲܝܬܝܼ ܪܵܒܵܐ ܒܘܫ ܡܸܢ ܒܲܝܬܘܟ.

"**Literal**: My house is bigger than your house."

To say "**more**" in Syriac, we say, ܒܘܫ ܓ̰ܝܼܙܵܐ. Where ܓ̰ܝܼܙܵܐ means (a lot). For example: Which city you like more? ܐܝܡܵܐ ܡܕܝܼܢܬܵܐ ܒܸܥܝܼܬ ܒܘܫ ܓ̰ܝܼܙܵܐ؟

Every /Each ܟܘܠ

ܟܘܠ uses for both, every and each in Syriac. For example:

Every

I drink tea every day (1st m).   ܐܢܐ ܫܵܬܹܝܢ ܟ̰ܵܝ ܟܘܠ ܝܘܡܵܐ.

He works every Tuesday and Friday   ܐܵܗܘ ܦܵܠܸܚ ܟܘܠ ܬܠܵܬ̣ܒܫܲܒܵܐ ܘܥܪܘܒ̣ܬܵܐ.

Each

Each kid has a book.   ܟܘܠ ܝܲܠܕܵܐ ܒܝܼܡܵܟܹܗ ܚܲܕ ܟܬܵܒ̣ܵܐ.

Each one of us has a job (1st f).   ܟܘܠ ܚܕܵܐ ܡܸܢܲܢ ܒܝܼܡܵܟܹܗ ܥܲܡܠܵܟ̣ܵܐ.

Each one of us has a bedroom.   ܟܘܠ ܚܲܕ ܡܸܢܲܢ ܒܝܼܡܵܟܹܗ ܡܘܼܬ̣ܒ̣ܵܐ ܕܕܲܡܟ̣ܵܐ.

Note: You say ܡܘܼܬ̣ܒ̣ܵܐ (room) first and them the type of the room. For example, to say:

Bedroom: ܡܘܼܬ̣ܒ̣ܵܐ ܕܕܲܡܟ̣ܵܐ (**Literal**: room of sleeping). Where ܕܲܡܟ̣ܵܐ is (sleep). You can just say ܡܘܼܬ̣ܒ̣ܵܐ, to refer to the bedroom, for example:

The socks are in your bedroom.   ܠܦܵܦܹܐ ܐܝܼܬܠܵܟ̣ ܒܡܘܼܬ̣ܒ̣ܵܟ̣ܘܿ.

Sitting room: ܡܘܼܬ̣ܒ̣ܵܐ ܕܝܼܬܵܒ̣ܵܐ (**Literal**: room of sitting).

---

[7] Also, you may say: ܟܠ ܚܲܕ (m), ܟܠ ܚܕܵܐ (f).

The Question Words in Syriac – ܟܘܚܬܐ

When ܐܡܬܝ

    Example: When your brother is coming? (2nd m) ܐܡܬܝ ܒܝܟ ܗܘܝܐ ܐܬܝܢܘܗܝ؟

Where ܐܝܟܐ

    Example: Where is your house? ܐܝܟܐ ܐܝܠܗ ܒܝܬܘܟ؟

What ܡܢܐ

    Example: What do you do for living? (2nd m) ܡܢܐ ܐܝܠܗ ܥܡܠܟܘ؟
                              Literal: What is your work?

Why ܡܛܠ

    Example: Why you did not come to wedding? (2nd m)

                  ܡܛܠ ܠܐ ܐܬܝܠܘܟ ܠܡܫܬܘܬܐ؟
                            Literal: Why you no come to wedding?

Also, ܩܐ is "why":

           Example: Why you are not doing your homework? (**2nd f**)

           ܩܐ ܠܝܬܘܢ ܒܥܒܕܐ ܦܠܚܘܬܐ ܕܘܪܫܝܟܝ؟

Who ܡܢ

    Example: Who ate the apple? ܡܢ ܚܝܠܗ ܚܒܘܫܐ؟

Whose ܕܡܢ

    Example: Whose comb is this? ܕܡܢ ܐܝܠܗ ܐܗܐ ܡܫܪܩܐ؟

How much ܟܡܐ

    Example: How much is the price of this book? ܟܡܐ ܐܝܠܗ ܟܘܡܐ ܕܐܗܐ ܟܬܒܐ؟

How many ܟܘܡܐ

    Example: How many books do you have? (2nd m) ܟܘܡܐ ܟܬܒܐ ܐܝܬܠܘܟ؟

How ܕܐܝܟ

    Example: How did you learn Syriac Language? (**2nd f**)

           ܕܐܝܟ ܒܠܝܦܠܝ ܠܫܢܐ ܕܐܬܘܪܝܐ؟

Note: ܐܬܘܪܝܐ or ܐܬܘܪܢܝܐ are used to refer to Syriac language.

Which   ܐܲܝܢܝܼ

> **Example**: Which one is an easy way to learn our language?
>
> ܐܲܝܢܝܼ ܐܝܼܬܵܗ̇ ܐܘܼܪܚܵܐ ܦܫܝܼܛܬܵܐ ܗܿܘ ܝܼܠܦܵܐ ܕܠܸܫܵܢܲܢ؟

How often   ܟܡܵܐ ܓܵܗܹܐ

> **Example**: How often do you go to Chicago? (2nd m)
>
> ܟܡܵܐ ܓܵܗܹܐ ܐܵܙܹܠܘܟ݂ ܠܫܝܼܟܵܓܘ؟

More Example using Questions words.

> Who wrote him a letter?   ܡܵܢ ܟܬܝܼܒ݂ܠܹܗ ܐܸܓܲܪܬܵܐ؟

Who had lunch at the Ishtar Restaurant?

> ܡܵܢ ܐܝܼܒ݂ܹܗ ܩܲܪܝܼܡܠܹܗ ܟ̰ܘܡܵܐ ܒܝܼ ܒܹܝܬ ܡܹܐܟ݂ܠܵܐ ܕܐܝܼܫܬܲܪ؟

> (**Literal**: who had lunch in restaurant of Ishtar?)

How many students in your class?

> ܟܡܵܐ ܬܲܠܡܝܼܕܹܐ ܐܝܼܬ ܒܓܵܘ ܨܸܦܵܐ ܕܝܼܘܟ݂ܘܿܢ (ܕܝܼܘܟ݂ܝ)؟

> When will he come and see us?   ܐܲܝܡܲܢ ܒܸܕ ܐܵܬܹܐ ܘܚܵܙܹܠܲܢ؟

> How long will she stay with them?   ܟܡܵܐ ܒܸܕ ܦܲܝܫܵܐ ܥܲܡܲܝܗܝ؟

> How long will he stay with them?   ܟܡܵܐ ܒܸܕ ܦܵܝܸܫ ܥܲܡܲܝܗܝ؟

How much he charged you for the shirt? (2nd m)

> ܟܡܵܐ ܥܒ݂ܝܼܕܠܹܗ ܡܸܢܘܟ݂ ܠܸܒܵܐ ܕܩܲܡܝܼܨܵܐ؟

How much she charged you for the shirt? (2nd f)

> ܟܡܵܐ ܥܒ݂ܝܼܕܠܵܗ̇ ܡܸܢܵܟ݂ ܠܸܒܵܐ ܕܩܲܡܝܼܨܵܐ؟

> How often do you go to church? (2nd f)   ܟܡܵܐ ܓܵܗܹܐ ܐܵܙܵܠܝ ܠܥܹܕܬܵܐ؟

> How often do you go to church? (2nd m)   ܟܡܵܐ ܓܵܗܹܐ ܐܵܙܵܠܘܟ݂ ܠܥܹܕܬܵܐ؟

> Why has she left early?   ܩܡܘܿܕܝ ܘܠܵܗ̇ ܦܠܝܼܛܬܵܐ؟

> Why has he left early?   ܩܡܘܿܕܝ ܘܠܹܗ ܦܠܝܼܛܵܐ؟

160

Chapter 6 Exercises

1. **Apply the possessive suffix on following Syriac nouns:**

	3rd		2nd		1st	
Group	Ind.	Group	Ind.	Group	Ind.	

Mountain ܛܘܪܐ

"Female" singer ܙܡܳܪܬܐ

Deacon ܡܫܡܫܢܐ

Farm ܚܩܠܐ

Donkey ܚܡܳܪܐ

Church ܥܕܬܐ

2. **Give the plural form of the following nouns.**

ܡܠܟܐ

ܚܡܐ

ܬܪܥܐ

ܘܪܕܐ

ܚܡܳܪܐ

ܬܠܡܝܕܐ

3. **Give the feminine form of the following nouns/adjectives. If the given noun/adjective is in the feminine form, leave it blank. If the given noun/adjective has no feminine form, explain why.**

ܚܬܐ

ܪܒܐ

ܡܠܟܐ

ܪܒܣܝܣ

ܛܘܪܐ

ܚܡܳܪܐ

5. **Parsing. Identify the gender and number of the following nouns.**

Number	Gender	Meaning	Transliterate	Syriac Word
Single	Feminine	Faith	Hay'ma'noo'tha	ܗܲܝܡܵܢܘܼܬ݂ܵܐ
				ܚܲܡܬ݂ܵܐ
				ܡܲܠܦܵܢܝܼܬ݂ܵܐ
				ܗܘܿܩܵܐ
				ܗܘܿܩܵܐ
				ܡܲܠܒܸܫܝܼܬ݂ܵܐ
				ܒܸܥܬ݂ܵܐ
				ܝܲܠܕܵܐ
				ܠܝܼܠܹܐ
				ܝܲܠܕܵܐ
				ܡܸܢܝܵܢܵܐ
				ܡܲܠܟܘܼܬ݂ܵܐ
				ܫܬ݂ܘܿܬ݂ܵܐ
				ܡܸܠܟ݂ܵܐ
				ܩܵܠܵܐ

6. **Translate the following statements to Syriac.**

    a. This is my shirt.
    b. That is my dad.
    c. How much you paid for this shirt?
    d. Those are my uncle kids.
    e. $23.50.
    f. My father went to Chicago last night.
    g. What is your phone number?
    h. What color is your car?
    i. This is your car.
    j. Why you are here so early.

Chapter 7

The Verbs: ܡܠܬܐ

Learning Objectives

In this chapter, you will learn:

- the First Person ܦܲܪܨܘܿܦܵܐ ܩܲܕܡܵܝܵܐ , Second Person ܦܲܪܨܘܿܦܵܐ ܬܪܲܝܵܢܵܐ, and Third Person ܦܲܪܨܘܿܦܵܐ ܬܠܝܼܬܵܝܵܐ of:
  - The simple present verb. ܙܲܒܢܵܐ ܕܗܵܫܵܐ ܦܫܝܼܛܵܐ.
  - The present continuous verb. ܙܲܒܢܵܐ ܕܗܵܫܵܐ ܡܘܼܬܲܪܟܵܢܵܐ.
  - The simple past verb ܙܲܒܢܵܐ ܕܥܒܼܝܼܪܵܐ ܦܫܝܼܛܵܐ.
  - The past continuous. ܙܲܒܢܵܐ ܕܥܒܼܝܼܪܵܐ ܡܘܼܬܲܪܟܵܢܵܐ.
  - The present perfect. ܙܲܒܢܵܐ ܕܗܵܫܵܐ ܓܡܝܼܪܵܐ.
  - The simple future verb. ܙܲܒܢܵܐ ܕܐܵܬܹܐ ܦܫܝܼܛܵܐ.
  - Future Perfect Tense. ܙܲܒܢܵܐ ܕܐܵܬܹܐ ܓܡܝܼܪܵܐ.
  - The "Used To" verb.
  - The imperative form. ܙܲܒܢܵܐ ܦܘܼܩܕܵܢܵܐ.
  - The Verb "To Have": ܐܝܼܬ
    - Present.
    - Future.
    - Past.
- Subject-Verb Agreement:
    - There is/there are. ܐܝܼܬ
    - There was/there were. ܐܝܼܬܘܵܐ
    - There will be, there is going to be. ܒܸܬ ܗܵܘܹܐ, ܒܸܕ ܗܵܘܹܐ
- The Permission Verbs- Let (ܫܒܘܿܩ and the special case: ܫܒܘܿܩܘܼ).
- The Modal Verbs:
  - Have to, Need to ܣܢܝܼܩܵܐ
  - Can/ be able to ܐܝܼܬܠܹܗ
  - Could ܡܘܼܨܝܵܐ

- o Should   ܟ݂ܘܕ
- o May (have) and Might (have) – Perhaps.   ܠܟ݂ܒܪ
- Conditional
  - o If   ܐܝܢ
  - o Unless/If not   (ܐܢ ܠܐ ܐܝܢ) ܐܝܢ ܠܐ
  - o In Case   ܒܠܐ

Unlike English language, the verb in Syriac, in the most cases, it is going to be different in spelling from the original (root) verb. We will try to make some simple rules to how we formed the verb from its original/root verb. In the meantime, try to make your own rules as a practice to learn more about Syriac verb. Also, take a close look how the vowels are represented when a verb, in any tense, is formed from the root.

The Simple Present Verb ܘܰܚܕܳܐ ܙܰܒ݂ܢܳܐ ܟܶܥܒ݂ܶܕ݂

Use the Simple Present to express the idea that an action is repeated or usual. The action can be a habit, a hobby, a daily event, a scheduled event, or something that often happens. It can also be something a person often forgets or usually does not do. In Syriac dialect, each simple present verb starts with a ܟ, and for:

First Person ܩܰܕ݂ܡܳܝܳܐ ܦܰܪ ܨܳܘܒܳܐ

Kih

Ends with ܝ and the vowel Zlama Psheeqa (O) on the preceding letter for first person masculine (single) and ܝ and the vowel Pthaha (Ȯ) on preceding letter for first person feminine (single). For first person plural, is the same for masculine and feminine and ends with ܚ.

ana

	Simple Present – 1st Person			English Meaning	Syriac Verb
Group/Plural		Female	Male		
echlooch ܟܶܐܟ݂ܠܺܝܚ	ܟܶܐܟ݂ܠܰܢ	ܐܰܢ ܟܶܐܟ݂ܠܰܢ	ܐܰܢ ܟܶܐܟ݂ܠܺܝ *Karran*	Eat	ܐܶܟ݂ܠܳܐ *eechala*
Kavooch	ܟܶܩܶܕ݂ܘܰܢ	ܐܰܢ ܟܶܩܶܕ݂ܰܢ *Kuryon*	ܐܰܢ ܟܶܩܶܕ݂ܺܝ *Karran*	Read	ܩܶܕ݂ܢܳܐ *Krya*
Jmah anvh	ܟܶܪܶܕ݂ܘܰܢ	ܐܰܢ ܟܶܪܶܕ݂ܰܢ *Kerann*	ܐܰܢ ܟܶܪܶܕ݂ܺܝ	Run	ܪܶܕ݂ܢܳܐ *gvatha*
Mahloo Uh	ܟܶܡܰܕ݂ܠܺܝܚ	ܐܰܢ ܟܶܡܰܕ݂ܠܰܢ	ܐܰܢ ܟܶܡܰܕ݂ܠܺܝ	Feed	ܡܰܕ݂ܠܳܐ *maholih*
	ܟܶܡܕ݂ܘܡܰܢ	ܐܰܢ ܟܶܡܕ݂ܘܡܰܢ	ܐܰܢ ܟܶܡܕ݂ܘܡܶܚ	Put to sleep	ܡܕ݂ܘܡܶܚ *Met moo heh*
	ܟܶܚܢܶܬ݂ܘܰܢ	ܐܰܢ ܟܶܚܢܶܬ݂ܰܢ	ܐܰܢ ܟܶܚܢܶܬ݂	Think	ܚܢܶܬ݂ܳܐ *Ch-Shawa*

Kidyomn achvoom Hchorr ana

Examples:
I eat one apple every day. (1st person male) ܐܰܢ ܟܶܐܟ݂ܠܺܝ ܚܕ݂ܳܐ ܚܰܒ݂ܘܫܬܳܐ ܚܘܕ݂ ܝܘܡܳܐ.
I read the Bible every morning. (1st person female)

ܐܰܢ ܟܶܩܶܕ݂ܰܢ ܟܬ݂ܳܒ݂ܩܘܕ݂ܫܳܐ ܚܘܕ݂ ܨܰܦܪܳܐ.

165

Kvaloue Koohka aymn Jseheym Kiyugign ana

We run 3 miles a day. ܐܢܚܢܲܢ ܚܕ݂ܝܣܡܘܝ ܡܝܠܹ̈ܐ ܒܟܠ ܝܘܡܵܐ.

I feed one apple every day. ܐܢܵܐ ܡܲܐܟ݂ܠܸܢ ܚܕ݂ ܫܬܘܼܚܹܐ ܚܕ݂ ܝܘܡܵܐ.

I put my kids to sleep at 9pm. ܐܢܵܐ ܡܲܕ݂ܡܸܟ݂ܢ ܝ̈ܠܕܝ ܕܝܼܡܹܐ ܬܡܵܢܹܐ ܒܠܲܝܠܹܐ.

I think it is going to rain this evening. ܐܢܵܐ ܚܵܫܒܹܢ ܘܸܒܟ ܐܹܙܹܐ ܡܝܼܚܠܵܐ ܐܸܕ݂ܝܘܼ ܒܪܲܡܫܵܐ.

Second Person ܦܲܪܨܘܿܦܵܐ ܬܪܲܝܵܢܵܐ

Ends with ܬ and Zlama Psheeqa (ܶ) vowel on preceding letter for masculine, and Pthaha (ܲ) vowel on preceding letter for feminine. For plural is the same and ends with ܝܬܘܿܢ.

ܝܬܘܿܢ

Simple Present – 2nd Person			English Meaning	Syriac Verb	
Group/Plural	Female	Male			
ܐܢ݇ܬܘܿܢ ܝܵܠܦܝܼܬܘܿܢ	ܐܢ݇ܬܝ ܝܵܠܦܲܬ	ܐܲܝ݇ܬ ܝܵܠܦܸܬ	Learn	ܝܠܦ	*eelapa*
ܐܢ݇ܬܘܿܢ ܡܲܠܦܝܼܬܘܿܢ	ܐܢ݇ܬܝ ܡܲܠܦܲܬ	ܐܲܝ݇ܬ ܡܲܠܦܸܬ	Teach	ܡܲܠܦܸܕ	*melopeh*
ܐܢ݇ܬܘܿܢ ܕܲܪܫܝܼܬܘܿܢ	ܐܢ݇ܬܝ ܕܲܪܫܲܬ	ܐܲܝ݇ܬ ܕܲܪܫܸܬ	Study	ܕܵܪܸܫ	*eedaraseh*
ܐܢ݇ܬܘܿܢ ܡܲܕ݂ܪܫܝܼܬܘܿܢ	ܐܢ݇ܬܝ ܡܲܕ݂ܪܫܲܬ	ܐܲܝ݇ܬ ܡܲܕ݂ܪܫܸܬ	Tutor/teach	ܡܲܕ݂ܪܸܫ	
ܐܢ݇ܬܘܿܢ ܚܵܫܒ݂ܝܼܬܘܿܢ	ܐܢ݇ܬܝ ܚܵܫܒܲܬ	ܐܲܝ݇ܬ ܚܵܫܒܸܬ	Think	ܚܵܫܸܒ	*kh-shawa*

Examples:

You learn Syriac at school (2nd m). ܐܲܝ݇ܬ ܝܵܠܦܸܬ ܐܵܬܘܿܪܵܐ ܒܡܲܕ݂ܪܲܫܬܵܐ.

You (all) study Church history. ܐܢ݇ܬܘܿܢ ܕܲܪܫܝܼܬܘܿܢ ܡܲܟܬܒ݂ܵܐ ܕܥܹܕܬܵܐ.

You teach the Syriac Language(2nd f). ܐܢ݇ܬܝ ܡܲܠܦܲܬ ܠܸܫܵܢܵܐ ܐܵܬܘܿܪܵܝܵܐ.

You tutor math every morning(2nd m). ܐܲܝ݇ܬ ܡܲܕ݂ܪܫܸܬ ܡܸܢܝܵܢܹܐ ܚܕ݂ ܡܲܨܪܲܚܬܵܐ.

Do you think it is big for me? (1st m or f to 2nd m)

ܚܵܫܒܸܬ ܐܲܝ݇ܬ ܪܲܒܠܹܐ ܕܵܟ݂ ܗܵܘܸܠܝ؟

166

Third Person ܩܕܝܘܬ݂ ܦܪ ܗܠܝܡܢܐ

Ends with ܐ and Ō (Sqapa) on the preceding letter to represent feminine. For masculine, the letter ܐ and the vowel Ō are omitted from the end of the verb. For plural, it is the same for both masculine or feminine plural and ends with ܝܼ when ܝ is silent.

Simple Present – 3rd Person			English Meaning	Syriac Verb
Group/Plural	Female	Male		
ܐܢܘܗ ܟܬ݂ܒ݂ܝ	ܐܗܘ ܟܬ݂ܒ݂ܐ	ܐܗܘ ܟܬ݂ܒ݂	Write	ܟܬ݂ܒ݂ܐ *Kthawa*
ܐܢܘܗ ܦܠܟܢܝ	ܐܗܘ ܦܠܟܢܐ	ܐܗܘ ܦܠܟܢ	Work	ܦܠܟܢܐ *glatha*
ܐܢܘܗ ܡܓܘܠܢܝ	ܐܗܘ ܡܓܘܠܢܐ	ܐܗܘ ܡܓܘܠܢ	Hire	ܡܓܘܠܢܐ *mechpocka*
ܐܢܘܗ ܕܢܝܐܝ	ܐܗܘ ܕܢܝܐܐ	ܐܗܘ ܕܢܝܐ	Walk	ܕܢܝܐ *medhhasha*
ܐܢܘܗ ܕܘܡܚܝ	ܐܗܘ ܕܘܡܚܐ	ܐܗܘ ܕܘܡܚ	Sleep	ܕܘܡܚܐ *mdha*
ܐܢܘܗ ܚܢܥܝ	ܐܗܘ ܚܢܥܐ	ܐܗܘ ܚܢܥ	Think	ܚܢܥܐ

Examples:

He writes every day in newspaper.   ܐܗܘ ܟܬ݂ܒ݂ ܟܠ ܢܘܡܐ ܒܓܗܢܘܡܐ. *Qwa*

She works by her uncle (mother side).   ܐܗܘ ܦܠܟܢܐ ܠܒܝܬ ܚܠܗ.

They hire teachers every summer.   ܐܢܘܗ ܡܓܘܠܢܝ ܡܠܦܢܐ ܟܠ ܒܝܬܐ.

He walks two miles every day.   ܐܗܘ ܕܢܝܐ ܗܕܡ ܡܝܠܐ ܟܠ ܢܘܡܐ.

My kids go to sleep at 9pm.   ܢܟܘܝ ܕܘܡܚܝ ܒܥܝܕܐ ܬܡܢܝܐ ܒܠܠܐ.

The Present Continuous Verb ܘܚܢܐ ܕܡܒܝܪ ܗܘܡܟܕܢܐ

In case of the Present Continuous, the verb is the same of the root verb for masculine, feminine, and plural with adding the letter ܒ at the beginning and adding the word ܐܗܐ (now – optional) at the end of the sentence.

ܐܗܐ (now) means: at the time of speaking, this second, today, this month, this year, this century, and so on. Sometimes, we use the present continuous to say that we are in the process of doing a longer action which is in progress; however, we might not be doing it at this exact second.

167

First Person ܦܪܨܘܦܐ ܩܕܡܝܐ

Play ܛܥܘܠܐ

Example: I am playing now (1st m). ܐܢܐ ܐܝܬܘܝ ܒܛܥܘܠܐ ܗܫܐ.

Buy ܙܒܢܐ

Example: I am buying a house (1st f). ܐܢܐ ܐܝܬܘܢ ܒܙܒܢܐ ܒܝܬܐ.

Sell ܡܙܒܘܢܐ

Example: I am selling my car. ܐܢܐ ܐܝܬܘܝ ܒܡܙܒܘܢܐ ܣܝܪܬܝ.

Sit ܝܬܘܒܐ

Example: We are sitting. ܐܚܢܢ ܐܝܬܘܚ ܒܝܬܘܒܐ.

Put (to put or to help sitting) ܡܘܬܘܒܐ

Example: I am helping my dad to sit on bed.

ܐܢܐ ܐܝܬܘܝ ܒܡܘܬܘܒܐ ܒܒܝ ܥܠ ܥܪܣܐ.

Second Person ܦܪܨܘܦܐ ܬܪܝܢܐ

Dig ܚܦܪܐ

Example: You are digging far from the house (2nd m).

ܐܢܬ ܐܝܬܘܬ ܒܚܦܪܐ ܪܚܝܩܐ ܡܢ ܒܝܬܐ.

Third Person ܦܪܨܘܦܐ ܬܠܝܬܝܐ

Learn ܝܠܦܐ

Example: They are learning Syriac. ܐܢܝ ܐܝܠܗܘܢ ܒܝܠܦܐ ܣܘܪܝܬ.

Gather ܟܢܫܐ

Example: He is gathering his staff from here.

ܐܗܘ ܐܝܠܗ ܒܟܢܫܐ ܚܦܬܗ ܡܢ ܕܐܟܐ.

The Simple Past Verb ܙܒܢܐ ܕܥܒܪܐ ܦܫܝܛܐ

In simple past verb, there is nothing to add at the beginning of the verb. Remove ܐ from the end and add the suffix:

First Person ܦܪܨܘܦܐ ܩܕܡܝܐ

Ends with ܠܝ for masculine and feminine, and ܠܢ for plural.

Syriac Verb	English Meaning	Simple Past – 1st Person: Male & Female	Group/Plural
ܡܣܘܚܒܐ	Speak	ܐܢܐ ܡܘܣܚܒܠܝ	ܐܚܢܢ ܡܘܣܚܒܠܢ
ܟܢܘܫܐ	Gather	ܐܢܐ ܟܢܫܠܝ	ܐܚܢܢ ܟܢܫܠܢ

We spoke with the teacher. ܐܚܢܢ ܡܘܣܚܒܠܢ ܥܡ ܕܡܠܦܢܐ.

Literal: we spoke with the teacher.

Second Person ܦܪܨܘܦܐ ܬܪܝܢܐ

Ends with ܠܘܟ for masculine, ܠܟܝ for feminine, and ܠܘܟܘܢ for plural.

Syriac Verb	English Meaning	Simple Past – 2nd Person: Male	Female	Group/Plural
ܡܫܕܘܪܐ	Send	ܐܢܬ ܡܫܘܕܪܠܘܟ	ܐܢܬܝ ܡܫܘܕܪܠܟܝ	ܐܢܬܘܢ ܡܫܘܕܪܠܘܟܘܢ

Did you send the money to your dad? (for female)

ܡܫܘܕܪܠܟܝ ܙܘܙܐ ܩܐ ܒܒܘܟܝ؟

Literal: (You) sent money to your dad? (ܐܢܬܝ is omitted)

Note: in some dialects, this verb (send) in past tense form, the letter ܠ is silent.

Third Person ܦܪܨܘܿܦܵܐ ܬܠܝܼܬܵܝܵܐ

Ends with ܠܹܗ to represent masculine and ܠܵܗ̇ to represent feminine. For plural ends with ܠ̈ܝ.

Simple Past – 3rd Person			English	Syriac
Group/Plural	Female	Male	Meaning	Verb
ܐܵܢܝܼ ܣܚܝܼܠ̈ܝ	ܐܵܗܝ ܣܚܝܼܠܵܗ̇	ܐܵܗܘ ܣܚܝܼܠܹܗ	Swim	ܣܚܵܝܵܐ
ܐܵܢܝܼ ܝܠܝܼܦܠ̈ܝ	ܐܵܗܝ ܝܠܝܼܦܠܵܗ̇	ܐܵܗܘ ܝܠܝܼܦܠܹܗ	Learn	ܝܵܠܵܦܵܐ

He swam last night. ܐܵܗܘ ܣܚܝܼܠܹܗ ܬܸܡܵܠ ܒܠܸܠܝܵܐ.

She learned how to drive the car. ܐܵܗܝ ܝܠܝܼܦܠܵܗ̇ ܕܹܐܟܼ ܐܵܝ ܡܵܬܘܿܪܵܐ ܣܵܩܵܐ.

Note: the sound of ܐܵܝ is ܕ when is used with a verb.

The Past Continuous ܙܒܼܢܵܐ ܥܒܼܝܼܪܵܐ ܡܫܲܡܠܝܵܢܵܐ

We use the past continuous to say that someone was in the middle of doing something at certain time. The action or situation had already started before this time but had not finished. The past continuous does not tell us whether an action was finished or not. Perhaps it was finished, perhaps not. The past continuous is: Pronoun + (was, were) + verb + ing.

First Person ܦܪܨܘܿܦܵܐ ܩܲܕܡܵܝܵܐ

Example:

This time 3 years ago, { m: I was / f: I was / we were } living in Iraq.

m: ܡܢ ܕܲܐܟܼܵܐ ܩܕܵܡ ܬܠܵܬܼ ܫܢܝ̈ܐ، ܐܵܢܵܐ ܗܘܹܐ ܗܘܵܐ ܝܵܬܼܒܼܵܐ ܒܒܹܝܬܼܢܲܗܪ̈ܝܢ.

f: ܡܢ ܕܲܐܟܼܵܐ ܩܕܵܡ ܬܠܵܬܼ ܫܢܝ̈ܐ، ܐܵܢܵܐ ܗܘܹܐ ܗܘܵܐ ܝܵܬܼܒܼܵܐ ܒܒܹܝܬܼܢܲܗܪ̈ܝܢ.

p: ܡܢ ܕܲܐܟܼܵܐ ܩܕܵܡ ܬܠܵܬܼ ܫܢܝ̈ܐ، ܐܲܚܢܲܢ ܗܘܲܝܚ ܗܘܵܐ ܝܵܬܼܒܼܵܐ ܒܒܹܝܬܼܢܲܗܪ̈ܝܢ.

Second Person ܦܪܨܘܦܐ ܬܪܝܢܐ

Example: I slept when you were playing.

2nd m: ܐܢܐ ܕܡܝܟܠܝ ܐܝܡܢ ܐܢܬ ܗܘܐ ܗܘܝܬܘܐ ܒܛܥܘܠܐ.
2nd f: ܐܢܐ ܕܡܝܟܠܝ ܐܝܡܢ ܐܢܬܝ ܗܘܐ ܗܘܝܬܝܘܐ ܒܛܥܘܠܐ.
2nd p: ܐܢܐ ܕܡܝܟܠܝ ܐܝܡܢ ܐܢܬܘܢ ܗܘܝܬܘܢ ܗܘܐ ܒܛܥܘܠܐ.

Third Person ܦܪܨܘܦܐ ܬܠܝܬܝܐ

Example:

Sargon was / Mariam was / They were — taking a bath when I arrived home.

m: ܣܪܓܘܢ ܗܘܐ ܗܘܐ ܒܣܚܝܐ ܐܝܡܢ ܐܢܐ ܡܛܝܠܗ ܠܒܝܬܐ.
f: ܡܪܝܡ ܗܘܐ ܗܘܐ ܒܣܚܝܐ ܐܝܡܢ ܐܢܐ ܡܛܝܠܗ ܠܒܝܬܐ.
p: ܐܗܘܢ ܗܘܐ ܗܘܐ ܒܣܚܝܐ ܐܝܡܢ ܐܢܐ ܡܛܝܠܗ ܠܒܝܬܐ.

The Present Perfect Verb ܙܒܢܐ ܕܩܐܡ ܠܡܥܒܪܐ

We form the present perfect verb with ܕܗܐ (now) + the past verb.

First Person ܦܪܨܘܦܐ ܩܕܡܝܐ

Example:

I / we — just had dinner.

m, f: ܐܢܐ ܕܗܐ ܐܟܠܝ ܥܫܝܐ.[8]
p: ܐܢܚܢ ܕܗܐ ܐܟܠܢ ܥܫܝܐ.

Also, you may hear people saying. ܐܚܢܢ ܗܕ ܕܗܐ ܐܟܠܢ ܥܫܝܐ.

---

[8] ܥܫܝܐ is a loaner word from Arabic. ܚܫܡܝܬܐ is in Syriac.

Second Person ܦܪܨܘܦܐ ܬܪܝܢܐ

Example:

You have just woke up.	m:	ܐܢܬ ܕܗܐ ܡܬܥܝܪܬ.
	f:	ܐܢܬܝ ܕܗܐ ܡܬܥܝܪܬܝ.
	p:	ܐܢܬܘܢ ܕܗܐ ܡܬܥܝܪܬܘܢ.

Third Person ܦܪܨܘܦܐ ܬܠܝܬܝܐ

Examples:

Yaqoo has	found a new job.	m:	ܝܥܩܘܒ ܕܗܐ ܫܟܝܚܠܗ ܫܘܓܠܐ ܚܕܬܐ.
Nahrain has		f:	ܢܗܪܝܢ ܕܗܐ ܫܟܝܚܠܗ̇ ܫܘܓܠܐ ܚܕܬܐ.
They have		p:	ܐܢܝ ܕܗܐ ܫܟܝܚܠܗܘܢ ܫܘܓܠܐ ܚܕܬܐ.

The Simple Future Verb ܙܒܢܐ ܕܐܬܝܐ ܦܫܝܛܐ

Simple Future has two different forms in Syriac: ܒܕ "**will**" and ܙܒܠ "**going to**." Although the two forms can sometimes be used interchangeably, they often express two very different meanings. These different meanings might seem too abstract at first, but with time and practice, the differences will become clear. Both "ܒܕ" and "ܙܒܠ" refer to a specific time in the future.

Note: the letter ܠ in ܙܒܠ is silent most the time. Especially when is used to ask or in the negative form. Therefore, we will have the slight line above the letter ܠ to make it silent.

First Person ܦܲܪܨܘܿܦܵܐ ܩܲܕܡܵܝܵܐ

Replace ܐ with ـܝ at the end and the vowel ܿ on the preceding letter for masculine, the vowel ܼ on preceding letter for feminine, and feminine, and ܘܿܚ for plural.

		Wait	ܗܲܟܹܐ

	I will wait.	I am going to wait.	
1st m:	ܐܵܢܵܐ ܒܸܕ ܗܲܟܹܝܢ.	ܐܵܢܵܐ ܘܸܠܟ ܗܲܟܹܝܢ.	ܗܲܟܹܝܢ
1st f:	ܐܵܢܵܐ ܒܸܕ ܗܲܟܹܝܢ.	ܐܵܢܵܐ ܘܸܠܟ ܗܲܟܹܝܢ.	ܗܲܟܹܝܢ
1st p:	ܐܲܚܢܲܢ ܒܸܕ ܗܲܟܹܐܘܿܚ.	ܐܲܚܢܲܢ ܘܸܠܟ ܗܲܟܹܐܘܿܚ.	ܗܲܟܹܐܘܿܚ

Example: I will wait for my dad here (1st m). ܐܵܢܵܐ ܒܸܕ ܗܲܟܹܝܢ ܗܵܐ ܬܵܚܒ ܒܵܒܝ.

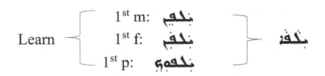

Learn

Example: I will learn Syriac (1st f). ܐܵܢܵܐ ܒܸܕ ܝܲܠܦܸܢ ܣܘܼܪܝܵܝܵܐ

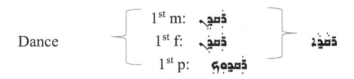

Dance

Example: We are going to dance at your wedding tomorrow (2nd m).

ܐܲܚܢܲܢ ܘܸܠܟ ܪܲܩܕܘܿܚ ܓܹܝܢܠܘܼܟܘܿܚ ܒܵܩܵܐ.

Second Person   ܦܳܪܘܿܦܳܐ ܬܪܰܝܳܢܐ

Replace ܐ with ܬ at the end and the vowel ◌ܘ on the preceding for masculine,
ܬ and the vowel ◌ܝ on preceding for feminine, and ܘܟ݂ܘ for plural.

			Sleep	ܕܡܟ݂ܐ
	You will sleep.	You are going to sleep.		
2nd m:	ܐܢܬ ܒܕ ܕܡܟ݂ܰܬ.	ܐܢܬ ܘܒܟ݂ ܕܡܟ݂ܰܬ.		ܕܡܟ݂ܰܬ
2nd f:	ܐܢܬܝ ܒܕ ܕܡܟ݂ܰܬ.	ܐܢܬܝ ܘܒܟ݂ ܕܡܟ݂ܰܬ.		ܕܡܟ݂ܰܬ
2nd p:	ܐܢܬܘܢ ܘܒܟ݂ ܕܡܟ݂ܘܬܘܢ.	ܐܢܬܘܢ ܒܕ ܕܡܟ݂ܘܬܘܢ.		ܕܡܟ݂ܘܬܘܢ

Example: You will sleep at your uncle's house (**2nd f**).

ܐܢܬܝ ܒܕ ܕܡܟ݂ܰܬ ܒܝܬܐ ܕܡܡܟ݂ܝ.

Third Person   ܦܳܪܘܿܦܳܐ ܬܠܝܬܳܝܐ

Remove the letter ܐ from the end and the Sqapa ◌ vowel from the preceding
letter for masculine and add the ܝ for plural.

			Sing	ܘܡܪܐ
	He/she/they will sing.	He/she/they Going to sing.		
3rd m:	ܐܵܗܘ ܒܕ ܘܡܪ.	ܐܵܗܘ ܘܒܟ݂ ܘܡܪ.		ܘܡܪ
3rd f:	ܐܵܗܒ ܒܕ ܘܡܪܐ.	ܐܵܗܒ ܘܒܟ݂ ܘܡܪܐ.		ܘܡܪܐ
3rd p:	ܐܢܕܵܗܒ ܒܕ ܘܡܪܝ.	ܐܢܕܵܗܒ ܘܒܟ݂ ܘܡܪܝ.		ܘܡܪܝ

Example: Yes, they are going to sing tonight.

ܐܝܢ، ܘܒܟ݂ ܘܡܪܝ ܒܝܘܡܐ ܠܠܝܐ.

Note: ܠ in ܘܒܟ݂ is not silent here to emphasize the verb.

Future Perfect Tense ܙܒܢܐ ܕܡܫܠܡ ܠܥܬܝܕܐ

The future perfect tense indicates that an action will have been completed at some point in the future. In Syriac, we use ܒܕ ܗܘܐ (m), ܒܕ ܗܘܝܐ (f) (will have). See how ܒܕ ܗܘܝܐ, ܒܕ ܗܘܐ and the verb (in past tense) spelling are formed base on who is/are talking to/from.

First Person ܦܪܨܘܦܐ ܩܕܡܝܐ

Examples: The verb to:

Walk: ܡܫܝܐ

- When I arrive to church, I will have walked the 5 miles. (1st m):
  ܐܝܡܢ ܕܡܛܝܢ ܠܥܕܬܐ، ܐܢܐ ܒܕ ܗܘܝܢ ܡܫܝܐ ܚܡܫܐ ܡܝܠܐ.

Buy: ܙܒܢܐ

- Before January, I will have bought the car. (1st f):

  ܩܕܡ ܟܢܘܢ ܐܚܪܝܐ، ܐܢܐ ܒܕ ܗܘܝܢ ܙܒܢܬܐ ܣܝܪܬܐ.

Move (from place to place): ܫܘܢܝܐ

- When summer comes, we will have moved to Michigan. (from group):
  ܐܝܡܢ ܕܐܬܐ ܩܝܛܐ، ܐܚܢܢ ܒܕ ܗܘܝܚ ܡܫܘܢܝܐ ܠܡܫܝܓܢ.

Second Person ܦܪܨܘܦܐ ܬܪܝܢܐ

Examples: The verb to:

Finish ܚܠܨܐ

- When he wakes up at 3pm, you will have finished your work. (2nd m)
  ܐܝܡܢ ܕܩܐܡ ܒܬܠܬ ܒܥܨܪܐ، ܐܢܬ ܒܕ ܗܘܝܬ ܚܠܨܐ ܥܒܕܘܟ.

See ܚܙܝܐ

- Before you go to Chicago, you will have seen your teacher. (**2nd f**)

  ܩܕܡ ܕܐܙܠܬ ܠܫܝܟܓܘ، ܒܕ ܗܘܝܬ ܚܙܝܐ ܡܠܦܢܬܟܝ.

Leave/get out   ܦܠܘܚ

- Before May, you will have been left the house. (to group)

ܩܲܕܡ ܝܲܪܚܵܐ ܕܡܵܝܼܣ، ܐܲܢ̄ܬܘܿܢ ܒܸܕ ܗܵܘܹܝܬܘܿܢ ܦܠܝܼܛܹܐ ܡܸܢ ܒܲܝܬܵܐ.

Literal: before month of May, you will have been left the house.

Third Person   ܦܲܪܨܘܿܦܵܐ ܬܠܝܼܬܵܝܵܐ

Examples: The verb to:

Work: ܦܠܵܚܵܐ

- Before he is getting married, Sargon will have worked at the hospital.

ܩܲܕܡܵܐ ܕܝܼܟܘܹܐ، ܣܵܪܓܘܿܢ ܒܸܕ ܗܵܘܹܐ ܦܠܝܼܚܵܐ ܒܬܸܒܝܼܬ̣ܚܘܿܠܡܵܢܹܐ.

Sleep: ܕܡܵܟ݂ܵܐ

- When finishes his work, she will have slept at least 3 hours.

ܐܝܼܡܲܢ ܕܫܲܠܝܼ ܥܵܘܵܕܗ، ܐܵܗܵܒ݂ ܒܸܕ ܗܵܘܝܵܐ ܕܡܝܼܟ݂ܬܵܐ ܒܵܨ ܗܲܠܲ ܬܠܵܬ݂ܵܐ ܣܵܥܲܬ̈ܵܐ.

Literal: When finishes his work, she will have slept a 3 hours.

Learn: ܝܠܵܦܵܐ

- Before teacher arrives, they will have learned the alphabet.

ܩܲܕܡܵܐ ܕܝܵܐܹܐ ܡܲܠܦܵܢܵܐ، ܐܲܢ̄ܢܝܼ ܒܸܕ ܗܵܘܝܼ ܝܠܝܼܦܹܐ ܐܵܠܲܦ ܒܲܝܬ.

176

The - Used to - Verb

We use **used to** with the simple present form and adding ܗܘܵܐ after the verb to say that something happened regularly in the past but no longer happens.

First Person

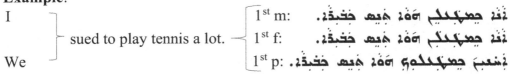

Example:

I ⎤
    ⎬ sued to play tennis a lot. ⎨
We ⎦

1ˢᵗ m:

1ˢᵗ f:

1ˢᵗ p:

Second Person

Example: You used to sleep over your uncle's house.

1ˢᵗ m:

1ˢᵗ f:

1ˢᵗ p:

Third Person

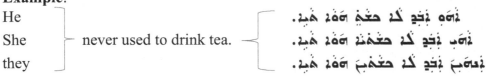

Example:

He ⎤
She ⎬ never used to drink tea. ⎨
they ⎦

The Imperative Form ܘܚܢ ܦܣܘܕܐ

The imperative form, in most cases, is the same in masculine and feminine in both singular and plural forms. There are no special rules to form the imperative from the root verb. You identify the imperative with the Rwassa vowel (ܘ) or Rwahha (ܘ) in the middle of the word in singular form. In plural form you will also see the imperative ends with (ܘܢ), where ܢ (noon) is silent in the most spoken accents.

Verb to:	Imperative Plural!	Imperative Singular!	Syriac Root
Sleep	ܕܡܘܟܘܢ	ܕܡܘܟ	ܕܡܟܐ
Look	ܚܘܪܘܢ	ܚܘܪ	ܚܘܪܐ
Go up	ܝܣܩܘܢ	ܝܣܩܘ	ܝܣܩܐ
Go down	ܟܢܘܣܘܢ	ܟܢܘܣ	ܟܢܣܐ
Eat	ܝܟܘܠܘܢ	ܝܟܘܠ	ܝܟܠܐ
Learn	ܝܠܘܦܘܢ	ܝܠܘܦ	ܝܠܦܐ
Study	ܕܪܘܫܘܢ	ܕܪܘܫ	ܕܪܫܐ
Dress up	ܝܠܒܫܘܢ	ܝܠܒܫ	ܝܠܒܫܐ
Shower	ܚܢܘܦܘܢ	ܚܢܘܦ	ܚܢܦܐ

The following imperative verbs are different for masculine and feminine in the singular form and they are the same in plural:

	2ⁿᵈ p	2ⁿᵈ f	2ⁿᵈ m	
Talk!	ܡܣܚܘܢ!	ܡܣܚܝ!	ܡܣܚܒ!	ܡܣܚܦܐ
See!	ܚܘܪܘܢ!	ܚܘܪ!	ܚܘܪ!	ܚܘܪܐ
Swim!	ܝܣܚܘܢ!	ܝܣܚܝ!	ܝܣܚܒ!	ܝܣܚܐ
Go!	ܗܘܢ!	ܗܝ!	ܗܒ!	ܝܒܘܠܐ

178

The Verb "To Have" – ܐܝܬ

Present: (Possessive + ܠ + ܐܝܬ)
Note: in the most accents, ܠ is silent in the present tense only.

First Person ܦܪܨܘܦܐ ܩܕܡܝܐ

Ends with the vowel ܝ for both masculine and feminine, and with ܢ for plural.

I have.	ܐܢܐ ܐܝܬܠܝ.
Do I have?	ܐܝܬܠܝ ܐܢܐ؟
I do not have.	ܐܢܐ ܠܐ ܕܐܝܬܠܝ.
We have.	ܐܚܢܢ ܐܝܬܠܢ.
Do we have?	ܐܝܬܠܢ ܐܚܢܢ؟
We do not have.	ܐܚܢܢ ܠܐ ܕܐܝܬܠܢ.

Example: We have a big house. ܐܚܢܢ ܐܝܬܠܢ ܒܝܬܐ ܪܒܐ.

Note: the negative form, is by adding the "ܠܐ" before the verb ܐܝܬ and the first letter "ܐ" and its vowel "ܝ" are silent for all tenses.

Second Person ܦܪܨܘܦܐ ܬܪܝܢܐ

Ends with ܘܟ for masculine, ܟܝ for feminine, and ܘܟܘܢ for plural.

To 2ⁿᵈ m:

You have.	ܐܝܬ ܐܝܬܠܘܟ.
Do you have?	ܐܝܬܠܘܟ ܐܝܬ؟
You do not have:	ܐܝܬ ܠܐ ܕܐܝܬܠܘܟ. or ܐܝܬ ܠܐ ܕܐܝܬܠܘܟ.

To 2ⁿᵈ f:

You have.	ܐܝܬܝ ܐܝܬܠܟܝ.
Do you have?	ܐܝܬܠܟܝ ܐܝܬܝ؟
You do not have	ܐܝܬܝ ܠܐ ܕܐܝܬܠܟܝ. or ܐܝܬܝ ܠܐ ܕܐܝܬܠܟܝ.

To 2nd p:

You have. ܐܲܢ̱ܬܘܿܢ ܐܝܼܬܠܘܿܟ݂ܘܿܢ.

Do you have? ܐܝܼܬܠܘܿܟ݂ܘܿܢ ܐܲܢ̱ܬܘܿܢ؟

You do not have. ܐܲܢ̱ܬܘܿܢ ܠܹܐ ܐܲܝܬܠܘܿܟ݂ܘܿܢ. or ܐܲܢ̱ܬܘܿܢ ܠܹܐ ܐܝܼܬܠܘܿܟ݂ܘܿܢ.

You have a nice car. (**2nd f**) ܐܲܢ̱ܬܝ ܐܝܼܬܠܵܟ݂ܝ ܣܲܝܵܪܵܐ ܫܲܦܝܼܪܬܵܐ.

Note: ܫܲܦܝܼܪܬܵܐ (f), and ܫܲܦܝܼܪܵܐ (m), means beautiful, nice, cute.

Third Person ܦܲܪܨܘܿܦܵܐ ܬܠܝܼܬܵܝܵܐ

Ends with ܗ for masculine, ܗ̇ for feminine, and the letter ܢ (silent in some accents) for plural.

He has. ܐܵܗܘܼ ܐܝܼܬܠܹܗ.

Does he have? ܐܝܼܬܠܹܗ ܐܵܗܘܼ؟

He does not have. ܐܵܗܘܼ ܠܹܐ ܐܝܼܬܠܹܗ. or ܐܵܗܘܼ ܠܹܐ ܐܲܝܬܠܹܗ.

She has. ܐܵܗܝܼ ܐܝܼܬܠܵܗ̇.

Does she have? ܐܝܼܬܠܵܗ̇ ܐܵܗܝܼ؟

She does not have. ܐܵܗܝܼ ܠܹܐ ܐܝܼܬܠܵܗ̇. or ܐܵܗܝܼ ܠܹܐ ܐܲܝܬܠܵܗ̇.

They have. ܐܵܢܝܼ ܐܝܼܬܠܗܘܿܢ.

Do they have? ܐܝܼܬܠܗܘܿܢ ܐܵܢܝܼ؟

They do not have. ܐܵܢܝܼ ܠܹܐ ܐܝܼܬܠܗܘܿܢ. or ܐܵܢܝܼ ܠܹܐ ܐܲܝܬܠܗܘܿܢ.

Example:

He has a long hair. ܐܵܗܘܼ ܐܝܼܬܠܹܗ ܣܲܥܪܵܐ ܐܲܪܝܼܟ݂ܵܐ.

Future: Possessive + ܬ + ܒܸܕ ܗܵܘܹܐ, Possessive + ܬ + ܒܸܬ ܗܵܘܹܐ

Note: some accents, you might hear ܒܸܕ ܐܵܘܹܐ, ܒܸܬ ܐܵܘܹܐ. Remember ܬ in ܒܸܬ is silent most the time ܒܸܬ݇ .

First Person ܦܲܪܨܘܿܦܵܐ ܩܲܕܡܵܝܵܐ

Ends with the vowel ܝܼ for both masculine and feminine, and ܢ for plural.
Same for masculine and feminine:

I will have.	ܐܵܢܵܐ ܒܸܕ ܗܵܘܹܐܠܝܼ.
Will I have?	ܒܸܕ ܗܵܘܹܐܠܝܼ ܐܵܢܵܐ؟
I will not have.	ܐܵܢܵܐ ܠܵܐ ܒܸܕ ܗܵܘܹܐܠܝܼ.
We will have.	ܐܲܚܢܲܢ ܒܸܕ ܗܵܘܹܐܠܲܢ.
Will we have?	ܒܸܕ ܗܵܘܹܐܠܲܢ ܐܲܚܢܲܢ؟
We will not have.	ܐܲܚܢܲܢ ܠܵܐ ܒܸܕ ܗܵܘܹܐܠܲܢ.
I am going to have.	ܐܵܢܵܐ ܒܸܬ ܗܵܘܹܐܠܝܼ.
Am I going to have?	ܒܸܬ ܗܵܘܹܐܠܝܼ ܐܵܢܵܐ؟
I am not going to have.	ܐܵܢܵܐ ܠܵܐ ܒܸܬ ܗܵܘܹܐܠܝܼ.
We are going to have.	ܐܲܚܢܲܢ ܒܸܬ ܗܵܘܹܐܠܲܢ.
Are we going to have?	ܒܸܬ ܗܵܘܹܐܠܲܢ ܐܲܚܢܲܢ؟
We are not going to have.	ܐܲܚܢܲܢ ܠܵܐ ܒܸܬ ܗܵܘܹܐܠܲܢ.

Examples: We will have a new house. (sometime in the future.)

ܐܲܚܢܲܢ ܒܸܕ ܗܵܘܹܐܠܲܢ ܚܲܕ ܒܲܝܬܵܐ ܚܲܕܬܵܐ.

We are going to have a new house. (near future.)

ܐܲܚܢܲܢ ܒܸܬ ܗܵܘܹܐܠܲܢ ܚܲܕ ܒܲܝܬܵܐ ܚܲܕܬܵܐ.

Note: in the negative form, Syriac speakers use ܒܸܬ instead of ܒܸܕ

Second Person ܦܲܪܨܘܿܦܵܐ ܬܪܲܝܵܢܵܐ

Ends with ܘܼܟ݂ for masculine, ܟ݂ܝ from feminine, and ܘܟ݂ܘܿܢ for plural.

To 2nd m:

You will have. ܐܲܢ̄ܬ ܒܸܕ ܗܵܘܹܐܠܘܼܟ݂.

Will you have? ܒܸܕ ܗܵܘܹܐܠܘܼܟ݂ ܐܲܢ̄ܬ؟

You will not have. ܐܲܢ̄ܬ ܠܵܐ ܒܸܕ ܗܵܘܹܐܠܘܼܟ݂.

You are going to have. ܐܲܢ̄ܬ ܕܒܸܠ ܗܵܘܹܐܠܘܼܟ݂.

Are you going to have? ܕܒܸܠ ܗܵܘܹܐܠܘܼܟ݂ ܐܲܢ̄ܬ؟

You are not going to have. ܐܲܢ̄ܬ ܠܵܐ ܕܒܸܠ ܗܵܘܹܐܠܘܼܟ݂.

To 2nd f:

You will have. ܐܲܢ̄ܬܝ ܒܸܕ ܗܵܘܹܐܠܵܟ݂ܝ.

Will you have? ܒܸܕ ܗܵܘܹܐܠܵܟ݂ܝ ܐܲܢ̄ܬܝ؟

You will not have. ܐܲܢ̄ܬܝ ܠܵܐ ܒܸܕ ܗܵܘܹܐܠܵܟ݂ܝ.

You are going to have. ܐܲܢ̄ܬܝ ܕܒܸܠ ܗܵܘܹܐܠܵܟ݂ܝ.

Are you going to have? ܕܒܸܠ ܗܵܘܹܐܠܵܟ݂ܝ ܐܲܢ̄ܬܝ؟

You are not going to have. ܐܲܢ̄ܬܝ ܠܵܐ ܕܒܸܠ ܗܵܘܹܐܠܵܟ݂ܝ.

To 2nd p:

You will have. ܐܲܚܬܘܿܢ ܒܸܕ ܗܵܘܹܐܠܘܟ݂ܘܿܢ.

Will you have? ܒܸܕ ܗܵܘܹܐܠܘܟ݂ܘܿܢ ܐܲܚܬܘܿܢ؟

You will not have. ܐܲܚܬܘܿܢ ܠܵܐ ܒܸܕ ܗܵܘܹܐܠܘܟ݂ܘܿܢ.

You are going to have. ܐܲܚܬܘܿܢ ܕܒܸܠ ܗܵܘܹܐܠܘܟ݂ܘܿܢ.

Are you going to have? ܕܒܸܠ ܗܵܘܹܐܠܘܟ݂ܘܿܢ ܐܲܚܬܘܿܢ؟

You are not going to have. ܐܲܚܬܘܿܢ ܠܵܐ ܕܒܸܠ ܗܵܘܹܐܠܘܟ݂ܘܿܢ.

Examples:

You will not have money (2nd m). ܐܲܢ̄ܬ ܠܵܐ ܒܸܕ ܗܵܘܹܐܠܘܼܟ݂ ܙܘܼܙܹܐ.

No, you are not going to have money (to 2nd p).

ܠܵܐ، ܐܲܚܬܘܿܢ ܠܵܐ ܕܒܸܠ ܗܵܘܹܐܠܘܟ݂ܘܿܢ ܙܘܼܙܹܐ.

Third Person ܦܪܨܘܦܐ ܬܠܝܬܝܐ

Ends with ܗ for masculine, ܗ̇ for feminine, and for plural ends with letter ܢ (silent in some accents).

To 2nd m:

He will have. ܐܗܘ ܒܕ ܗܘܝܠܗ.
Will he have? ܒܕ ܗܘܝܠܗ ܐܗܘ؟
He will not have. ܐܗܘ ܠܐ ܒܕ ܗܘܝܠܗ.

He is going to have. ܐܗܘ ܕܒܥ ܗܘܝܠܗ.
Is he going to have? ܕܒܥ ܗܘܝܠܗ ܐܗܘ؟
He is not going to have. ܐܗܘ ܠܐ ܕܒܥ ܗܘܝܠܗ

To 2nd f:

She will have. ܐܗܝ ܒܕ ܗܘܝܠܗ̇.
Will she have? ܒܕ ܗܘܝܠܗ̇ ܐܗܝ؟
She will not have. ܐܗܝ ܠܐ ܒܕ ܗܘܝܠܗ̇.
She is going to have ܐܗܝ ܕܒܥ ܗܘܝܠܗ̇.
Is she going to have? ܕܒܥ ܗܘܝܠܗ̇ ܐܗܝ؟
She is not going to have. ܐܗܝ ܠܐ ܕܒܥ ܗܘܝܠܗ̇.

To 2nd p:

They will have. ܐܢܝ ܒܕ ܗܘܝܠܗܘܢ.
Will they have? ܒܕ ܗܘܝܠܗܘܢ ܐܢܝ؟
They will not have. ܐܢܝ ܠܐ ܒܕ ܗܘܝܠܗܘܢ.

They are going to have. ܐܢܝ ܕܒܥ ܗܘܝܠܗܘܢ.
Are they going to have? ܕܒܥ ܗܘܝܠܗܘܢ ܐܢܝ؟
They are not going to have. ܐܢܝ ܠܐ ܕܒܥ ܗܘܝܠܗܘܢ.

Example:
They will have a wedding next month.
ܐܢܝ ܒܕ ܗܘܝܠܗܘܢ ܫܠܘܠܐ ܒܝܪܚܐ ܕܐܬܝܐ ܒܬܪܟܐ.

Past (had): ܒܝܼܡܵܗܘܵܐ

Note: with the past tense, also means: there was, there were. See subject-verb agreement.

First Person ܦܲܪܨܘܿܦܵܐ ܩܲܕܡܵܝܵܐ

Ends with the vowel ـܠܝܼ for both masculine and feminine, and ܠܲܢ for plural.
Same for masculine and feminine

I had.	ܐܵܢܵܐ ܒܝܼܡܵܗܘܵܠܝܼ.
Did I have?	ܒܝܼܡܵܗܘܵܠܝܼ ܐܵܢܵܐ؟
I did not have.	ܐܵܢܵܐ ܠܹܐ ܒܝܼܡܵܗܘܵܠܝܼ. or ܐܵܢܵܐ ܠܹܐ ܝܼܒܹܡܵܗܘܵܠܝܼ.
We had.	ܐܲܚܢܲܢ ܒܝܼܡܵܗܘܵܠܲܢ.
Did we have?	ܒܝܼܡܵܗܘܵܠܲܢ ܐܲܚܢܲܢ؟
We did not have	ܐܲܚܢܲܢ ܠܹܐ ܒܝܼܡܵܗܘܵܠܲܢ. or ܐܲܚܢܲܢ ܠܹܐ ܝܼܒܹܡܵܗܘܵܠܲܢ.

Example: I had a small house (1st m/f) ܐܵܢܵܐ ܒܝܼܡܵܗܘܵܠܝܼ ܒܲܝܬܵܐ ܘܥܝܼܩܵܐ.

Second Person ܦܲܪܨܘܿܦܵܐ ܬܸܪܝܵܢܵܐ

Ends with ـܠܘܿܟ for masculine, ـܠܵܟܝ from feminine, and ـܠܵܘܟܘܿ for plural.

For male:	You had.	ܐܲܝܬ ܒܝܼܡܵܗܘܵܠܘܿܟ.
	Did you have?	ܒܝܼܡܵܗܘܵܠܘܿܟ ܐܲܝܬ؟
You did not have.		ܐܲܝܬ ܠܹܐ ܒܝܼܡܵܗܘܵܠܘܿܟ. or ܐܲܝܬ ܠܹܐ ܝܼܒܹܡܵܗܘܵܠܘܿܟ.
For female:	You had.	ܐܲܝܬܝ ܒܝܼܡܵܗܘܵܠܵܟܝ.
	Did you have?	ܒܝܼܡܵܗܘܵܠܵܟܝ ܐܲܝܬܝ؟
You did not have.		ܐܲܝܬܝ ܠܹܐ ܒܝܼܡܵܗܘܵܠܵܟܝ or ܐܲܝܬܝ ܠܹܐ ܝܼܒܹܡܵܗܘܵܠܵܟܝ.
For group:	You had.	ܐܲܚܬܘܿܢ ܒܝܼܡܵܗܘܵܠܵܘܟܘܿ.
	Did you have?	ܒܝܼܡܵܗܘܵܠܵܘܟܘܿ ܐܲܚܬܘܿܢ؟
You did not have.		ܐܲܚܬܘܿܢ ܠܹܐ ܒܝܼܡܵܗܘܵܠܵܘܟܘܿ. or ܐܲܚܬܘܿܢ ܠܹܐ ܝܼܒܹܡܵܗܘܵܠܵܘܟܘܿ.

Example: You had a white horse (2nd p).

ܐܲܚܬܘܿܢ ܒܝܼܡܵܗܘܵܠܵܘܟܘܿ ܣܘܼܣܵܐ ܚܘܵܪܵܐ ܣܢܝܼܩܵܐ.

Third Person　　ܩܕܝܡܘܬ ܡܟܢܝܐ

Ends with ܘܠ for masculine, ܠܗ for feminine, and for plural ends with letter
ܠܢ (silent in some accents).

	He had.	ܗܘܐ ܒܝܬܘܬܠܗ.
	Did he have?	ܒܝܬܘܬܠܗ ܗܘܐ؟
He did not have.	ܗܘܐ ܠܐ ܒܝܬܘܬܠܗ. or ܗܘܐ ܠܐ ܒܝܬܘܬܠܗ.	
	She had	ܗܘܒ ܒܝܬܘܬܠܗ.
	Did she have?	ܒܝܬܘܬܠܗ ܗܘܒ؟
She did not have.	ܗܘܒ ܠܐ ܒܝܬܘܬܠܗ. or ܗܘܒ ܠܐ ܒܝܬܘܬܠܗ.	
	They had	ܢܘܗܒ ܒܝܬܘܬܠܢ.
	Did they have?	ܒܝܬܘܬܠܢ ܢܘܗܒ؟
They did not have.	ܢܘܗܒ ܠܐ ܒܝܬܘܬܠܢ. or ܢܘܗܒ ܠܐ ܒܝܬܘܬܠܢ.	

Example: She had a brother worked for government.

ܗܘܒ ܒܝܬܘܬܠܗ ܚܘܢܐ ܦܠܚܢܘܗ ܗܘ ܣܘܟܡܐ.

185

Subject-Verb Agreement

There is/are: ܐܝܬ

ܐܝܬ (or ܐܝܼܬ for emphasize) use for both singular and plural.

Example:

There is a bird in the sky.   ܐܝܬ ܚܕܳ ܛܲܝܪܳܐ ܒܫܡܲܝܳܐ.

There are two doves in the cage.   ܐܝܬ ܬܪܝܢ ܝܘܿܢ̈ܐ ܒܩܦܣܳܐ.

In the negative form "there is no", is by adding ܠܐ before ܐܝܬ and silent the ܐ letter. This is also true for "there was/were". **For example**:

There is no school tomorrow.   ܠܐ ܐܝܬ ܡܕܪܫܬܳܐ ܩܘܕܡܐ.

There was/were: ܐܝܬܗܘܳܐ

Same for both singular and plural

Examples:

There was a game yesterday.   ܐܝܬܗܘܳܐ ܚܕ ܛܘܼܥܒܳܐ ܐܬܡܠ.

There was no party last night.   ܠܐ ܐܝܬܗܘܳܐ ܚܲܓܳܐ ܒܠܠܝܐ ܕܒܬܪܳܐ.

There will be.   ܒܕ ܗܘܐ

There is going to be.   ܒܠ ܗܘܐ

Examples:

There will be a wedding this coming Sunday.

ܒܕ ܗܘܐ ܚܕܳ ܡܫܬܘܼܬܳܐ ܚܕܒܫܒܳܐ ܕܐܬܝܵܢܳܐ ܕܥܬܝܕ.

It is not going to rain tomorrow.

ܠܐ ܒܠ ܗܘܐ ܡܛܪܳܐ ܩܘܕܡܐ.

Literal: There is going to be no rain tomorrow. (the letter ܠ in ܒܠ is not silent)

The Permission Verb - Let (ܫܒܘܩ)

The verb "let - ܫܒܘܩ" is used for making invitations, requests, and giving permission.

First Person ܩܕܡܝܐ ܒܪ ܢܝܫܐ

Note: the pronoun (first, second, and third person) ܐܢܐ, ܐܢ̰ܬ, ܐܢ̰ܬܝ, ܐܢܚܢ, etc. just like we learned before, is also optional when using with the permission verb.

- From 1ˢᵗ person to 2ⁿᵈ person: it is the same for male and female:

$$\text{ܐܢܐ ܫܒܘܩ + ܠܝ}$$

Example: Let me sleep.

1ˢᵗ m: ܐܢܐ ܫܒܘܩܠܝ ܗܘ ܕܕܡܟ.

(**Literal**: I let me to sleep, ܗܘ is sounds ܕ before verb)

1ˢᵗ f: ܐܢܐ ܫܒܘܩܠܝ ܗܘ ܕܕܡܟ.   or   ܐܢܐ ܫܒܘܩܠܝ ܗܘ ܕܕܡܟ.

Or:

ܫܒܘܩ ܗܘ ܕܕܡܟ.   or: ܐܢܐ ܫܒܘܩ ܗܘ ܕܕܡܟ.

ܫܒܘܩ ܗܘ ܕܕܡܟ.   or: ܐܢܐ ܫܒܘܩ ܗܘ ܕܕܡܟ.

Example: Let me go home.

1ˢᵗ m & f: ܫܒܘܩ ܗܘ ܘܠܝ ܠܒܝܬܐ.

(**Literal**: let me to go to home.)

- From 1ˢᵗ person to 2ⁿᵈ person plural: ܫܒܘܩܘܢܠܝ, for example:

Example: Let me speak.

1ˢᵗ m: ܫܒܘܩܘܢܝ ܗܘ ܗܡܙܡܝ.   or   ܫܒܘܩܘܢܠܝ ܗܘ ܗܡܙܡܝ.

1ˢᵗ f: ܫܒܘܩܘܢܝ ܗܘ ܗܡܙܡܢܝ.   or   ܫܒܘܩܘܢܠܝ ܗܘ ܗܡܙܡܢܝ.

- 1ˢᵗ person plural to 2ⁿᵈ person plural. Same for male and female:

ܫܒܘܩܘܢܠܢ

Example: Let us talk.   ܫܒܘܩܘܢܝ ܗܘ ܗܡܙܡܘܚ.   or   ܫܒܘܩܘܢܠܢ ܗܘ ܗܡܙܡܘܚ.

Special Case ܥܒܘܕ

In the first-person case, you can just merge the two words, ܥܒܘܕ and ܗܝ, in one-word ܥܒܘܕ for example:

Let me eat (1st m) .	ܥܒܘܕ ܢܐܟܠܝ
Let me eat (1st f).	ܥܒܘܕ ܢܐܟܠܝ
Let us go.	ܥܒܘܕ ܘܟ

Second Person ܩܕܡܝܐ ܕܬܪܝܢܐ

It is by adding the letter ܒ at the beginning and ends with the second person possessive:

1st m to 2nd m: I let you go.	ܒܥܒܘܕܝܢܘܗܝ ܗܝ ܘܟܘܝ
1st m to 2nd f: I let you study.	ܒܥܒܘܕܝܢܝ ܗܝ ܕܕܩܐ
1st m to 2nd p: I let you work.	ܒܥܒܘܕܝܢܘܟܘܢ ܗܝ ܦܠܚܘܟܘܢ
1st f to 2nd m.	ܒܥܒܘܕܝܢܘܗܝ
1st f to 2nd f.	ܒܥܒܘܕܝܢܝ
1st f to 2nd p.	ܒܥܒܘܕܝܢܘܟܘܢ

Example: I let you swim. (**2nd f**). ܒܥܒܘܕܝܢܝ ܗܝ ܗܢܝܐ.

1st p to 2nd m.	ܒܥܒܘܕܝܢܘܟܘܗܝ
1st plural to 2nd f.	ܒܥܒܘܕܝܢܘܟܠܝ
1st p to 2nd p.	ܒܥܒܘܕܝܢܘܟܠܘܟܘܢ

Example: We let you sleep (2nd p). ܒܥܒܘܕܝܢܘܟܠܘܟܘܢ ܗܝ ܕܡܟܘܟܘܢ.

Third Person ܩܕܝ̇ܡܵܝܵܐ ܡܬܐܡܪܵܢܵܐ

It is by adding the letter ܒ at the beginning and ends with the third person possessive:

1st m to 3rd m.	ܒܬܦܘܩܝܢ
1st m to 3rd f.	ܒܬܦܘܩܝܢ
1st m to 3rd p.	ܒܬܦܘܩܝܢ

Example: I let her sit with us (1st m).   ܒܬܦܘܩܝܢ ܗܿܝ ܢܷܬܘܵ ܥܲܡܲܢ.

1st f to 3rd m.	ܒܬܦܘܩܝܢ
1st f to 3rd f.	ܒܬܦܘܩܝܢ
1st f to 3rd p.	ܒܬܦܘܩܝܢ

Example: I let him speak (1st f).   ܒܬܦܘܩܝܢ ܗܿܘ ܗܲܡܙܸܡ.

1st p to 3rd m.	ܒܬܦܘܩܡܘܚܠܹܗ
1st p to 3rd f.	ܒܬܦܘܩܡܘܚܠܵܗ
1st p to 3rd p.	ܒܬܦܘܩܡܘܚܠܗ

Example: We let her drive.   ܒܬܦܘܩܡܘܚܠܵܗ ܗܿܝ ܟܵܠܢܵܐ.

Seeking Permission

This is used widely with the **Condition** ܐܸܢ. See more options and examples in Condition section.

• **From Second Person:** same for male and female

1st m/f seeking permission from 2nd m.	ܒܬܦܘܩܝܘܟ
1st m/f seeking permission from 2nd f.	ܒܬܦܘܩܝܘܟܝ
1st m/f seeking permission from 2nd p.	ܒܬܦܘܩܝܘܟܘܢ
1st p seeking permission from 2nd m.	ܒܬܦܘܩܝܟ
1st p seeking permission from 2nd f.	ܒܬܦܘܩܝܟܝ
1st p seeking permission from 2nd p.	ܒܬܦܘܩܡܘܟܘܢ

189

- **From Third Person**

1st m/f seeking permission from 3rd m.	ܫܒܘܩܠܝ
1st m/f seeking permission from 3rd f.	ܫܒܘܩܠܝ
1st m/f seeking permission from 3rd p.	ܫܒܘܩܢܠܝ
1st p seeking permission from 3rd m.	ܫܒܘܩܠܢ
1st p seeking permission from 3rd f.	ܫܒܘܩܠܢ
1st p seeking permission from 3rd p.	ܫܒܘܩܢܠܢ

The Modal Verbs
The Verbs (Have to, Need to) ܣܢܝܩܐ

The verb ܣܢܝܩܐ / ܣܢܝܩܬܐ / ܣܢܝܩܝܢ is used to express certainty, necessity, and obligation. It has two meanings depending on its subject.

1. **Need to: noun + ܠ + ܣܢܝܩܐ**

ܣܢܝܩܐ / ܣܢܝܩܬܐ / ܣܢܝܩܝܢ means "need" when it is followed by a noun preceded by the letter ܠ, for example:

I need a house (1st m).	ܐܢܐ ܐܝܘܢ ܣܢܝܩܐ ܠܒܝܬܐ.
I need a car (1st f).	ܐܢܐ ܐܝܘܢ ܣܢܝܩܬܐ ܠܡܝܢܕܐ.
He needs money.	ܐܗܘ ܐܝܠܗ ܣܢܝܩܐ ܠܙܘܙܐ
She needs job.	ܐܗܝ ܐܝܠܗ ܣܢܝܩܬܐ ܠܥܘܒܕܐ
They need a house.	ܐܢܝ ܐܝܠܝ ܣܢܝܩܝܢ ܠܒܝܬܐ.

2. **Have to, Has to, Had to, Must verb + ܬܐ + ܣܢܝܩܐ**

ܣܢܝܩܐ / ܣܢܝܩܬܐ / ܣܢܝܩܝܢ means "have to" "must" when it is followed by a verb preceded by ܬܐ (to). For example:

I must sleep. (1st m).	ܐܢܐ ܐܝܘܢ ܣܢܝܩܐ ܬܐ ܕܡܟܢ.
I had to walk. (1st f).	ܐܢܐ ܣܢܝܩܬܐ ܗܘܝܢ ܗܘܐ ܬܐ ܡܫܓܐ.
I think you must sleep here. (2nd m)	ܐܢܐ ܒܚܫܒܢ ܐܝܘܬ ܣܢܝܩܐ ܬܐ ܕܡܟܬ ܐܟܐ.
They must go home.	ܐܢܝ ܐܝܠܝ ܣܢܝܩܝܢ ܬܐ ܐܙܠܝ ܠܒܝܬܐ.

Remember that ܬܐ sounds ܕ with a verb.

Can/ be able to (Suffix + ܡܵܨܹܐ)

ܡܵܨܹܐ is one of the most commonly used modal verbs in Syriac It can be used to express ability or opportunity, to request or offer permission, and show possibility or impossibility.

We use (suffix + ܡܵܨܹܐ) to say that something is possible or that someone has the ability to do something.

First Person   ܦܲܪܨܘܿܦܵܐ ܩܲܕܡܵܝܵܐ

I can   ܐܵܢܵܐ ܡܵܨܹܝܢ

        Example: I can swim very good. (1ˢᵗ f).   ܐܵܢܵܐ ܡܵܨܝܵܢ ܗܵܐ ܒܵܣܝܵܡ ܕܵܪܹܓ.

Can I?   ܡܵܨܹܝܢ ܐܵܢܵܐ؟

        Example: Can I go now?   ܡܵܨܹܝܢ ܐܵܢܵܐ ܗܵܐ ܙܵܠܟ ܕܝܵܘ؟

I can not   ܐܵܢܵܐ ܠܵܐܡܵܨܹܝܢ or ܐܵܢܵܐ ܠܵܐ ܡܵܨܹܝܢ.

Example: I cannot see you tonight (1st m/f to 2ⁿᵈ f).

     ܐܵܢܵܐ ܠܵܐܡܵܨܹܝܢ ܗܵܐ ܚܵܙܹܢ ܠܝܵܬܘܿܟ ܒܝܼܘܡܵܐ ܒܠܹܠܝܵܐ.

We can   ܐܲܚܢܲܢ ܡܵܨܹܚ

Example: We can go to movie tomorrow at night.

     ܐܲܚܢܲܢ ܡܵܨܹܚ ܗܵܐ ܙܵܠܟ ܠܣܝܼܢܹܡܵܐ ܩܵܕܡ ܒܠܹܠܝܵܐ.

Can We?   ܡܵܨܹܚ ܐܲܚܢܲܢ؟

        Example: Can we sleep here?   ܡܵܨܹܚ ܐܲܚܢܲܢ ܗܵܐ ܕܵܡܚܲܚ ܐܵܟܵܐ؟

We can not   ܐܲܚܢܲܢ ܠܵܐܡܵܨܹܚ or ܐܲܚܢܲܢ ܠܵܐ ܡܵܨܹܚ.

Example: We cannot sleep because of mosquito.

     ܐܲܚܢܲܢ ܠܵܐܡܵܨܹܚ ܗܵܐ ܕܵܡܚܲܚ ܡܸܛܠ ܕܝܼܬ ܒܵܩܵܐ.

        Literal: (we) cannot sleep because there is mosquito.

I was able to.	ܐܵܢܵܐ ܡܨܹܐܠܝܼ.
Was I able to?	ܡܨܹܐܠܝܼ ܐܵܢܵܐ؟
I was not able to.	ܐܵܢܵܐ ܠܵܐܡܨܹܐܠܝܼ.

We were able to.	ܐܸܢܲܚܢܲܢ ܡܵܨܹܝܗܘܵܐ.
Were we able to?	ܡܵܨܹܝܗܘܵܐ ܐܸܢܲܚܢܲܢ؟
We were not able to.	ܐܸܢܲܚܢܲܢ ܠܵܐܡܵܨܹܝܗܘܵܐ.

Example: I was not able to eat because I was so tired.

ܐܵܢܵܐ ܠܵܐܡܵܨܹܝܗܘܵܐ ܗ݇ܘܹܐ ܐ݇ܵܟ݂ܠܝܼܬܹܗܘܵܐ ܡܸܛܘܿܠ ܕܝܼ ܗܵܘܹܐ ܚܠܝܼܨ ܓ݂ܵܢܵܐ

I will be able to.	ܐܵܢܵܐ ܒܸܕ ܗܵܘܹܐ ܡܵܨ.
Will I be able to?	ܒܸܕ ܗܵܘܹܐ ܡܵܨ ܐܵܢܵܐ؟
I will not be able to.	ܐܵܢܵܐ ܠܵܐ ܒܸܕ ܗܵܘܹܐ ܡܵܨ.
We will be able to.	ܐܸܢܲܚܢܲܢ ܒܸܕ ܗܵܘܹܐ ܡܵܨ.
Will we be able to?	ܒܸܕ ܗܵܘܹܐ ܡܵܨ ܐܸܢܲܚܢܲܢ؟
We will not be able to.	ܐܸܢܲܚܢܲܢ ܠܵܐ ܒܸܕ ܗܵܘܹܐ ܡܵܨ.
I am going to be able to.	ܐܵܢܵܐ ܘܝܼܟ݂ ܗܵܘܹܐ ܡܵܨ.
Am I going to be able to?	ܘܝܼܟ݂ ܗܵܘܹܐ ܡܵܨ ܐܵܢܵܐ؟
I am not going to be able to.	ܐܵܢܵܐ ܠܵܐ ܘܝܼܟ݂ ܗܵܘܹܐ ܡܵܨ.
We are going to be able to.	ܐܸܢܲܚܢܲܢ ܘܝܼܟ݂ ܗܵܘܹܐ ܡܵܨ.
Are we going to be able to.	ܘܝܼܟ݂ ܗܵܘܹܐ ܡܵܨ ܐܸܢܲܚܢܲܢ؟
We are not going to be able to.	ܐܸܢܲܚܢܲܢ ܠܵܐ ܘܝܼܟ݂ ܗܵܘܹܐ ܡܵܨ.

Example: We are not going to be able to finish by tomorrow.

ܐܸܢܲܚܢܲܢ ܠܵܐ ܘܝܼܟ݂ ܗܵܘܹܐ ܡܵܨ ܗ݇ܵܐ ܫܲܠܡܘܿܗ ܩܘܕܡ.

Second Person   ܦܲܪܨܘܿܦܵܐ ܬܪܲܝܵܢܵܐ

To 2ⁿᵈ m:

You can.	ܐܲܢ݇ܬ ܡܵܨܹܝܬܘܿܗܝ.
Can you?	ܡܵܨܹܝܬܘܿܗܝ ܐܲܢ݇ܬ؟
You cannot.	ܐܲܢ݇ܬ ܠܵܡܵܨܹܝܬܘܿܗܝ or ܐܲܢ݇ܬ ܠܵܐ ܡܵܨܹܝܬܘܿܗܝ.
You were able to.	ܐܲܢ݇ܬ ܡܵܨܹܬܘܿܗܝ.
Were you able to?	ܡܵܨܹܬܘܿܗܝ ܐܲܢ݇ܬ؟

You were not able to.　　　　　　　　　ܐܲܢ݇ܬ ܠܵܐ ܒܸܡܨܵܝܬܘܼܟ.

You will be able to.　　　　　　　　　ܐܲܢ݇ܬ ܒܸܕ ܗܵܘܝܵܐܘܼܟ.

Will you be able to?　　　　　　　　　ܒܸܕ ܗܵܘܝܵܐܘܼܟ ܐܲܢ݇ܬ؟

You will not be able to.　　　　　　　　ܐܲܢ݇ܬ ܠܵܐ ܒܸܕ ܗܵܘܝܵܐܘܼܟ.

You are going to be able to.　　　　　　ܐܲܢ݇ܬ ܘܸܠܟ ܗܵܘܝܵܐܘܼܟ.

Are you going to be able to?　　　　　ܘܸܠܟ ܗܵܘܝܵܐܘܼܟ ܐܲܢ݇ܬ؟

You are not going to be able to.　　　　ܐܲܢ݇ܬ ܠܵܐ ܘܸܠܟ ܗܵܘܝܵܐܘܼܟ.

To 2nd f:

edon ryit

You can.　　　　　　　　　　　ܐܲܢ݇ܬܝ ܒܸܡܨܵܝܬܝ.

Can you?　　　　　　　　　　　ܒܸܡܨܵܝܬܝ ܐܲܢ݇ܬܝ؟

You cannot.　　ܐܲܢ݇ܬܝ ܠܲܝܬܸܢ or ܐܲܢ݇ܬܝ ܠܵܐ ܒܸܡܨܵܝܬܝ.

You were able to.　　　　　　　ܐܲܢ݇ܬܝ ܒܸܡܨܵܝܬܝ.

Were you able to?　　　　　　　ܒܸܡܨܵܝܬܝ ܐܲܢ݇ܬܝ؟

You were not able to.　　　　　ܐܲܢ݇ܬܝ ܠܵܐ ܒܸܡܨܵܝܬܝ.

You will be able to.　　　　　　ܐܲܢ݇ܬܝ ܒܸܕ ܗܵܘܝܵܬܝ.

Will you be able to?　　　　　　ܒܸܕ ܗܵܘܝܵܬܝ ܐܲܢ݇ܬܝ؟

You will not be able to.　　　　ܐܲܢ݇ܬܝ ܠܵܐ ܒܸܕ ܗܵܘܝܵܬܝ.

You are going to be able to.　　ܐܲܢ݇ܬܝ ܘܸܠܟ ܗܵܘܝܵܬܝ.

Are you going to be able to?　ܘܸܠܟ ܗܵܘܝܵܬܝ ܐܲܢ݇ܬܝ؟

You are not going to be able to.　ܐܲܢ݇ܬܝ ܠܵܐ ܘܸܠܟ ܗܵܘܝܵܬܝ.

To 2nd p:

You can.　　　　　　　　　　ܐܲܢ݇ܬܘܿܢ ܒܸܡܨܵܬܘܿܢ.

Can you?　　　　　　　　　ܒܸܡܨܵܬܘܿܢ ܐܲܢ݇ܬܘܿܢ؟

You cannot.　ܐܲܢ݇ܬܘܿܢ ܠܲܝܬܸܢ or ܐܲܢ݇ܬܘܿܢ ܠܵܐ ܒܸܡܨܵܬܘܿܢ.

You were able to.　　　　　ܐܲܢ݇ܬܘܿܢ ܒܸܡܨܵܝܬܘܿܢ.

Were you able to?　　　　ܒܸܡܨܵܝܬܘܿܢ ܐܲܢ݇ܬܘܿܢ؟

You were not able to.　　ܐܲܢ݇ܬܘܿܢ ܠܵܐ ܒܸܡܨܵܝܬܘܿܢ.

You will be able to.　　　ܐܲܢ݇ܬܘܿܢ ܒܸܕ ܗܵܘܝܵܬܘܿܢ.

193

Will you be able to?	ܒܕ ܡܨܝܬܘܢ ܐܚܬܘܢ؟
You will not be able to.	ܐܚܬܘܢ ܠܐ ܒܕ ܡܨܝܬܘܢ.

You are going to be able to.	ܐܚܬܘܢ ܒܝܬ ܡܨܝܬܘܢ.
Are you going to be able to?	ܒܝܬ ܡܨܝܬܘܢ ܐܚܬܘܢ؟
You are not going to be able to.	ܐܚܬܘܢ ܠܐ ܒܝܬ ܡܨܝܬܘܢ.

Example:
You cannot stay by your uncle's house (2nd p).

ܐܚܬܘܢ ܠܐ ܝܡܨܝܬܘܢ ܩܝܡܬܘܢ ܠܐ ܒܝܬܐ ܕܕܕܘܟܘܢ

Third Person ܦܪܨܘܦܐ ܬܠܝܬܝܐ

He can.	ܐܗܘ ܝܡܨܐ[9]
Can he?	ܝܡܨܐ ܐܗܘ؟
He cannot.	ܐܗܘ ܠܐܝܡܨܐ or ܐܗܘ ܠܐ ܝܡܨܐ
He was able to.	ܐܗܘ ܝܡܨܝܠܗ.
Was he able to?	ܝܡܨܝܠܗ ܐܗܘ؟
He was not able to.	ܐܗܘ ܠܐ ܝܡܨܝܠܗ.

He will be able to.	ܐܗܘ ܒܕ ܡܨܐ.
Will he be able to?	ܒܕ ܡܨܐ ܐܗܘ؟
He will not be able to.	ܐܗܘ ܠܐ ܒܕ ܡܨܐ.

He is going to be able to.	ܐܗܘ ܒܝܬ ܡܨܐ.
Is he going to be able to?	ܒܝܬ ܡܨܐ ܐܗܘ؟
He is not going to be able to.	ܐܗܘ ܠܐ ܒܝܬ ܡܨܐ.

Example: He is not going to be able to come to the wedding party?

ܐܗܘ ܠܐ ܒܝܬ ܡܨܐ ܗܐ ܕܐܬܐ ܠܚܠܘܠܐ.

---

[9] Also means "it has" for contains something. For example: **The cup has a water in it**.

ܟܣܐ ܝܡܨܐ ܡܝܐ ܓܘܗ.

She can	ܗܿܘ ܡܵܨܹܐ.
Can she?	ܡܵܨܹܐ ܗܿܘ؟
She can not	ܗܿܘ ܠܵܐܡܵܨܹܐ or ܗܿܘ ܠܵܐ ܡܵܨܹܐ
She was able to	ܗܿܘ ܡܨܹܐܘܵܗ.
Was she able to?	ܡܨܹܐܘܵܗ ܗܿܘ؟
She was not able to	ܗܿܘ ܠܵܐ ܡܨܹܐܘܵܗ.
She will be able to	ܗܿܘ ܒܸܕ ܡܵܨܝܵܐ.
Will she be able to?	ܒܸܕ ܡܵܨܝܵܐ ܗܿܘ؟
She will not be able to	ܗܿܘ ܠܵܐ ܒܸܕ ܡܵܨܝܵܐ.
She is going to be able to	ܗܿܘ ܘܸܠܹܐ ܡܵܨܝܵܐ.
Is she going to be able to?	ܘܸܠܹܐ ܡܵܨܝܵܐ ܗܿܘ؟
She is not going to be able to	ܗܿܘ ܠܵܐ ܘܸܠܹܐ ܡܵܨܝܵܐ.

Example: She can come and sleep over: ܗܿܘ ܡܵܨܹܐ ܕܵܐ ܐܵܬܝܵܐ ܘܕܵܡܟܵܐ ܠܓܹܒܲܢ

They can	ܐܵܢܝܼ ܡܵܨܝܼ
Can they?	ܡܵܨܝܼ ܐܵܢܝܼ؟
They can not	ܐܵܢܝܼ ܠܵܐܡܵܨܝܼ or ܐܵܢܝܼ ܠܵܐ ܡܵܨܝܼ
They were able to	ܐܵܢܝܼ ܡܨܹܐܠܗܘܿܢ.
Were they able to?	ܡܨܹܐܠܗܘܿܢ ܐܵܢܝܼ؟
They were not able to	ܐܵܢܝܼ ܠܵܐ ܡܨܹܐܠܗܘܿܢ.
They will be able to	ܐܵܢܝܼ ܒܸܕ ܡܵܨܝܼ.
Will they be able to?	ܒܸܕ ܡܵܨܝܼ ܐܵܢܝܼ؟
They will not be able to	ܐܵܢܝܼ ܠܵܐ ܒܸܕ ܡܵܨܝܼ.
They are going to be able to	ܐܵܢܝܼ ܘܸܠܹܐ ܡܵܨܝܼ.
Are they going to be able to?	ܘܸܠܹܐ ܡܵܨܝܼ ܐܵܢܝܼ؟
They are not going to be able to	ܐܵܢܝܼ ܠܵܐ ܘܸܠܹܐ ܡܵܨܝܼ.

Example: Will he be able to come next week?

ܒܸܕ ܡܵܨܝܵܐ ܗܿܘ ܕܵܐ ܐܵܬܹܐ ܒܸܫܲܒ݂ܬܵܐ ܕܐܵܬܝܵܢܵܐ؟

195

Could   (Suffix + ܡܵܨܹܐ)

ܡܵܨܹܐ is a modal verb used to express possibility or past ability or future ability as well as to make suggestions and requests. ܡܵܨܹܐ is also commonly used in conditional sentences as the conditional form of ܝܵܕܥ

First Person   ܩܲܕܡܵܝܵܐ ܦܲܪܨܘܿܦܵܐ

This is the same for both male and female in First Person.

Present:

I could	ܐܵܢܵܐ ܡܵܨܘܼܒ
Could I?	ܡܵܨܘܼܒ ܐܵܢܵܐ؟
(in negative form, we replace ܒ with ܚ) I could not	ܐܵܢܵܐ ܠܲܐ ܡܵܨܘܼܚ
We could	ܐܲܚܢܲܢ ܡܵܨܘܼܚ
Could we?	ܡܵܨܘܼܚ ܐܲܚܢܲܢ؟
We could not	ܐܲܚܢܲܢ ܠܲܐ ܡܵܨܘܼܚ

Future: we use ܒܸܕ and ܘܸܠ with (suffix + ܡܵܨܹܐ) in Syriac

Literal	Will	Going to
I will /I am going to could.	ܐܵܢܵܐ ܒܸܕ ܡܵܨܹܢ	ܐܵܢܵܐ ܘܸܠ ܡܵܨܹܢ
Will I?/Am I going to could?	ܒܸܕ ܡܵܨܹܢ ܐܵܢܵܐ؟	ܘܸܠ ܡܵܨܹܢ ܐܵܢܵܐ؟
I will not/I am not going to could.	ܐܵܢܵܐ ܠܲܐ ܒܸܕ ܡܵܨܹܢ	ܐܵܢܵܐ ܠܲܐ ܘܸܠ ܡܵܨܹܢ
We will/we are going to could.	ܐܲܚܢܲܢ ܒܸܕ ܡܵܨܲܚ	ܐܲܚܢܲܢ ܘܸܠ ܡܵܨܲܚ
Will we/Are we going to could?	ܒܸܕ ܡܵܨܲܚ ܐܲܚܢܲܢ؟	ܘܸܠ ܡܵܨܲܚ ܐܲܚܢܲܢ؟
We will not/we are not going could	ܐܲܚܢܲܢ ܠܲܐ ܒܸܕ ܡܵܨܲܚ	ܐܲܚܢܲܢ ܠܲܐ ܘܸܠ ܡܵܨܲܚ

Past: Unlike English, in Syriac, we can use (Suffix + ܡܨܹܠܹܗ) to talk about single events that happened in the past. Also, we can use (can/be able to: Suffix + ܝܵܕܥ). This applies to 2ⁿᵈ and 3ʳᵈ person too.

I could have	ܐܵܢܵܐ ܡܨܹܠܝܼ
Could have I?	ܡܨܹܠܝܼ ܐܵܢܵܐ؟

196

I could not have	ܐ݂ܢܵܐ ܠܵܐ ܗܘܹܐܠܝܼܒ
We could have	ܐ݂ܢܲܚܢ ܗܘܹܐܠܲܢ
Could have we?	ܗܘܹܐܠܲܢ ܐ݂ܢܲܚܢَ؟
We could have not	ܐ݂ܢܲܚܢَ ܠܵܐ ܗܘܹܐܠܲܢ

Example:

ܥܘܼܕܬܵܐ ܗܵܘܹܐ ܗܵܘܹܐ ܚܠܝܼܒ ܠܵܐ ܬܲܗܝܼܡܬܲܐ. ܐ݂ܢܵܐ ܠܵܐ ܗܘܹܐܠܝܼܒ ܗܵܐ ܓܲܠܹܐ ܡܹܐܚܕܲܒ ܬܲܗ ܡܸܠܚܵܐ.

The soup was terrible. I could taste nothing but salt.

Second Person   ܦܲܪܨܘܿܦܵܐ ܬܸܪ ܗܲܕܵܢܵܐ

Present

	Plural	Female	Male
You could	ܐ݂ܢܬܘܿܢ ܕܡܵܨܝܼܬܘܿܢ	ܐ݂ܢܬܝ ܕܡܵܨܝܼܬ	ܐ݂ܢܬ ܕܡܵܨܝܼܬ
Could you?	ܕܡܵܨܝܼܬܘܿܢ ܐ݂ܢܬܘܿܢ؟	ܕܡܵܨܝܼܬ ܐ݂ܢܬܝ؟	ܕܡܵܨܝܼܬ ܐ݂ܢܬ؟
You could not	ܐ݂ܢܬ ܠܵܐ ܕܡܵܨܝܼܬܘܿܢ	ܐ݂ܢܬܝ ܠܵܐ ܕܡܵܨܝܼܬ	ܐ݂ܢܬ ܠܵܐ ܕܡܵܨܝܼܬ

Future: one example is given in masculine singular form. Practice the other forms.

Literal	Will	Going to
You will /you are going to could	ܐ݂ܢܬ ܒܸܕ ܡܵܨܝܼܬ	ܐ݂ܢܬ ܘܸܠ ܡܵܨܝܼܬ

Past: one example is given in masculine singular form. Practice the other forms.

You could have	ܐ݂ܢܬ ܗܘܹܐܠܘܿܟ

Example:

ܝܼܡܵܐܬܒ ܐ݂ܢܵܐ ܗܵܐ ܐ݂ܙܵܠ ܥܲܡ ܚܲܒܪܵܘܵܬܝܼ ܠܨܝܼܢܵܐ ܐ݂ܒܝܼܘܵܐ ܠܝܼܡܵܐܬܒ؟
ܗܹܐ، ܒܸܕ ܡܵܨܝܼܬ.

Can I go with my friends to movie this evening? ... Yes, you could.

Third Person ܩܕܝ̈ܘܿܦ̇ܵܐ ܗ̇ܠܝ̈ܡ̈ܢܵܐ

Present: one example is given. Try the other forms.

~~They could~~	She could	He could
ܒܹܬ݂ܠܘܿܗܹ̈ܐ	ܒܹܬ݂ܠܘܿܗ̇ܵܐ	ܒܹܬ݂ܠܘܿܗܹ̇

(handwritten: "Same but add these" with bracket, and "silba")

Future: one example is given in masculine singular form. Practice the other forms.

Literal	Will	Going to
He will /he is going to could	ܒܹܬ݂ ܒܸܕ ܗܵܘܹ ܒܹܬ݂	ܒܹܬ݂ ܘܹܠܹ ܗܵܘܹ ܒܹܬ݂

Past: one example is given in masculine singular form. Practice the rest forms.

He could have   ܗ̇ܘܹ ܗ̇ܘܵܐ ܒܹܬ݂

Example:

ܡܲܪܝܲܡ ܘܝܲܩܘ̇ ܗ̇ܘܵܐ ܒܓܵܘܹܗ . ܒܹܬ݂ܠܘܿܗܹ̈ ܗ̇ܘܵܐ ܫܲܡܥܝ ܠܩܵܠܵܝ̈ܗܝ ܠܓܵܘܵܐ.

Mariam and Yaqoo were in there. They could hear their voices inside.

Should   Verb + ܗ̇ܘܹ + ܠܵܙܸܡ

(handwritten above: ܗܵܘܹ)   *(handwritten: lzim above ܠܵܙܸܡ)*

Just like English, ܠܵܙܸܡ is a modal verb most commonly used to make recommendations, advice, obligation, or expectation. ܠܵܙܸܡ does not take the possessive or suffix in any form. No masculine or feminine forms. The possessive or suffix will apply to the verb is used with it. It uses also in meaning of: have to, has to, had to, and must.

Examples: in these examples, the pronoun is omitted.

ܚܵܠܘܿܟ݂ ܒܝܼܠܹܗ ܡܲܪܥܝܼܵܢܵܐ . ܠܵܙܸܡ ܗ̇ܵܐ ܘܲܚܙܹܐ ܘܸܡܢܘܼܘܲܗ.

Your uncle is sick. You should go and see him. (recommendation).

ܠܵܙܸܡ ܐܵܬ݂ ܕܵܪܹܢܬ ܚܲܝܠܘܼܟ݂ ܒܝܼܫ ܒܩܪܵܝܬܵܐ ܕܝܼܕܘܼܟ݂.
You should focus more on your study. (advice)
ܒܫܲܪܝܼܪܘܼܬ݂ܵܐ ܠܵܙܸܡ ܐܵܢܵܐ ܗܵܘܹܝܢ ܒܥܹܕܬܵܐ ܒܐܲܪܒܲܥ ܒܫܵܥܬܵܐ.
I really should be in the church by 4pm. (obligation)
ܐܵܢܝܼ ܕܗܵܐ، ܠܵܙܸܡ ܐܵܢܝܼ ܗܵܘܹܐ ܒܒܹܝܬ݂ܢܲܗܪܝܼܢ.
They should already be in Iraq. (expectation)

May (have) and Might (have) - Perhaps ܒܲܠܟܵܐ

We use ܒܲܠܟܵܐ to say that something is possible happenings or possible actions in the future.

Examples:

I may go to Iraq this Easter. ܒܲܠܟܵܐ ܐܵܢܵܐ ܒܸܕ ܐܵܙܸܠ ܠܒܹܝܬ݂ܢܲܗܪܝܼܢ ܒܥܹܐܕܵܐ ܕܩܝܵܡܬܵܐ.

It might snow this night. ܒܲܠܟܵܐ ܒܸܕ ܐܵܬ݂ܹܐ ܬܲܠܓܵܐ ܒܠܸܠܝܵܐ.

He might be at church. ܒܲܠܟܵܐ ܐܵܗܘ ܐܝܼܠܹܗ ܒܥܹܕܬܵܐ.

The negative form is ܒܲܠܟܵܐ ܕܠܵܐ

Examples:

Mariam may not be at church. ܡܲܪܝܲܡ ܒܲܠܟܵܐ ܕܠܵܐ ܐܝܼܠܵܗ̇ (ܕܝܼܠܵܗ̇) ܒܥܹܕܬܵܐ.

There might not be a party this Friday.
ܒܲܠܟܵܐ ܕܠܵܐ ܐܝܼܬ݂ (ܕܝܼܬ݂) ܡܸܫܬܘܼܬ݂ܵܐ ܐܵܕܝܼ ܥܪܘܼܒ݂ܬ݂ܵܐ.

Conditional

IF ܐܢ

Examples:

ܐܢ ܨܒܝܬ ܗܿܬ ܕܐܙܠܬ ܠܣܚܬܐ ܦܘܕܪ، ܡܣܕܪ ܡܘܟܬ ܣܚܝܬ.

If you want to go to swimming tomorrow, pack your swimming things
tonight. (2nd m)

ܐܢ ܝܘܡܐ ܕܡܚܪ ܝܘܡܐ ܛܒܝܒܐ، ܐܫܟܚ ܕܡܨܝܢ ܗܿܬ ܐܙܠܢ ܠܥܕܬܐ.

If tomorrow is a nice day, we could go to the church.

ܐܢ ܐܢܐ ܗܘܝܬ ܥܣܪܝ ܫܢܐ ܒܨܘ ܫܚܝܒ ܒܬ، ܐܢܐ ܒܕ ܚܒܩܢܐ ܐܢܝܟܗ.

If I were twenty years' younger, I would marry her.

ܐܢ ܐܢܐ ܫܐܠܩܝ ܗܘܐ ܗܿܐ ܐܚܢܐ، ܐܘܗܐ ܒܕ ܡܙܕܩܠܒ ܡܘܐ ܗܿܐ ܚܬܝ ܗܘܐ.

If I had asked the doctor, he would have advised me on what to do. (1st m)

If you need assistance, press here. (2nd f)   ܐܢ ܨܒܝܬ ܣܝܥܬܐ، ܕܘܣ ܐܟܐ.

ܐܢ ܐܢܐ ܝܘܕܥܗܘܐ ܠܟ ܗܘܕܒ ܡܥܚܘܗܐ ܡܩܕܡ ܙܘܥܐ، ܐܢܐ ܒܕ ܗܘܝܕܡܗܘܐ ܘܒܠܟ.

If I had known about the party earlier, I would have gone.

Seeking permission examples:

ܐܢ ܥܒܦܨܚܝܒ ܗܿܐ ܘܠܟ ܕܐܢܐ، ܐܢܐ ܒܕ ܚܒܝܢܝ ܚܬܚܐ ܕܐܗܢܐ.

If you let me go now, I will help you next week. (1st m to 2nd f)

ܥܒܦܨܚܝܒ ܗܿܐ ܣܢܚܘܗܝ، ܐܫܟܚ ܒܕ ܒܣܘܗܝ ܠܝܟܐ.

If you let us swim, we will cut the grass. (1st p to 2nd m)

ܐܢ ܥܒܦܨܒܠܐ ܗܿܐ ܘܡܩܐ، ܐܘܗܐ ܒܕ ܐܗܢܐ ܒܨܛ ܠܚܡܚܘܗܐ.

If they let her sing, she will come with them to the party.

ܐܢ ܥܒܦܨܒܠܟ ܗܿܐ ܕܡܚܒ ܕܐܢܐ، ܐܕܘܗܐ ܒܕ ܡܚܠܠܟ ܕܒܘܐ ܝܘܦܨܐ.

If they let them sleep now, they will play good tomorrow.

ܐܢ ܐܢܐ ܒܗܚܠܟܘܗܝ ܡܚܥܡܗܐ، ܒܕ ܥܒܦܨܚܝܒ ܗܿܐ ܘܠܟ ܠܚܬܝܪ؟

If I give you a kiss, would you let me go out? (1st f to 2nd m)

200

Unless/If not ܐܸܢ ܠܵܐ (ܐܸܠܵܐ)

Examples:

ܠܵܐ ܡܲܚܟܹܝܬ ܠܹܗ ܡܲܪܩܘܿܣ ܡܵܢܵܐ ܡܹܪܝܼ ܠܝܼ ܐܸܢ ܠܵܐ ܐܵܗܘ ܡܲܫܐܸܠܠܘܼܟ.

Do not tell Mark what I said unless he asks you.

We will be late unless we hurry. ܒܸܕ ܡܲܬܘܼܚܪܸܚܠܘܼܟ ܐܸܢ ܠܵܐ ܕܵܗܸܒܘܼܟ ܡܲܠܘܼܟܵܐ.

ܠܵܐ ܫܵܩܠܲܬ ܕܲܪܡܵܢܵܐ ܐܸܢ ܠܵܐ ܐܵܡܸܪܠܘܼܟ ܐܵܣܝܵܐ ܥܒܘܼܕܠܹܗ.

Do not take the medicine if the doctor does not tell you to do so.

In Case ܕܲܠܵܐ

Examples:

ܒܵܒܝ ܠܲܟܝܼܪܵܐ ܕܐܵܬܹܐ ܐܲܕܝܼܘܿܡ ܒܠܲܝܠܹܐ. ܐܵܢܵܐ ܠܵܐ ܒܥܵܝܵܢ ܕܐܵܙܹܠ ܠܲܒܵܪܵܐ ܕܠܵܐ ܐܵܬܹܐ.

My dad might come tonight. I do not want to go out in case he comes.

- **In case** ܕܲܠܵܐ is not the same as **if** ܐܸܢ. Compare these sentences:

I will buy more food if Yosip comes.

ܐܵܢܵܐ ܒܸܕ ܙܵܒܢܸܢ ܒܝܼܫ ܟܡܵܐ ܕܡܲܐܟܠܵܐ ܐܸܢ ܐܵܬܹܐ ܝܘܿܣܸܦ.

I will by more food in case Yosip comes.

ܐܵܢܵܐ ܒܸܕ ܙܵܒܢܸܢ ܒܝܼܫ ܟܡܵܐ ܕܡܲܐܟܠܵܐ ܕܲܠܵܐ ܐܵܬܹܐ ܝܘܿܣܸܦ.

- You can use ܕܲܠܵܐ to say why someone did something in the past:

ܐܵܢܵܐ ܙܒܸܢܠܝܼ ܚܕܵܐ ܒܝܼܫ ܟܡܵܐ ܕܡܲܐܟܠܵܐ ܕܲܠܵܐ ܐܵܬܹܐܘܵܐ ܝܘܿܣܸܦ.

I bought some more food in case Yosip came.

Chapter 7 Exercises

Q1. give the First-Person past tense form for the following Syriac verbs:

Write   ܟܬܒܐ

Kneel   ܒܪܟܐ

Kill   ܩܛܠܐ

Q2. give the Second Person past tense form for the following Syriac verbs:

Sleep   ܕܡܟܐ

Read   ܩܪܢܐ

Walk   ܪܫܥܐ

Q3. Give the Simple Future Verb form of the following verbs:

Eat   ܐܝܟܠܐ

Dig   ܚܦܪܐ

Pray   ܨܠܝܢܐ

Q4. Present Continues verb: Put the verb into the correct form:

    a. Why are you looking at me like that? Did I say something wrong?

ܚܕ ܕܡܝܐ ܠܐ ܡܝܕܝ ܒܩܣܝܡ ܐܘܕܝ؟ ܐܘܝܗ ܕܟܡܒ (ܣܢܕܐ - ܒܪܘܘܗ) -------------- ܡܝ

    b. Listen! Are you hearing next door people? They are yelling at each other again.

ܫܝܥܗ! ܒܪܘܘܗ ܒܥܡܦܠܐ ܥܬܩܝ؟ ܐܒܠܟ -------------- (ܡܒܢܦܠܐ) ܚܪܐ ܐܢܩܕܐܐ.

202

Q5. **Simple Present verb:** Put the verb into the correct form:

    a.   What time the bank closes here?

    b.   Water boils at 100 degree Celsius.

    c.   It takes me an hour to get to work. How long it takes you?

    d.   Read and correct this sentence. The Syriac is correct, but the
           information is wrong. Write two correct sentences in Syriac.

           The sun rises in the west   ܝܡܥܐ ܕܪܗܡܐ ܡܢ ܡܝܕܕܢܐ.

Q6. Read carefully and find all verbs in the following paragraph. Draw one
line under simple verb, two lines under simple past verb, three lines under
simple future verb, draw a square shape around present continuous, and a
circle around imperative verb.

Q7. Read aloud and translate the following Syriac conversation.

Q8. Complete the sentences with ܢܥܢܐ and (ܝܝ or ܘܒܟ) plus an appropriate verb.

Q9. Write whether the underlined verb is telling us about the past or present.

Q10. **Complete each sentence by changing the given verb in parentheses into past tense.**

a. Sara ate all the walnuts.

b. My friend helped me washing my dad's car.

c. Last night I forgot to put my food in my bag.

204

Q11. Write this passage in past tense.

ـ(ܢܒܠܗ) --------- ܠܒܠܕ ܝܢܥܚܝܐ ܘܡܪܒܝܬܐ ܘܐܢܐ (ܝܩܬܐ) --------- ܚܠܘܐ ܘܚܬܐ. ܐܢܐ
ـ(ܢܒܘܝܐ) ܝ. (ܣܩܠܐ) --------- ܐܢܐ ܝܘ ܐܡܢܐ ܝܥܡܒ ܘܝܕ ܘܡܚܝ. ܐܢܐ (ܚܝܢܐ) ---------
ܗܐ ܘܚܩܝ ܝܗܘܢ ܠܬܒܝܐ. ܐܢܐ (ܥܡܝܐ) --------- ܝܠܐ ܘܐܢܡܠܟܝܐ ܘܝܢܝ ܚܕܫܝܐ. ܐܢܐ ܚܬܒܝܐ
ـ(ܘܙܝܐ) ܘ(ܗܝܐ) --------- ܝܘܩܝܒ ܘܢܝ (ܥܙܢܐ) --------- ܘ(ܢܒܘܝܐ) ---------
ܘ(ܢܒܠܗ) --------- ܝܢܘܠܡܐ.

Dark	ܝܢܥܚܐ
Forest	ܠܚܐ
Stop	ܣܩܠܐ
Frighten	ܘܙܝܐ
Lose	ܗܝܐ
Shake	ܥܙܢܐ

Chapter 8

The Conversations   ܕܡܡܠܠܬܐ

Learning Objectives

In this chapter, you will learn how to talk and answer to people in the form of conversations:

- Daily statements   ܦܘܠܚܢܐ ܕܗܘ ܘܥܕܐ
- Conversations
  - The Greetings   ܫܠܡܐ
  - **These** and **Those** conversation
  - **This** and **That** Conversation
  - **Sweet** and **Sour** conversation.
  - **They** and **Are they** conversation.
  - **Few**, **Little**, and **Lots** conversation.
  - Introducing People
  - In Classroom conversation   ܝܘܠܦܐ
  - At Supermarket conversation   ܫܘܩܐ
  - Traditional Marriage   ܙܘܘܓܐ ܕܥܝܕܐܬܐ
  - New couple and the priest   ܒܠܬܐ ܘܟܗܢܐ
  - At The Clinic   ܡܣܝܪܐ
  - Human Body (Internal Organs and Human Profile)

    ܐܘܪܓܢܐ ܕܒܪܢܫܐ
  - Learn about traditional Syriac Food   ܡܐܟܠܬܐ
  - At Restaurant   ܒܝܬ ܡܐܟܠܬܐ
  - Building The House   ܒܢܝܐ ܕܒܝܬܐ
  - Going Outside   ܦܠܛܐ ܠܒܪ
  - Looking for Job   ܒܥܝܐ ܕܦܘܠܚܢܐ

206

ܦܘܠܬܟܐ ܚܘܒ ܗܕܟܐ

Good morning	ܨܘܪܗܐܕ ܚܕܝܓܐܝ.
Good morning (2nd f)	ܨܘܪܗܐܚܒ ܚܕܝܓܐܝ.
Good morning (2nd m)	ܨܘܪܗܐܘܩ ܚܕܝܓܐܝ.
Good morning (2nd p)	ܨܘܪܗܐܘܚܘ ܚܕܝܓܐܝ.
What are you doing? (2nd m)	ܡܢܐ ܒܝܥܘܡܐ ܚܥܬܕܝܝ؟	ܡܢܘܡܐ ܚܥܬܕܝܝ؟
What do you do for living? (2nd f)	ܡܢܐ ܚܦܠܟܝܢܐ ܦܢܡܒܝ؟
Good day (2nd m)	ܢܘܡܘܩ ܚܕܝܓܝ.
Good evening (2nd f)	ܒܡܥܓܚܒ ܠܠܝܝ.
What is your name? (2nd m)	ܡܢܐ ܒܝܠܟܗ ܥܡܘܩ؟	ܡܒܠܟܗ ܥܡܘܩ؟
What is your name? (2nd f)	ܡܢܐ ܒܝܠܟܗ ܥܡܚܒ؟	ܡܒܠܟܗ ܥܡܚܒ؟
Good to see you (2nd m)	ܒܪܝܟܐ ܕܓܡܥܢܘܒܘܩ.
In peace you come (2nd p)	ܒܥܝܢܐ ܦܢܡܠܦܘܚܘ.
God bless you (2nd m)	ܡܪܢܐ ܡܬܒܝܥ ܓܠܘܩ.
Happy birthday (2nd m)	ܒܝܡ ܒܠܕܘܒܩ ܗܘܝ ܚܕܝܓܐ.
Happy birthday (2nd f)	ܒܝܡ ܒܠܕܝܚܒ ܗܘܝ ܚܕܝܓܐ.
It is nice day today	ܒܝܘܡܘܡܓ ܒܝܠܟܗ ܢܘܡܐ ܒܗܝܥܐ.
Merry Christmas	ܠܕܝܕܐ ܕܒܝܢܟܠܕܐ ܚܕܝܓܐ.	ܗܘܡܠܟܗ ܡܪܝ
Happy Easter	ܠܕܝܕܐ ܕܡܢܩܡܐ ܚܕܝܓܐ.	ܝܡܠܟܗ ܡܪܝ
Happy New Year	ܒܪܐ ܕܥܬܟܐ ܚܕܝܓܐܝ.

Conventions

Greetings

ܒܥܝܢ ܢܘܣܦ: ܕܝܟ ܝܬܘܡܐ؟
Hello Yosip. How are you?

ܥܠܟܢ ܝܠܟܡ ܡܪܬܐ!
Peace upon you (Hello!) Martha

Yosip: I am very good. How are you?

ܢܘܣܦ: ܐܢܐ ܚܠܒ ܡܬܪ ܝܬܘܡܐ، ܐܢܬܡ ܕܝܟ ܝܬܘܡܐ؟

Martha: Thank you, I am doing great.

ܡܪܬܐ: ܟܢܘܡܝ ܬܫܒܚܡܐ: ܐܢܐ ܚܠܒ ܡܬܒܐ ܝܬܘܡܐ..

Yosip: How is your family?

ܢܘܣܦ: ܕܝܟ ܝܒܠܕ ܐܢܬܕ ܕܬܒܐ؟

Martha: They are good! Thank you. How are you guys?

ܡܪܬܐ: ܡܬܪ ܝܒܠܕ، ܟܢܘܡܝ ܬܫܒܚܡܐ — ܕܝܟ ܝܬܘܡܘܡܝ ܐܢܬܘܡܐ؟

Yosip: We are going fine. Thank you! Say hi to your family.

ܢܘܣܦ: ܝܬܘܡܘܩ ܡܬܪ -ܟܢܬܒ ܬܫܒܚܡܐ! ܘܩܪ ܥܠܟܢ ܠܐܢܬܕ ܕܬܒܐ. ܟܦܒ ܬܥܠܟܢ ܡܪܬܐ

Martha: Goodbye Yosip

ܡܪܬܐ: ܟܦܒ ܬܥܠܟܢ ܢܘܣܦ.

These and Those Conversation

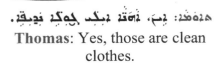

ܬܐܘܡܐܣ: ܗܹܐ، ܐ݇ܢܵܝ ܕܝܼ݇ܠܹܗ ܠܒ݂ܘܼܟܹ̈ܐ ܢܕ݂ܝܼܩܹ̈ܐ.

Thomas: Yes, those are clean
clothes.

ܡܵܪܩܘܿܣ: ܐ݇ܢܵܝ ܕܝܼ݇ܠܲܝ ܠܒ݂ܘܼܟܹ̈ܐ ܢܕ݂ܝܼܩܹ̈ܐ؟

Marcus: Are these clean
clothes?

ܬܐܘܡܐܣ: ܠܵܐ، ܐ݇ܢܵܝ ܠܵܐ ܕܝܼ݇ܠܹܗ (ܠܝܼ݇ܠܹܗ) ܟ̰ܲܪ̈ܒܹܐ
ܥܸܢܩܹ̈ܐ.

Thomas: No, those are not dirty
socks.

ܡܵܪܩܘܿܣ: ܐ݇ܢܵܝ ܕܝܼ݇ܠܲܝ ܟ̰ܲܪ̈ܒܹܐ ܥܸܢܩܹ̈ܐ؟

Marcus: Are these dirty socks?

This and That Conversation

Sargon: Is this coat long or short? ܗܕܟܦܝ: ܐܝܠܗ ܐܗܝܐ ܦܬܘܗܐ ܝܪܝܟܐ ܝܢ ܟܪܝܐ؟

Mariam: That coat is long. ܡܪܝܡ: ܐܗܘܐ ܦܬܘܗܐ ܐܝܠܗ ܝܪܝܟܐ.

Sargon: Is this glove left, or right? ܗܕܟܦܝ: ܐܝܠܗ ܐܘܝ ܚܦܐ ܕܝܣܡܝܐ ܝܢ ܕܝܡܝܢܐ؟

Mariam: That glove is right. ܡܪܝܡ: ܐܗܢܐ ܚܦܐ ܐܝܠܗ ܕܝܡܝܢܐ.

Nada: Is this necklace old or new? ܢܕܐ: ܐܝܠܗ ܐܘܝ ܚܠܩܐ ܥܬܝܩܐ ܝܢ ܚܘܕܬܐ؟

Hanna: That necklace is old. ܚܢܐ: ܐܗܢܐ ܚܠܩܐ ܐܝܠܗ ܥܬܝܩܐ.

Luke: Is this your black comb? ܠܘܩܐ: ܐܝܠܗ ܐܗܝܐ ܡܣܪܩܘܟ ܟܘܡܐ؟

Peter: No, that is not my black comb. That is my sister's.
ܦܝܛܪܘܗ: ܠܐ، ܐܗܘܐ ܠܝܠܗ ܕܝܒܝ، ܐܗܘܐ ܐܝܠܗ ܕܚܬܝ.

Luke: Is this your white shirt? ܠܘܩܐ: ܐܝܠܗ ܐܘܝ ܣܘܣܘܟ ܚܘܪܐ؟

Peter: Yes, it is. ܦܝܛܪܘܗ: ܗܝ، ܐܝܠܗ.

Sweet and sour Conversation

Yaqoo: What is very sweet? ܝܩܘ: ܡܘܕܝ ܐܝܠܗ ܚܝܠܟ ܚܠܝܐ؟

Mariam: Honey and baklava are very sweet. ܡܪܝܡ: ܕܘܫܐ ܘܬܣܠܟܐ ܐܝܠܟ ܚܝܠܟ ܚܠܝܬܐ.

Yaqoo: What is very sour? ܝܩܘ: ܡܘܕܝ ܐܝܠܗ ܚܝܠܟ ܚܡܘܨܐ؟

Mariam: Lemons and green apples are sour. ܡܪܝܡ: ܠܝܡܘܢ ܘܚܬܘܚܐ ܝܘܪܩܐ ܐܝܠܟ ܚܡܘܨܐ.

They and Are They Conversation

Ilya: Are beer and wine cold drinks? ܐܝܠܝܐ: ܐܝܠܟ ܚܒܐ ܘܚܡܪܐ ܡܫܬܝܢܐ ܩܪܝܪܐ؟

John: Yes, beer and wine are cold drinks.
ܝܘܚܢܢ: ܗܝ، ܚܒܐ ܘܚܡܪܐ ܐܝܠܟ ܡܫܬܝܢܐ ܩܪܝܪܐ.

Ilya: Is the fish in or out of the water? ܐܝܠܝܐ: ܐܝܠܟ ܢܘܢܬܐ ܓܘܝܐ ܝܢ ܠܒܪ ܕܡܝܐ؟

John: It is out of the water. ܝܘܚܢܢ: ܐܝܠܟ ܠܒܪ ܕܡܝܐ.

210

Few, Little, and Lots Conversation

John: Let us go eat outside.

ܣܘܿܚܢܢ: ܥܒܘܿܕ ܘܠܢ ܢܐܟܠܘܿܗ ܟܕܸܝܐ.

Nahrain: No, I cannot. I have little money.

ܢܲܗܪܹܝܢ: ܠܵܐ. ܠܵܐܡܵܨܹܐܒ. ܐܝܼܒܝܼ ܚܲܕ ܡܝܼܢ ܙܘܼܙܹܐ.

John: How much do you have?

ܣܘܿܚܢܢ: ܟܡܵܐ ܐܝܼܒܟܸܕ ܐܝܼܢܵܐ؟

Nahrain: I have a few dollars.

ܢܲܗܪܹܝܢ: ܐܵܢܵܐ ܐܝܼܒܝܼܟܸܒ ܡܸܕܪܸܡܵܐ ܕܘܿܠܵܪܹܐ.

John: It is Ok. I have $100. Let us call Mariam to come with us.

ܣܘܿܚܢܢ: ܠܵܐ ܐܝܼܒܐܟܸܕ ܟܹܐܛ! ܐܵܢܵܐ ܐܝܼܒܐܟܸܒ ܐܸܡܵܐ ܕܘܿܠܵܪܹܐ. ܥܒܘܿܕ ܘܩܲܕܘܿܗ ܡܲܪܝܲܡ ܕܐܸܬܝܵܐ ܥܲܡܲܢ.

Nahrain: No. She talks to much.

ܢܲܗܪܹܝܢ: ܠܵܐ. ܐܵܗܹܒ ܚܲܡܣܲܚܢܵܐ ܟܬܸܒܵܐ.

Introducing People

He is my nephew (brother side).

ܐܵܗܹܘ ܐܝܼܠܹܗ ܒܪܵܐ ܕܐܲܚܘܿܢܒ.

She is my niece (sister side).

ܐܵܗܹܒ ܐܝܼܠܵܗ ܒܪܵܬܵܐ ܕܚܵܬܒ.

Shamiran is my daughter-in-law.

ܫܲܡܝܼܪܵܢ ܐܝܼܠܵܗ ܟܲܠܵܒ.

Solomon is my son-in-law.

ܫܠܹܝܡܘܿܢ ܐܝܼܠܹܗ ܚܲܬܢܒ.

Abraham is my cousin (mother side).

ܐܲܒܪܵܗܲܡ ܐܝܼܠܹܗ ܒܪܵܐ ܕܝܼܢܵܐܟܒ.

Farah is Elijah's daughter-in-law.

ܦܲܪܲܚ ܐܝܼܠܵܗ ܟܲܠܬܵܐ ܕܐܹܠܝܼܵܐ.

Yaqoo is Isaiah's son-in-law.

ܝܲܩܘܿ ܐܝܼܠܹܗ ܚܲܬܢܵܐ ܕܐܹܫܲܥܝܵܐ.

Thomas is my cousin (father side).

ܬܐܘܿܡܵܐ ܐܝܼܠܹܗ ܒܪܵܐ ܕܐܲܡܒ.

That is Yaqoo's grandson. (daughter side).

ܐܵܗܵܐ ܐܝܼܠܹܗ ܒܪܵܐ ܕܒܪܵܬܵܐ ܕܝܲܩܘܿ. also ܢܲܒܝܼܪܵܐ ܕܝܲܩܘܿ

She is my granddaughter (son side).

also ܢܲܒܝܼܪܬܒ, ܐܵܗܹܒ ܐܝܼܠܵܗ ܒܪܵܬܵܐ ܕܒܪܘܿܢܒ.

Peter is my sister in law's husband.

also ܢܲܝܒܒ, ܦܸܛܪܘܿܣ ܐܝܼܠܹܗ ܓܲܘܪܒ.

Sargon is my father-in-law.

ܣܲܪܓܘܿܢ, ܐܝܼܠܹܗ ܚܡܵܢܒ.

Shooshan is my mother-in-law

ܫܘܿܫܲܢ ܐܝܼܠܵܗ ܚܡܵܬܒ.

Matthew is Mark's brother.

ܡܲܬܲܝ ܐܝܼܠܹܗ ܐܲܚܘܿܢܵܐ ܕܡܲܪܩܘܿܣ.

She is my sister-in-law (spouse's sister).

ܐܵܗܹܒ ܐܝܼܠܵܗ ܚܵܬܵܐܫܸܓܲܒܒ.

He is my brother-in-law (spouse's brother).

ܐܵܗܹܘ ܐܝܼܠܹܗ ܚܸܙܢܵܐܢܒ.

Yaqoo is my first cousin.

ܝܲܩܘܿ ܐܝܼܠܹܗ ܒܪܵܐ ܕܐܲܡܒ ܟܸܣܵܐ.

This is Nahrain. She is my first cousin.

ܐܵܘܵܐ ܐܝܼܠܵܗ ܢܲܗܪܹܝܢ، ܐܝܼܠܵܗ ܒܪܵܬܵܐ ܕܝܼܢܵܐܟܒ ܟܸܣܵܐ.

211

Classroom ܟܠܤܐ

ܗܕܟܐ: ܪܒܝ ܝܡܠܦܢܐ... ܘܗܫܐ ܦܬܚܘܢ ܦܬܘܬܐ ܕܝ ܝܫܝܐ ܐܝ؟

ܪܒܝ ܝܡܠܦܢܐ: ܡܬܠ ܦܬܘܬܐ ܡܢ ܩܡܬܐ ܕܐܕܝܡ ܘܙܥܬܠ ܡܢ ܩܡܬܐ ܕܐܠܟܐ.

ܝܥܘܕ: ܠܡܠܟ ܚܙܝܬܐ ܙܘܬܐ ܪܒܝ ܝܡܠܦܢܐ؟

ܪܒܝ ܝܡܠܦܢܐ: ܚܙܝܬܐ ܙܝܠܟ ܐܝ ܗܠܥܒܝܬܐ ܘܠܟܠ ܘܚܝܠܟ ܡܝܐ ܐܝ ܗܠܥܒܝܬܐ ܚܒܝܬܐ.

ܥܘܬ: ܠܢܢܘܝ ܬܗܒܝܫܐ ܪܒܝ: ܝܫܘܘܐ ܬܥܠܐܩ ܝܡܬܐ ܐܝ ܤܘܠܩܢܐ.

ܪܒܝ ܝܡܠܦܢܐ: ܗܠܥܒܝܒ ܠܘܬܘܙ ܦܠܝܡܐ ܝܠܠ ܘܡܢܥܬܘܝ ܤܘܠܩܢܐ ܘܠܓܘܡܝܗ ܠܩܕܝܢܝܘܡܐ.

ܠܠܝܘܒ: ܐܢܐ ܙܝܡܐܠܟ ܥܒܝܘܬܐ ܐܢܐ ܬܠܟܘܡܝ ܪܒܝ، ܘܠܚܝܒ ܐܢܐ ܙܝܠܟܐ ܙܙܝܤܘܦ ܬܪܝܩܘܝ.

English	Syriac	English	Syriac
Teacher	ܪܒܝ	Smart – active	ܚܒܝܬܐ
Pages	ܦܬܘܬܐ	Thank you (m)	ܠܢܢܘܝ ܬܗܒܝܫܐ
Exam	ܝܫܝܐ	Respect	ܝܤܬܐ
Chapter	ܩܡܬܐ	Duty – Responsibility	ܦܠܝܡܐ
To many	ܚܒܝܬܐ	Civilization	ܩܕܝܢܝܘܡܐ
Lazy	ܘܠܟܠ	Lucky	ܠܚܝܒ

Shopping at the Supermarket ܫܘܩܐ

ܒܲܟ݂ܬܵܐ: ܫܠܵܡܵܐ ܥܠܘܟ݂ܝ... ܐܵܢܝ ܛܡܵܛܹܐ ܘܚܝܵܪܹܐ ܚܲܕ݇ܬܹܐ ܐܝܼܢܵܐ؟
ܡܵܪܵܐ ܕܟܘܼܢܵܐ: ܟܠܗ ܐܲܕܝܘܡ ܐܵܬܹܝܠܗ ܥܲܡ ܕܩܲܪܕܠܘܐ ܘܦܫܛܝ̈ܢܐ ܘܫܡܙܘ̈ܬܐ.
ܒܲܟ݂ܬܵܐ: ܒܲܣ ܐܵܢܝ ܚܘܟ݂ܝ̈ܐ ܘܐܠܘܟ݂ܝ̈ܐ ܠܲܝܬܲܝ ܚܲܕ݇ܬܹ̈ܐ ܐܘܦ ܚܲܒܘ̈ܫܐ.
ܡܵܪܵܐ ܕܟܘܼܢܵܐ: ܐܵܬܹܝܢ ܐܝܠܗ ܕܐܲܬܡܵܠܝ. ܒܲܣ ܗܵܢܝ ܦܪܬܩܵܠ̈ܐ ܘܥܸܢܒ̈ܐ ܚܲܕ݇ܬܹ̈ܐ ܝܢܵܐ.
ܒܲܟ݂ܬܵܐ: ܗܲܒ݇ܠܝ ܚܕܵܐ ܦܵܘܢܬܵܐ ܓܘܵܙܵܐ ܘܬܲܪ̈ܬܹܝ ܦܵܘܢ̈ܬܹܐ ܒܘܼܕܩܹ̈ܐ ܘܚܲܡܫܵܐ ܦܵܘܢ̈ܬܹܐ ܦܸܣܬܩܹ̈ܐ.
ܡܵܪܵܐ ܕܟܘܼܢܵܐ: ܣܢܝܼܩܵܬܝ ܚܲܕ ܡܸܕܸܡ؟ ܐܝܬܠܲܢ ܡܵܘܙܹ̈ܐ ܘܬܘܼܡܪ̈ܐ ܘܫܲܒܠܘܼܛܹ̈ܐ ܘܡܲܥܕܲܢܘܣ.
ܒܲܟ݂ܬܵܐ: ܚܲܢܘܢ ܒܣܝܼܡܵܐ، ܣܢܝܼܩܵܠܝ ܫܸܬܵܐ ܦܵܘܢ̈ܬܹܐ ܩܲܡܚܵܐ ܘܬܡܵܢܝܵܐ ܫܲܟܲܪ.

Lady: Hello! Are these tomatoes and cucumbers fresh?
Business owner: All came today with wild cucumbers, cantaloupes, and watermelons.
Lady: But these peaches and plums are not fresh, and neither the apples!
Business owner: They came in yesterday; but the oranges and grapes are fresh.
Lady: Give me one pound of walnuts, two pounds of nuts, and five pounds of pistachio.
Business owner: Do you need anything else? We have bananas, dates, chestnuts, and parsley.
Lady: Thank you; I want six pounds of flour and eight pounds of sugar.

Traditional Marriage ܙܘܘܓܐ ܥܬܝܩܐ

ܠܥܒܪܐ: ܫܠܡܐ ܥܠܝܟ ܝܡܐ.

ܝܡܐ: ܒܫܝܢܐ ܬܝܬ.. ܕܝܢ ܐܝܠܗ ܡܘܕܥܡܬܘܟ؟

ܠܥܒܪܐ: ܒܪܝܟܐ ܝܡܐ.. ܐܝܘܡܐ ܐܢܐ ܐܬܝܘܕܠܝ ܚܕ ܒܪܬܐ ܛܒܬܐ ܝܣܝܩܬܐ.

ܝܡܐ: ܚܢܝܬܝ ܒܣܝܡܬܐ ܬܬܝܬ، ܐܢܐ ܘܐܒܘܟ ܚܬܒܬܐ ܙܝܡܟܟ ܥܬܝܩܬܐ ܬܠܟܘܬܝ.

ܬܕܡܝܬ ܚܒܬܝ ܗܐ ܡܣܚܝ ܝܡܐܝܬ.. ܐܒܘܡܐ، ܝܡܐ ܘܩܠܬܘܗ ܡܘܡܣܓܝܠܟܐ ܝܡܒ
ܘܚܒܬܝܕ ܕܝܠܟܬܒܠܝ ܗܐ ܬܕܘܡܣܝܒ ܡܥܒ. ܦܥܒ ܫܘܠܗ ܥܡܟܝܠܟ ܫܘܗܐ ܘܗܠܟܬ
ܘܚܒܬܝܕ ܗܐ ܟܘܗ ܘܩܥܝܢ ܬܝܗܐ ܫܘܗܐ.

ܠܥܒܪܐ: ܝܡܐ!!! ܬܡ ܐܢܐ ܠܗܘܦ ܚܠܝܗܐ ܡܘܕܥܡܒ ܘܩܥܠܝܠܟ ܫܘܙ ܥܬܥܐ ܘܚܠܝܐ.

ܝܡܐ: ܗܘ ܐܢܐ ܗܘܙܝ ܙܐܡܣܕܟܒ ܗܐܢܟܐ ܬܬܝܬ، ܬܡ ܙܐܡܣܕܟܗ، (ܚܕ ܗܩܕܘܗ ܘܕ ܗܐ ܚܠܝܢܐ
ܡܝ ܡܘܕܥܡܗܐ)...ܘܐܢܐ ܚܢܥܬܝ ܢܬ ܬܕܗܒ، ܦܥܒ ܬܕܘܢܐ ܗܠܬܐ ܘܩܠܫܢܐ ܐܝܠܗ، ܘܐܢܥܥܦܐܗܐ
ܗܘ ܗܠܬܐ ܐܝܠܟܐ ܘܗܚܒܬܐ ܚܛܝܠܟ. ܗܘ ܬܬܬܬ ܚܬܒܬܐ ܩܝܥܠܟܗ ܐܝܦ ܘܥܡܓܟܗ
ܘܗܘܡܣܓܝܠܟ ܬܢܫܦܚ. ܘܐܢܐ ܚܢܥܬܝ ܟܐ ܐܝܬܐ ܡܝܕܒ ܘܩܠܠܟܗ ܝܡܓܗ ܘܗܣܚܗܐܗܐܗ
ܐܝܫܘܙܝܒ.

ܠܥܒܪܐ: ܗܘ ܐܢܐ ܚܒܘܝܠ ܡܥܒ ܐܝܠܗ ܢܠܘܙܐ ܗܠܬܐ ܘܐܝܗܠܟܗ ܘܗܘܡܣܓܝܠܟܗ ܝܡܒ ܬܐܘܒ

ܬܝܣܗ: ܬܡ ܠܟܐ ܙܐܡܣܕܟܒ ܡܝܕܒ ܗܐܢܟܗ...ܐܢܐ ܚܕ ܩܠܠܟܝ ܝܡܓܗ ܘܐܝܫܥܝܒ
ܚܕ ܡܣܚܘܗ.

Vocabulary

Fiancé	ܚܠܝܒܬܐ	Proud of you (1st p to 2nd f)	ܙܝܡܟܟ ܥܬܥܐܘܬܐ ܬܠܟܘܬܝ	(He) wants	ܚܒܬܝܕ
Good	ܛܒܬܐ	(she) talked	ܡܣܓܝܠܟܐ	(I) Think (1st f)	ܚܢܥܬܝ
Test	ܝܣܝܩܬܐ	(He) found	ܫܘܠܗ		

214

Priest: How is it going with you?

Fiancé: Very good Rabbi; I am so happy with this lady.

Priest: What do you say young lady?

Fiancée: Since I have met this person, I am filled with happiness.

Priest: So, you have many things in common.

Fiancée: yes, Rabbi because we are from the same nation and have the same culture.

Fiancé: Also, our personalities are similar.

Priest: I am so happy for both of you. You are wise and know what makes you happy in life. Congratulations!.

Vocabulary

My back	ܫܝܒ	Cracked	ܚܕܟܝܠܗ
Hurting	ܟܡܐܕܟܐ	Medicine, Medication	ܘܕܘܡܢܐ
I lift	ܟܠܝܒ	Say hello to your family	ܘܩܒ ܥܠܟܐ ܠܐܢ̈ܬܐ̇ ܕܬܝܡ̈ܐ
Sofa, couch	ܩܢܩܐ		

216

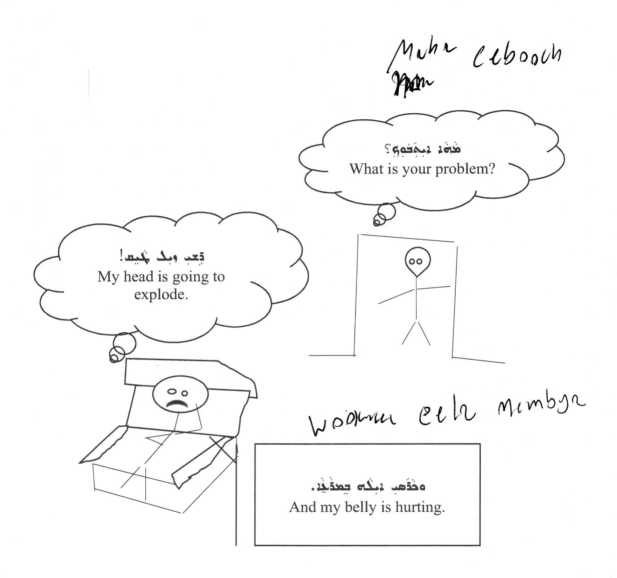

217

Internal Organs: ܗܕ̈ܡܐ ܕܓܘܫ̈ܡܐ ܓܘ̈ܝܐ

Brain	ܡܘܚܐ	Gallbladder	ܡܪܪܬܐ	Liver	ܟܘܡܬܐ -ܟܒܕܐ
Pharynx	ܩܠܘܥܝܬܐ	Kidney	ܟܘܠܝܬܐ	Pancreas	ܥܠܘܣܬܐ
Larynx	ܓܓܪܬܐ	Skeleton	ܫܠܕܐ ܓܪܡܢܐ	Muscle	ܥܠܬܐ
Rib	ܥܠܥܐ	Intestines	ܡܥܝܬܐ	Vein	ܘܪܝܕܐ
Lung	ܪܐܬܐ	Spleen	ܛܚܠܐ	Artery	ܥܪܩܐ
Heart	ܠܒܐ	Bone marrow	ܡܘܚܐ ܕܓܪܡܐ	Stomach	ܟܪܣܐ

ܝܠܕܐ: ܣܒܝ ܐܝܡܢܐ ܗܕܡܐ ܐܝܬܝ ܒܦܓܪܐ ܕܒܪܢܫܐ؟
ܣܒܐ: ܟܒܝܪܐ ܐܝܬܠܢ ܒܓܘܢ، ܐܝܟ ܡܘܚܐ ܕܡܚܫܒܬܐ ܘܠܒܐ ܕܡܫܕܪܢܐ ܕܡܐ ܠܦܓܪܐ.
ܝܠܕܐ: ܒܪܡ ܟܪܣܐ ܘܪܐܬܐ ܗܡ ܡܘܢܐ ܐܝܬܠܢ؟
ܣܒܐ: ܟܪܣܐ ܒܦܠܚܐ ܠܐܟܠܐ ܘܪܐܬܐ ܒܫܩܠܐ ܦܘܚܐ ܗܡ ܠܓܘܫܡܐ.
ܝܠܕܐ: ܟܗ ܐܢܝ ܐܝܬܠܢ! ܝܡܐ ܐܡܝܪܬܠܗ ܕܐܝܬܠܢ ܟܘܡܬܐ ܘܟܘܠܝܬܐ.
ܣܒܐ: ܐܝܢ ܟܗ ܟܘܡܬܐ ܘܟܘܠܝܬܐ ܗܡ ܐܝܬܠܢ ܡܥܝܬܐ ܘܚܨܪܐ.
ܝܠܕܐ: ܘܐܢܝ ܡܘܢܐ ܒܥܒܕܝ ܒܪܡ؟
ܣܒܐ: ܡܥܝܬܐ ܒܡܫܡܫܝ ܕܐܟܠܐ ܠܓܘܦܐ ܘܚܨܪܐ ܒܣܢܕ ܟܠܗ ܓܘܫܡܐ.

ܚܨܪܐ ܒܣܢܕ ܟܠܗ ܓܘܫܡܐ.
The spine supports all body.

The Outside Members of The Human Body

Wrist	ܐܘܪܟܬܐ ܕܐܝܕܐ	Fingers	ܨܒܥܬܐ ܕܐܝܕܐ	Hair	ܣܥܪܐ
Belly	ܟܪܣܐ	Thigh	ܥܛܡܐ	Head	ܪܫܐ
Breast	ܕܝܕܐ	Knee	ܒܘܪܟܐ	Ear	ܢܬܐ
Chest	ܨܕܪܐ	Ankle	ܐܘܪܟܬܐ ܕܐܩܠܐ	Lip	ܣܦܬܐ
Mouth	ܦܘܡܐ	Foot	ܦܘܕܐ	Neck	ܦܩܪܬܐ
Nose	ܦܘܩܐ	Heel	ܥܩܒܐ	Shoulder	ܟܬܦܐ
Eye	ܥܝܢܐ	Toes	ܨܒܥܬܐ ܕܐܩܠܐ	Arm	ܕܪܥܐ
Eyebrow	ܓܒܝܢܐ	Leg	ܐܩܠܐ	Elbow	ܣܘܟܐ
Eyelashes	ܡܠܦܦܐ	Nail	ܛܦܪܐ	Belly button	ܫܘܪܬܐ
Forehead	ܦܚܕܐ	Thumb	ܟܠܬܐ	Hand	ܐܝܕܐ
		Butt	ܥܪܡܐ	Back	ܚܨܐ

The Mouth Parts

The gums	ܠܟܐ
Upper lip	ܣܦܬܐ ܥܠܝܬܐ
Tongue	ܠܫܢܐ
Lower lip	ܣܦܬܐ ܬܚܝܬܐ
Chin	ܕܩܢܬܐ
Tooth	ܟܟܐ

For more about human body, see Appendix G.

Challenging Quiz:

1. Give the plural form for each of the following outside member of the human body:

Plural	Member	Plural	Member *begvinn*
ܐܝܼܕ݂ܵܐ		ܬܝܼܠܬܝܼܢܵܐ	
ܚܕ݂ܵܕܵܐ		ܢܵܐ *ch*	
ܟܦܵܢܵܐ		ܗܩܵܐ	
ܚܘܼܡܵܐ		ܥܘܼܕ݂ܵܐ	
ܚܸܢܵܐ		ܐܝܼܕ݂ܵܐ	
ܕܝܼܕ݂ܵܐ		ܝܼܠܬܵܐ	
		ܝܘܼܩܵܐ	

2. Give the singular form of the following outside members of the human body:

ܝܲܬܬܵܐ

ܚܘܼܕ݂ܚܵܐ

ܟܦܵܬܵܐ

ܝܘܼܩܵܐ

ܐܝܼܠܟܵܐ

ܝܲܟܕܵܐ

3. Multiple choice

ܐ – ܬܲܝܟܵܐ ܕ ------ ܚܢܘܼ.

   a. ܟܦܵܐ   b. ܚܸܢܵܐ   c. ܚܘܼܡܵܐ   d. ܢܵܐ

ܒ – ܡܵܢܵܐ ܐܝܼܡ ܠܵܐܸܢܵܐ ܕܝܼܝܘܼܡܗ؟

   a. ܚܵܢܵܐ   b. ܟܦܵܐ   c. ܡܸܥܕܵܐ   d. ܚܘܼܡܵܐ

220

Food ܡܐܟ݂ܘܠܬܐ

Rice	ܩܘܪܐ
Kubba	ܚܩܬܒ
Staffed Grapes Leaves	ܕܘܠܟ݂ܐ
Turkey	ܣܠܡܝܠܗ
Fish	ܩܘܢܝܐ
Pacha	ܚܕܩܐ
Barley	ܩܣܘܗܐ
Cracked wheat	ܠܟ݂ܘܩܠܘܕ
Lamb	ܚܡܐ ܕܝܠܘܕܐ

221

At Restaurant ܒܝܬ ܡܐܟܠܬܐ

What do you like to eat?	ܡܘܢܐ ܟܒܥܝܬ ܐܬ ܐܟܠܬ؟
I want rice and soup with lamb.	ܟܒܥܝܢ ܪܘܙܐ ܘܡܪܩܐ ܥܡ ܕܒܣܪܐ ܕܐܡܪܐ.
We have lamb with yellow rice.	ܐܝܬܠܢ ܒܣܪܐ ܕܐܡܪܐ ܥܡ ܕܪܘܙܐ ܨܘܦܪܐ.
Do you have French fries?	ܐܝܬܠܘܟܘܢ ܦܬܬܐ ܡܬܓܢܐ؟
We do have French fries with eggs.	ܐܝܬܠܢ ܦܬܬܐ ܡܬܓܢܐ ܥܡ ܕܒܥ̈ܐ.
Bring me well done eggs with bread.	ܡܝܬܝܠܝ ܒܥ̈ܐ ܡܟܝܟܐ ܪܒܬܐ ܥܡ ܕܠܚܡܐ.
Do you like tea with sugar and milk?	ܟܒܥܝܬ ܟܝ ܥܡ ܕܫܟܪܐ ܘܚܠܒܐ؟
How does much the food cost?	ܟܡܐ ܐܝܬܠܗ ܛܝܡܐ ܕܐܟܠܐ؟
Twenty-three dolor.	ܥܣܪܝܢ ܘܬܠܬܐ ܕܘܠܪܐ.

Building The House ܒܢܝܢܐ ܕܒܝܬܐ

ܒܲܢܵܝܵܐ : ܐܲܪܥܘܼܟ݂ܘܿܢ ܪܲܒܬܵܐ ܝܠܵܗ̇! ܕܵܟ݂ܝ ܒܸܛܠܵܒ݂ܘܼܬ݂ܘܿܢ ܝܠܵܗ̇ ܒܲܝܬܘܼܟ݂ܘܿܢ؟
ܒܲܟ݂ܬܵܐ : ܒܸܛܠܵܒ݂ܘܼܚ ܗܵܘܹܐ ܠܲܢ ܐܵ ܡܲܗܠܲܠܬܵܐ ܪܲܒܬܵܐ ܕܝܲܠܘܿܕܹ̈ܐ ܓܵܚܟܝ ܘܒܸܛܠܵܒ݂ܘܼܚ ܕܗܵܘܹܐ ܠܲܢ ܡܲܛܒܲܚ ܪܲܒܵܐ ܘܡܲܟ݂ܣܲܢܬܵܐ ܦܲܠܓܵܝܬܵܐ.
ܒܲܢܵܝܵܐ : ܐܲܝܡܵܢ ܩܘܼܛܵܘܵܬܵܐ ܒܸܛܠܵܒ݂ܘܼܬ݂ܘܿܢ ܘܕܵܟ݂ܝ ܒܸܛܠܵܒ݂ܘܼܬ݂ܘܿܢ؟
ܓܲܒ݂ܪܵܐ : ܒܸܛܠܵܒ݂ܘܼܚ ܐܲܪܒܲܥ ܩܘܼܛܵܘܵܬܵܐ ܬܲܚܬܵܝܵܐ: ܘܬܠܵܬ݂ ܠܥܸܠ ܥܲܡ ܟܬܵܒ݂ܵܢܵܝܬܵܐ.
ܒܲܟ݂ܬܵܐ : ܩܘܼܛܵܐ ܕܠܥܸܠ ܓܲܘܵܐ ܗܵܘܹܐ ܪܲܒܬܵܐ ܘܥܲܡ ܗܵܘܹܐ ܦܲܠܓܵܝܬܵܐ ܘܟܬܵܒ݂ܵܢܵܝܬܵܐ ܙܥܘܿܪܬܵܐ.
ܒܲܢܵܝܵܐ : ܟܡܵܐ ܕܪܵܬ݂ܵܐ ܘܡܲܫܩܲܦܬܵܐ ܩܲܕܵܐ ܪܲܒܵܐ ܒܸܛܠܵܒ݂ܘܼܬ݂ܘܿܢ ܝܠܵܗܘܿܢ؟ ܘܐܵܗ ܩܘܼܛܵܐ ܐܲܪܵܚܵܐ ܕܵܟ݂ܝ
ܒܸܛܠܵܒ݂ܘܼܬ݂ܘܿܢ ܝܠܵܗ̇؟
ܒܲܟ݂ܬܵܐ : ܡܲܫܩܲܦܬܵܐ ܓܲܘܵܐ ܗܵܘܹܐ ܦܲܠܓܵܝܬܵܐ ܘܕܵܪܬܵܐ ܘܩܘܼܛܵܐ ܐܲܪܵܚܵܐ ܪܲܒܵܐ.

Builder: You have a big lot! How do you like your house to look like?
Wife: We would like to have a big corridor, so the kids can play, and we would like to have a big kitchen and medium size pantry.
Builder: How many bedrooms would you like to have and how do you like them to be?
Husband: We want four bedrooms on the first floor and three bedrooms upstairs including the library.
Wife: The upstairs bedroom should be big with medium size closet and a small library.
Builder: what about the basement and the attic? How big do you want them to be? What about the guest room, how do you want it to be?
Wife: Attic should be medium size and basement and the guest room should be big.

On exam

Going Outside ܦܠܛܐ ܠܒܪܐ

ܐܕܝܘܡ ܐܝܠܗ ܝܘܡܐ ܒܣܝܡܐ، ܫܒܘܩ ܙܠܚ ܕܝܬܒܚ ܒܪܐ.
ܡܢܐ ܡܚܒܝܬܘܢ ܗܐ ܕܐܟܠܝܬܘܢ ܐܕܝܘܡ ܒܚܫܡܬܐ؟
ܫܒܘܩ ܡܫܒܘܚ ܒܣܪܐ ܘܟܬܝܬܐ ܘܫܬܝܚ ܚܡܪܐ ܘܒܝܪܐ.
ܠܐ ܟܚܫܒܢ ܕܐܝܬܠܢ ܒܣܪܐ ܘܒܝܪܐ!
ܫܒܘܩ ܗܐ ܙܠܚ ܠܫܘܩܐ ܗܐ ܕܙܒܢܚ ܒܣܪܐ ܘܒܝܪܐ ܘܗܡ ܠܚܡܐ.
ܗܡ ܚܕܐ ܓܙܪܐ ܘܦܠܦܠܐ ܘܦܬܬܐ ܘܒܨܠܐ ܚܘܪܐ.
ܠܐ ܦܫ ܚܠܒܐ ܘܓܘܒܬܐ ܘܛܚܝܢ.

Today is a nice day, let us go sit outside.
What do you like to eat for dinner?
Let us BBQ beef and chickens and drink wine and beer.
I do not think we have beef and beer!
Let us go to the supermarket to buy beef, beer, and bread.
Also, some carrots, green pepper, potato, and white onions.
No milk, cheese, and Tahin left.

Looking for Job   ܒܥܝܐ ܕܥܒܕܐ

---

1. Who ܢܘܗܝ wanted to meet with?

    a. Doctor   b. Business owner   c. Teacher   d. Friend

2. What ܢܘܗܝ was looking for?

    a. Her brother   b. car   c. work   d. house

3. Did ܡܪܝܡ give/help ܢܘܗܝ with what she was looking for?

    Yes   No

4. What day(s) is/are mentioned in this conversation?

5. What number(s) is/are mentioned in this conversation?

225

Chapter 9

The Cultural Stories – ܟ̈ܬܒܼ̈ܐ

Learning Objectives

In this chapter, you will learn how to use the verbs using short stories:

- Helping The Blind Man.   ܣܡܝܐ ܡܣܥܪܬܐ
- The Fortune.   ܓܕܐ
- My School.   ܡܕܪܫܬܝ
- The Rope.   ܚܒܠܐ
- The Heart.   ܠܒܐ
- The Family.   ܒܝܬܐ ܕܒܝܬܐ
- The Winter.   ܣܬܘܐ
- The Fall.   ܬܫܪܝܢ
- The Cow and The Frog.   ܬܘܪܬܐ ܘܐܘܪܕܥܐ
- The Ant and The Cockroach.   ܫܘܫܡܢܐ ܘܨܪܨܘܪܐ

Helping The Blind Man ܟܬܒܐ ܣܡܝܐ

Practice ܘܘܩܬܐ

1. Who was going to school?

a. ܗܩܟܠܗ،   b. ܗܡܢܐ   c. ܟܗܡܩܡܐܕ   d. ܟܒܕܬܐ

2. What does ܐܘܕܝ mean in English?

a. See you later   b. Bye   c. Thanked   d. None of these

4. The blind man wanted to _____.

a. sits in car   b. cross the road   c. use the phone   d. walk with his friend

4. The word ܒܘܪܐ means a(n) _____ in English:

a. Nose   b. Head   c. Ear   d. None of the choices

Vocabulary

Sons	ܚܡܦܬܐ	Gold	ܪܘܘܡܐ
Energetic (plural)	ܚܪܝܬܐ	They started	ܗܣܥܘܪܝܠܕ
Able to	ܗܘܠܝܬܐ	They dig	ܝܢܩܕܒ
nearness	ܗܕܝܠܗ	A Lot of fruits	ܩܝܪܐ ܚܚܒܬܐ
Teach them	ܗܘܠܝܩܠܕ	Richer	ܠܚܡܝܬܐ

228

learn Class Subjects

My School ܡܕܪܫܬܝ

ܐܢܐ ܫܡܝ ܐܝܠܗ ܡܪܝܡ. ܐܢܐ ܐܝܘܢ
ܝܠܘܦܬܐ ܒܝܦܐ ܒܡܕܝܢܬܐ (ܕܝܗܘܕܐ)
ܘܒܝܠܦܢ ܡܕܢܐ ܘܚܡܫܐ ܒܫܢܝ ܠܫܢܐ:
ܐܬܘܪܝܐ ܘܐܢܓܠܝܙܝܐ ܥܡ ܕܡܝܢܘܬܐ
ܘܟܝܡܝܐ ܘܡܬܡܐܛܝܩܝ ܘܬܐܘܠܘܓܝܐ
ܘܫܪܟܐ.
ܐܢܐ ܚܒܝܒܬܐ ܒܝܬܝ ܕܝܠܦܢ ܠܫܢܝ
ܐܬܘܪܝܐ - ܠܫܢܐ ܕܐܒܗ̈ܬܢ ܘܠܝܕܗ
ܘܡܟܝܢ ܐܝܠܗ ܠܫܢܐ ܕܡܫܝܚܝܠܗ
ܒܠܘܗ ܡܪܢ ܘܦܪܘܩܢ ܝܫܘܥ
ܡܫܝܚܐ.
ܐܝܬܠܝ ܒܠܘܗ ܝܪܬܘܬܐ ܥܬܝܪܬܐ
ܕܬܐܘܠܘܓܝܐ ܘܚܟܡܬܐ ܘܦܝܠܣܘܦܘܬܐ ܘܫܪܟܐ ܕܝܘܠܦܢܐ.
ܐܘܦ ܠܫܢܝ ܚܠܝܐ ܘܫܦܝܪܐ ܐܝܠܗ ܢܝܫܐ ܕܐܘܡܬܢܐ ܩܛܪܐ ܠܒܢܝ ܐܘܡܬܝ ܒܢܘܗܪܐ ܐܚܪܐ
ܕܐܝܬܐ ܒܟܠܗ ܥܠܡܐ.

Vocabulary

Chemistry	ܟܝܡܝܐ	Wisdom	ܚܟܡܬܐ
Theology	ܬܐܘܠܘܓܝܐ	Philosophy	ܦܝܠܣܘܦܘܬܐ
Our fathers	ܐܒܗ̈ܬܢ	Satin, pretty	ܫܦܝܪܐ
Our savior	ܦܪܘܩܢ	Symbol – target	ܢܝܫܐ
Legacy, fortune	ܝܪܬܘܬܐ	Ties	ܩܛܪ̈ܐ
Rich	ܥܬܝܪܬܐ	To children of	ܠܒܢ̈ܝ

The Rope ܣܩܠܐ

ܗܘܝܡ ܢܟܘܿܕܹ ܘܝܼܩܘܿܕܹ ܫܘܒܟܕ ܫܒܟܕ ܒܚܡܝܬܐ. ܘܡܥܘܩܒܝܟܕ ܚܩܠܩܝܕ ܒܝܠܗ. ܘܚܕ ܡܢܹ ܡܢܝܘܿܡ ܒܩܒܝܠܗ ܚܕܹܢܕ ܕܫܒܟܕ ܘܡܥܘܩܒܝܟܕ ܢܝܩܘܿܙܗ ܚܢܢܟܕ ܘܣܘܝܠܝܠܗ ܫܒܟܕ ܘܢܩܠܕ ܗܘܿܦܹܢܝܘܿܡ ܬܒܝܢܬܐ.

(signature)

Vocabulary

Two little boys	ܗܘܝܡ ܢܟܘܿܕܹ ܘܝܼܩܘܿܕܹ
Rope	ܫܒܟܕ
Old	ܒܚܡܝܬܐ
Arguing	ܚܩܠܩܝܕ
Held (p)	ܒܩܒܝܠܗ
Pulling it	ܢܝܩܘܿܙܗ
To hard	ܚܢܢܟܕ
Cut (past)	ܣܘܝܠܝܠܗ
Fell (plural)	ܢܩܠܕ
Mud	ܒܝܢܬܐ

The Heart ܠܒܐ

ܠܒܟܕ ܚܢܩܝܬ ܘܝܼܩܕ ܠܚܠܕ ܠܘܿܥܩܕ. ܘܝܼܩܕ ܚܩܠܝ ܢܝܒܟܕ ܘܩܘܿܫܕ. ܢܝܡ ܗܘܝܡ ܩܘܿܩܟܕ ܡܝ ܢܝܟܘܿܩܕ ܘܝܼܩܕ. ܢܝܟܘܿܩܕ ܕܘܿܩܕ ܢܩܒ ܘܚܩܟܝܬܒ ܘܝܼܩܕ ܡܝ ܠܝܟܕ ܢܝܠܟܕ ܥܩܢܝܕ. ܢܝܗܘܿܬ ܘܚܩܟܝܬܒ ܘܝܼܩܕ ܠܝܟܕ ܢܝܠܟܕ ܘܩܒܘܿܕ.

Artery	ܥܩܢܝܕ	Oxygen/air	ܩܘܿܫܕ
Vein	ܘܩܒܝܕ	Blood vessels	ܢܝܟܘܿܩܕ ܕܘܿܩܕ

6 peple, 4 Kids

The Family ܒܢܝ̈ܐ ܕܒܝܬܐ

ܒܐܡܪ ܢܡܪܘܕ ܒܢܝ̈ܐ ܕܒܝܬܝ ܝܢܐ ܠܫܬܬܐ
ܐܝܠܝ. ܒܒܐ ܘܝܡܐ ܘܬܪܝܢ ܐܚ̈ܘܢܐ ܘܬܪ̈ܬܝܢ
ܚܬ̈ܘܬܐ. ܒܒܝ ܐܝܠܗ ܐܟܪܐ ܒܙܪܥ ܚܛ̈ܐ ܘܡܫܚ̈ܬܐ
ܒܚܩܠܐ. ܝܡܝ ܒܫܡܫܐ ܟܠ ܕܒܢ̈ܝܐ ܕܒܝܬܐ
ܘܡܒܫܠܐ ܘܡܚܘܪܐ ܘܡܢܛܪܐ ܠܗ ܠܐܚܘܢܝ
ܘܒܪܬܐ. ܚܬ̈ܘܬܝ ܒܐܙܠܝ ܠܡܕܪܫܬܐ ܟܠ ܚܕܐ
ܒܨܦܐ ܕܝܠܗ̇. ܐܚܘܢܝ ܙܥܘܪܐ ܐܝܠܗ ܛܦܠܐ ܒܡܝܨ
ܚܠܒܐ. ܐܢܐ ܐܝܘܢ ܝܠܘܦܐ ܒܨܦܐ ܬܠܝܬܝܬܐ. ܒܢ̈ܝܐ
ܕܒܝܬܝ ܐܝܠܝ ܒܚܘܒܐ ܘܫܝܢܐ ܥܡ ܕܚܕ̈ܕܐ.

Vocabulary

He Says	ܒܐܡܪ	Laundry	ܡܚܘܪܐ
Family	ܒܢܝ̈ܐ ܕܒܝܬܝ	Class (grade)	ܨܦܐ
Brothers	ܐܚ̈ܘܢܐ	My brother	ܐܚܘܢܝ
Sisters	ܚܬ̈ܘܬܐ	Sucking milk (infant)	ܒܡܝܨ ܚܠܒܐ
She does laundry	ܒܚܘܪܐ	Together	ܥܡ ܕܚܕ̈ܕܐ

ܫܘܐ̈ܠܐ

ܐ: ܚܕܟܡܐ ܐܚ̈ܘܢܐ ܘܚܬ̈ܘܬܐ ܐܝܬܘܠܗ ܠܢܡܪܘܕ؟
ܐ. ܫܬܐ ܒ. ܚܡܫܐ ܓ. ܬܠܬܐ ܕ. ܐܪܒܥܐ

ܒ: ܡܘܢܐ ܒܦܠܚ ܒܒܐ ܕܢܡܪܘܕ؟
ܐ. ܐܣܝܐ ܒ. ܡܠܦܢܐ ܓ. ܟܬܒܐ ܕ. ܐܟܪܐ

ܓ: ܒܐܡܪ ܢܡܪܘܕ: ܝܡܝ ܥܘܒܕܢܗ̇ ܐܝܠܗ -----.
ܐ. ܡܠܦܢܘܬܐ ܒ. ܒܫܡܫܐ ܟܠ ܕܒܢ̈ܝܐ ܕܒܝܬܐ ܘܡܒܫܠܐ
ܓ. ܐܚܘܢܝ ܙܥܘܪܐ ܐܝܠܗ ܛܦܠܐ ܒܡܝܨ ܚܠܒܐ ܕ. ܝܠܘܦܘܬܐ ܒܨܦܐ ܬܡܝܢܝܬܐ

ܕ: ܢܡܪܘܕ ܝܠܘܦܐ ܒܨܦܐ -----.
ܐ. ܩܕܡܝܬܐ ܒ. ܬܠܝܬܝܬܐ ܓ. ܬܪܝܢܝܬܐ ܕ. ܐܪܒܥܝܬܐ

The Fall　　　　ܐܬܪܥܠܐ

Vocabulary

According to Syriac year ܚܡܘܥܟܝܬ ܕܝܥܢܥܐ ܕܝܐܗܘܕܢܝܐ, also ܒܝ ܥܢܥܐ ܕܝܐܗܘܕܢܝܐ	
Day becomes shorter.	ܢܘܗܕ ܝܨ ܚܩܝܨ ܝܚܕܐܢܐ
Fruits	ܩܝܕܐܝ
Leaves	ܠܗܕܩܝ
Before leaves fall.	ܝܘܓܐܢܐ ܗܐ ܢܗܕܝ ܠܗܕܩܝ
And fruits ripe, harvest, and cut from trees.	ܘܩܝܕܝ ܚܕܟܥܠܝ ܘܚܩܝܥܥܒܝ ܫܘܒܝܘܒܝ ܘܥܗܠܒܝܩܒܝ ܡܢ ܕܝܠܟܬܐ

232

The Winter ܣܬܘܐ

ܝܘܡܢܐ ܕܣܬܘܐ ܩܪܝܪܐ ܝܢܐ ܣܓܝ
ܦܐܫܐ ܩܪܝܪܐ ܝܠܗ ܘܬܠܓܐ ܒܟܒܝܪܐ
ܒܢܚܬ ܒܣܬܘܐ.
ܐܪܥܐ ܒܦܝܫܐ ܚܘܪܬܐ ܟܠ ܕܘܟܐ
ܘܐܘܪܚܬܐ ܘܢܗܪܐ ܕܡܝܐ ܒܓܠܕܝ.
ܘܛܪܦܐ ܕܐܝܠܢܐ ܒܟܒܝܪܐ ܩܫܝܐ ܒܢܦܠܝ.
ܘܐܝܠܢܐ ܒܫܠܚܝ ܒܬܠܓܐ ܘܒܗܘܝܐ
ܐܝܟ ܚܘܪܐ ܫܦܝܪܐ.

ܒܡܫܪܝܬܐ ܣܬܘܐ ܒܠܒܫܝ ܘܐܝܟ ܟܠܗܘܢ ܩܪܝܪܐ ܘܫܠܚܝ ܒܠܒܫܝ ܒܟܘܬܢܐ ܕܥܡܪܐ. ܝܘܡܐ ܒܟܝܪ ܒܢܘܗܪܐ ܒܝܬܐ ܒܝܬܐ ܘܠܒܫܝ ܒܟܘܬܢܐ ܕܣܘܝܬܐ.
ܐܢܫܐ ܒܥܩܝ ܡܢ ܣܬܘܐ ܣܓܝ ܐܝܠܗ ܩܪܝܪܐ ܘܥܪܝܩܐ ܘܝܘܡܢܐ ܟܪܝܐ ܝܢܐ، ܟܐ ܐܝܬ ܒܨܘܪܐ ܐܢܫܐ ܒܟܝܦܝ ܣܬܘܐ ܘܢܛܪܐ ܒܡܫܬܠܛܝ ܒܬܠܓܐ ܘܒܡܚܕܝ ܦܠܛܐ ܕܐܢܫܐ ܡܢ ܬܠܓܐ.

ܣܬܘܐ ܐܝܠܗ ܥܘܣܠܦܐ ܕܒܝܬܐ (ܕܐܪܒܥܐ) ܕܫܢܬܐ ܘܐܪܒܥܝܗ ܐܝܢܐ: ܨܝܦܐ، ܩܝܛܐ، ܨܝܦܐ ܐܪܒܥܐ، ܘܣܬܘܐ. ܘܐܝܬ ܥܐܕܐ ܪܒܐ ܒܕܥܟܠ ܒܣܬܘܐ، ܥܐܕܐ ܕܒܪ ܝܠܕܐ ܘܥܐܕܐ ܕܪܫܐ ܕܫܢܬܐ ܕܡܫܝܚܝܐ. ܘܐܝܬ ܥܐܕܐ ܕܣܘܒܪܐ.

ܐܝܟ ܚܕ ܝܘܡܐ ܕܣܬܘܐ ܠܐܢܬܬ ܬܠܓܐ ܘܠܐ ܐܝܠܗ ܩܪܝܪܐ، ܒܐܡܪܘܚ (ܗܐ ܝܘܡܐ ܟܐܝܢܐ ܐܝܠܗ ܘܕܡܝܐ ܝܘܡܐ ܕܒܗܪܐ.)

Vocabulary

Winters' days	ܝܘܡܢܐ ܕܣܬܘܐ	Beautiful (m)	ܫܦܝܪܐ
A lot	ܒܟܒܝܪܐ	People get upset	ܐܢܫܐ ܒܥܩܝ
Falls (literal; gets down) (m)	ܒܢܚܬ	Few	ܒܨܘܪܐ
Becomes (f)	ܒܦܝܫܐ	face	ܦܠܛܐ
(They) freeze	ܒܓܠܕܝ	Looks like (m)	ܕܡܝܐ
Hard - tough	ܩܫܝܐ	We say	ܒܐܡܪܘܚ

The Cow and The Frog   ܬܘܪܬܐ ܘܐܘܪܕܥܐ

Vocabulary

Pond	ܢܩܒܐ	Increase (f)	ܘܝܕܐ
Comes (f)	ܚܕܥܡܐ	Get bigger (f)	ܩܘܡܥܐ
Steers (f)	ܚܥܝܓܡܩܐ	Listened (f)	ܡܘܝܗܠܟܐ
Surprised (f)	ܚܝܗܩܗܐ	Blew up (f)	ܩܥܝܠܟܐ
To blow	ܡܩܢܐ	Shake (f)	ܥܢܥܕܐ

ܟܘܕ ܣܬܘܝܬܐ ܗܘܐ ܦܪܝܩܬܐ ܙܐܒܝܨܘܦܬܐ ܩܝܟܐ ܘܩܢܫܟܐ ܓܠܟ ܦܠܝܠܕ. ܘܚܕ ܡܢ ܦܠܝܠܕ ܒܝܕܐ ܘܒܟܘܕܪܬܐ ܕܘܡܕܐ ܘܬܒܒܒܨܘܦܬܐ ܘܦܕܐ ܡܥܣܟܐ ܓܕܘܕܐ ܟܓܢܬܝ ܘܚܣܘܝܘܦܐ ܥܓܕܐ ܟܘܕ ܢܘܐܕ ܚܓܟܢܐ ܘܣܓܟܡܘܝܕ ܣܝܟܐ ܡܝܩܐ ܕܘܦܘܝܐ ܗܐ ܗܩܘܦܐ ܘܘܦܐ ܗܘܙ ܟܓܢܫܟܝ ܝܠܗ ܘܢܐܚܕ ܗܘܦܠܗ ܦܕ ܚܢܘܡ ܡܝ ܩܝܟܐ ܙܐ ܥܚܘܦܐ؟ ܗܕ ܚܢܘܗܘܐ ܟܓܢܫܟܐ ܙܒܚܟܐ ܘܟܐ ܝܗܟܘܝ ܝܝܙܢܐ ܗܐ ܬܗܬܝ ܚܙܐܩ ܩܝܟܐ ܦܩܢܐ ܕܝܩܨܘܦܐ!

ܩܝܗ ܗܘܐ ܥܚܘܦܐ ܘܟܐ ܡܣܚܐ ܗܘܐ. ܘܚܕ ܣܬܘܝܬܐ ܩܝܟܐ ܙܐܬܝܠܕ ܘܙܐܒܝܠܕ ܗܩܘܦܐ ܟܩܘܕܐ ܘܒܝܬܝܕ ܦܢܫܗ ܣܢܗ ܕܝܪܕܝܢܐ ܒܝܘܩܕܐ ܗܘܐ ܗܘܐ ܟܝܓܕ ܕܝܟܐ ܒܙܒܚܟܐ ܘܘܝܟܐ ܘܡܟܝܬܟܝܐ ܒܢܐ ܩܝܨܐ ܙܒܚܟܐ ܡܝ ܥܚܘܦܐ. ܘܣܝܗܘܬܟܐ ܥܚܘܦܐ ܘܩܝܨܐ ܗܙܟܝܐ، ܚܟܝ ܣܝܟܐ ܙܒܝܨܘܗܐ ܗܘܐ ܟܓܢܫܟܐ ܝܠܝ ܘܘܝܐ ܚܒܬܝܟܐ ܣܓܘܟܟܐܙ، ܢܘܒ ܟܕܐ ܟܢܘܒܓܘܗܝ ܙܙܟܐ ܟܕܐ ܢܙܩܐ ܣܙܩܐ ܣܥܝܒ ܟܐ ܚܢܘܗ ܡܥܒ. ܗܘܘܗ ܗܘܐ ܙܘܦܕܐ ܚܟܝ ܩܝܟܐ ܘܟܐ ܦܠܝܢܠܩܝ ܗܐ ܗܩܘܦܐ، ܣܘܒ ܩܕܐ ܝܓܕܘܟܐ ܦܗܟܢܘܗܙ ܟܟܚܘܗܝ. ܘܩܡܐ ܗܟܐܙ ܣܘܩܗܙ ܣܒܣܘܦܬܐ ܒܝܕܐ ܡܝ ܩܩܢܐ.

Vocabulary

When winter was over	ܟܘܕ ܣܬܘܝܬܐ ܗܘܐ ܦܪܝܩܬܐ
Insects	ܩܝܟܐ
Got out (p)	ܦܠܝܠܕ
Got out (s - m)	ܦܠܝܠܗ
Prides himself	ܡܢܩܟܐ ܥܓܕܘܕܐ ܕܓܢܬܝܗ
Laughs on him	ܟܓܢܫܟܐ ܝܠܗ
Severe winter	ܗܩܘܦܐ ܚܩܘܦܐ
Under ground	ܣܢܗ ܕܝܪܕܝܢܐ
Next time will get nothing from me	ܙܟܐ ܟܕܐ ܣܙܩܐ ܣܥܝܒ ܟܐ ܚܢܘܗ ܡܥܒ
And you did not plan for winter	ܘܟܐ ܦܠܝܢܠܩܝ ܗܐ ܗܩܘܦܐ
Poverty	ܩܩܢܐ

Chapter 10

The Vocabulary   ܠܘܼܩܛܐ

Relatives   ܐܚܝܵܢܘܼܬܐ

Male	ܕܸܟܪܐ	Female	ܢܸܩܒܐ
Best Man	ܐܙܒܝܼܢܐ	Maid of honor	ܐܙܒܝܼܢܬܐ
Grandfather/Oldman	ܣܵܒܐ	Grandmother/old woman	ܣܵܒܬܐ
Dad	ܒܵܒܐ	Mom	ܝܸܡܐ
Male	ܙܵܘܘܿܕܐ	Female	ܒܲܝܬܐ
Husband/Man	ܓܲܒܪܐ	Wife/Woman	ܒܲܟܬܐ
Boy/son	ܒܪܘܿܢܐ	Girl/daughter	ܒܪܵܬܐ
Uncle (Fathers side)	ܥܲܡܐ	Aunt (Father's side)	ܥܲܡܬܐ
Uncle (Mother's side)	ܚܵܠܐ	Aunt (Mother's side)	ܚܵܠܬܐ
Brother	ܐܲܚܘܿܢܐ	Sister	ܚܵܬܐ
Groom	ܚܸܬܢܐ	Bride	ܟܲܠܘܿ/ܟܲܠܬܐ
Father-in-law	ܚܸܡܝܵܢܐ	Mother-in-law	ܚܸܡܬܐ
Spouse's brother	ܐܲܚܘܿܢܝܼܢܐ	Spouse's sister	ܒܲܪܚܡܝܵܢܬܐ
Grand son	ܢܸܬܝܼܐ	Grand daughter	ܢܸܬܝܼܬܐ
Sister-in-law's husband	ܐܵܕܝܼܫܐ/ܢܲܝܒܝܼܫܐ	Brother-in-law's wife	ܝܵܘܡܬܐ
Friend	ܚܲܒܪܐ		ܚܲܒܪܬܐ

Food   ܡܹܐܟܘܼܠܬܐ

Garlic	ܬܘܿܡܐ	Milk	ܚܲܠܒܐ/ܚܲܠܒܐ
Wine	ܚܲܡܪܐ	Yogurt	ܡܸܣܬܐ
Beer	ܒܸܥܪܐ / ܩܘܿܝ	Cheese	ܓܘܼܦܬܐ
Sour	ܚܲܡܘܼܨܐ	Bread	ܠܲܚܡܐ
Onion	ܒܸܨܠܐ	Vermicelli	ܪܸܫܬܐ
Salt	ܡܸܠܚܐ	Honey	ܕܘܼܒܫܐ
Vinegar	ܚܲܠܐ	Honey	ܓܲܪܘܿܬܐ

236

Classroom ܣܕܪܐ

Pencil	ܩܠܡܐ/ܩܢܝܐ	Notebook	ܟܘܪܣܐ/ܟܪܟܐ
Sharpener	ܡܓܝܪܦܢܐ	Bag	ܟܝܣܐ
Eraser	ܓܪܦܬܐ	Ruler	ܡܣܛܪܬܐ
Paper	ܛܪܦܐ	Board	ܠܘܚܐ
Book	ܟܬܒܐ	Chair	ܟܘܪܣܐ

Animals Sound ܩܠ ܕܚܝܘܬܐ

Scream	ܩܥܝܐ ܝܥܪܐ	Bellow	ܓܥܝܬ ܬܘܪܐ
Crow	ܩܪܐ ܕܝܟܐ	Barking	ܢܒܚ ܟܠܒܐ
Whinny	ܨܗܠ ܣܘܣܐ	Bleat	ܦܥܝ ܥܪܒܐ
Bird	ܨܝܪܐ ܨܘܠܨܘܠ	Bray	ܢܗܩ ܚܡܪܐ
Lion Roar	ܢܗܡ ܐܪܝܐ	Meow	ܢܘܐ ܫܘܢܪܐ

States Of Water ܓܢܣܘܬܐ ܕܡܝܐ

Frozen	ܓܡܘܕܐ	Cold	ܩܪܝܪܐ
Warm	ܦܫܘܪܐ	Cool/Chilly	ܦܫܘܪܐ
Hot	ܚܡܝܡܐ	Very hot	ܫܚܝܢܐ
Boiling	ܪܬܚܐ	Ice	ܓܠܝܕܐ
Steam	ܗܘܠܐ		

Time Of The Day ܙܒܢܐ ܕܝܘܡܐ

Evening	ܪܡܫܐ	Day	ܝܘܡܐ
Dark	ܚܫܟܐ	Dawn	ܥܘܪܬܐ/ܥܝܘܪܬܐ
After noon	ܦܢܝܬܐ	Morning	ܨܦܪܐ/ܩܕܡܬܐ
Nightfall	ܥܨܪܐ	Midday	ܛܗܪܐ
Night	ܠܠܝܐ		

The Fingers   ܨܒ̈ܥܬܐ ܕܐܝܕܐ

Thumb	ܟܪܘܬܐ
Index finger	ܦܘܫܟܣܝܐ
Ring finger	ܩܪܨܐ
Forefinger	ܨܪܝܬܐ
Little finger/Pinky	ܒܨܪܐ

The Stages Of Human Life   ܡܫܘܚ̈ܬܐ ܕܚܝܐ ܕܒܪܢܫܐ

Youth	ܥܠܝܡܐ	Embryo	ܥܘܠܐ
Teenager	ܒܥܘܕܐ/ܓܕܘܕܐ	Premature	ܢܣܦܐ
Young man	ܥܠܝܡܐ	Infant	ܢܘܦܐ
Man	ܓܒܪܐ	Child	ܝܠܘܕܐ
Old man	ܣܒܐ	Boy	ܛܠܝܐ

238

Appendix A

English Equivalent	Letter	Number Value
A	�	1
B		2
G		3
D		4
H		5
W		6
Z		7
KH*		8
TD*		9
Y		10
K		20
L		30
M		40
N		50
S		60
E*		70
P		80
SS*		90

Q*	ڍ	100
R	ܪ	200
SH	ܫ	300
T	ܬ	400

*This is the closest English equivalent for this letter.

Letter Alignment Connections

Final	Medial	Initial
ܐ	ـܐ	ـܐ
ܒ	ـܒ	ܒ
ܓ	ـܓ	ܓ
ܕ	ـܕ	ـܕ
ܗ	ـܗ	ـܗ
ܘ	ـܘ	ـܘ
ܙ	ـܙ	ـܙ
ܚ	ـܚ	ܚ
ܛ	ـܛ	ܛ
ܝ	ـܝ	ܝ
ܟ	ـܟ	ܟ
ܠ	ـܠ	ܠ
ܡ	ـܡ	ܡ
ܢ	ـܢ	ܢ
ܣ	ـܣ	ܣ
ܥ	ـܥ	ܥ
ܦ	ـܦ	ܦ

Sounds

Labials	ܦܒܡܝܬܐ
	ܒ . ܘ . ܦ . ܡ
Sibilants	ܡܫܘܩܢܝܗܐ
	ܙ . ܣ . ܨ . ܫ
Velars	ܟܝܟܢܝܗܐ
	ܐ . ܗ . ܚ . ܟ . ܩ
Palatal	ܠܥܢܐ ܘܥܡ ܟܘܡܐ
	ܓ . ܝ . ܟ . ܩ
Lingual	ܠܥܢܐ ܘܢܬܐ
	ܕ . ܠ . ܢ . ܪ . ܬ

Un-Joined Letters: ܐ ، ܕ ، ܘ ، ܙ ، ܨ ، ܪ

Weakest Letters: ܐܘܝ

Preposition Letters: ܒ . ܕ . ܘ . ܠ

ܟ	ܟܼ	ܟܼ
ܩ	ܩ	ܩ
ܨ	ܨ	ܨ
ܚ	ܚ	ܚ
ܗ	ܬܗ	ܗ

241

Vowels

Sqapa	$\overset{\circ}{\text{ܐ}}$ ܐ	AH	ܘܩܬܐ
Pthaha	ܐ ܐ	UH	ܩܡܨܐ
Zlama Psheeqa	ܐ ܐ	IH	ܘܐܬܐ ܟܥܝܬܐ
Zlama Qishya	ܐ ܐ	EH	ܘܐܬܐ ܡܥܢܐ
Rwahha	ܐ	OH	ܕܘܡܐ
Rwassa	ܘ	OO	ܕܬܝܐ
Hwassa	ܐ	EE	ܣܬܝܐ

242

Appendix B

Punctuation

Period	ܣܢܕ ܕܘܡܨܐ	.
Exclamation mark	ܢܗܐ ܕܝܘܡܚܒܐ	!
Comma	ܘܢܕ	،
Semicolon	ܘܢܕ ܘܕܘܡܨܐ	؛
Colon	ܗܩܒ ܕܘܡܨܐ	:
Quotation marks	ܣܥܡܐ ܗܘܩܢܢܐ	" "
Question Mark	ܢܗܐ ܕܥܘܐܠܐ	؟
Dash	ܗܩܒܠܐ	-
Parentheses	ܣܥܡܐ ܣܢܘܡܐ	( )
Paragraph Marker	ܢܗܐ ܕ ܚܕܘܐ	◆

Special Characters and Ligatures

Final Simkath	ܣ	
Dot less Dalath/Resh	ܕ	
Garshouni Gamal	ܠ	
Reverse Peh	ܩ	
Garshouni Teth	،	
Yah	ܡܝ	Symbol for God. The three dots represent the Holy Trinity. The single dot means One God.
Subscript Alap	ܐ	
Taw Alap	ܠܐ	ܐ ܣ

243

Modifiers

Pronunciation	Letter
B	ܒ
W	ܒ݂
G	ܓ
GH	ܓ݂
J	ܔ
D	ܕ
TH	ܕ݂
W	ܘ
U	ܘ݂
O	ܘ݁
Y	ܝ
EE	ܝ݂
CH	ܟ
K	ܟ݁
KH	ܟ݂
P	ܦ
F	ܦ݂
W	ܦ
V	ܦ
SH	ܫ
CH	ܫ݂
T	ܬ
TH	ܬ݂

244

Appendix C

The Hard and Soft Letters Rules

These rules are for those seeking more in learning the classical Syriac language.

Hard Letters: Each letter of these five letters (ܒ ܓ ܕ ܟ ܦ ܬ) gives hard sound if:

1. when falls at the beginning of the word, like in:

House	ܒܲܝܬܵܐ
Man	ܓܲܒ݂ܪܵܐ
Religion	ܕܼܝܢܵܐ
Bride	ܟܲܠܬ݂ܵܐ
Rooster	ܬܲܪܢܵܓ݂ܠܵܐ

2. has a vowel after Pthaha ◌ܲ, like in:

Big	ܪܲܒܵܐ
Carpenter	ܢܲܓܵܪܵܐ
Choir, Division (army)	ܟܲܟܵܐ
Wise man	ܚܲܟܼܝܡܵܐ

3. when falls silent (no vowel) at the end of the word after silent, like in: ܠܵܐ "No, Not"

4. when falls thirdly and first letter has Pthaha ◌ܲ, like in:

Spear, war, Sword	ܣܲܝܦܵܐ
Snow	ܬܲܠܓܵܐ
Flower	ܘܲܪܕܵܐ
King	ܡܲܠܟܵܐ

Soft Letter: Each of these letters ܗ ܟ ܘ ܓ ܒ ܬ gives soft sound if:

1. when falls at the beginning of the word and proceed by one of the preposition letter ܟ ܒ ܘ ܕ and group of letters ܗܔ ܒ ܒ ܗ like in:

Of man	ܕܟܬ݂ܪ
And blood	ܘܕܡܐ
He heals	ܡܬ݂ܗܡ
We translate	ܒܡܬ݂ܩܠܡ

2. when falls silent (no vowel) at the end of word or after the first letter, like in:

Write in	ܟܬ݂ܘܒ
Desired(c)	ܨܒ݂ܐ
For you (c)	ܠܟ݂
Man	ܟܬ݂ܪܐ
Body	ܦܓ݂ܪܐ
Stupid	ܗܓ݂ܠܐ

3. when it is vowel and falls after:

a. Sqapa ܵ, like in:

Good	ܛܒ݂ܐ
Old man	ܣܒ݂ܐ
Crown	ܟܠܝܠܐ
Light	ܢܗ݂ܝܪܐ

b. Rwahha ܘ like in:

Writer	ܟܬ݂ܘܒ݂ܐ
Worker	ܟܕ݂ܘܕ݂ܐ

c. Hwassa ܝ like in:

Cross	ܙܩܝܦ݂ܐ

Congratulations حڌیخ؛

Asleep (f) هلڬبۀ؛

d. After first silent letter, like in:

Corruption (c) سٮٚٮڭڍ

Neck سوۡڭڍ

Walking (c) دٚڬڍڍ

e. After two silent letters, like in:

Rabbit ؛ٚٚڍخ؛

Queen ؛هلڬخۀ؛

4. When falls after silent Alap (ٍ) or Yod (ـ) and preceded Zlama Qishya (◌), like in:

Wolf دٍڌخ؛

Holiday بڌوۡ؛

Trembling (c) دهبۀ؛

Notes:

1. At the end of word, the letter Taw ٰ pronounces "Th" ٰ as in "Three" if:

a. proceeded by Rwassa ه "oo" like in:

Stupidly هجلهۀ؛

slavery بٚدوهۀ؛

Grace بٮٚتهۀ؛

b. after silent letter proceeded by Pthaha ◌ like in:

Gospel (c) هٚٚدۀ؛

Expense (c) دفٚبۀ؛

247

Appendix D

The Preposition Letter Rules

These rules are for those seeking more in learning the classical Syriac language.

1. If the first letter of the name has vowel, like in ܟܬܒܐ and :
   a. a preposition letter added at the beginning of that name, then the preposition letter must be silent (no vowel) like ܒܟܬܒܐ and ܕܟܬܒܐ .
   b. If two preposition letters were added, then the first preposition letter must have vowel **Pthaha** "ܦܬܚܐ", and silent the second, like in, ܕܠܟܬܒܐ and ܘܠܟܬܒܐ
   c. If three preposition letters were added, then the first and the third propositional letters must be silent and the second has the vowel **Pthaha** "ܦܬܚܐ", like in, ܠܕܒܟܬܒܐ and ܘܕܒܟܬܒܐ
   d. If four of them were added together, then the first and third preposition letters are vowel with **Pthaha** "ܦܬܚܐ", and second and fourth are silent, like in, ܘܠܕܒܟܬܒܐ
2. If the first letter of the name is silent, like in ܡܫܝܚܐ and:
   a. a preposition letter is added must have vowel **Pthaha** "ܦܬܚܐ", like in, ܡܫܝܚܐ، ܒܡܫܝܚܐ، ܕܡܫܝܚܐ
   b. If two preposition letters are added, silent the first and vowel the second with **Pthaha** "ܦܬܚܐ", like in, ܒܕܡܫܝܚܐ، ܘܠܡܫܝܚܐ
   c. If three preposition letters are added, the first and third will have **Pthaha** "ܦܬܚܐ", and silent the second, like in, ܠܕܒܡܫܝܚܐ، ܘܕܒܡܫܝܚܐ
   d. If four preposition letters are added, then the second and the fourth letters will have **Pthaha** "ܦܬܚܐ", and silent the first and third, like in, ܘܠܕܒܡܫܝܚܐ

Appendix E

Silent Letters
These rules are for those seeking more in learning the classical Syriac language.

There are twelve letters that are written but not pronounced regardless of the dash line above it:

Note: Most of the following words are in Classical Syriac language and it marked with "c" for classical.

ܐ ܂ ܓ ܂ ܗ ܂ ܘ ܂ ܚ ܂ ܝ ܂ ܟ ܂ ܠ ܂ ܡ ܂ ܢ ܂ ܥ ܂ ܦ

English	Words	Syriac Letters
Secret, mass	ܐ̄ܪܵܙܵܐ	ܐ
Person, man	ܐ̄ܢܵܫܵܐ	
Last, final(m)	ܐ̄ܚܵܪ̈ܵܝܵܐ	
New, modern	ܚܲܕ̄ܬܵܐ	ܓ
Church	ܥܹܕ̄ܬܵܐ	
Romans	ܖ̈ܘܿܡܵܝܹ̈ܐ	ܗ
Jewish (c)	ܝܗ̄ܘܿܕܵܝܵܐ	
Knowledge (c)	ܝܼܕܲܥܬܵܐ	ܘ
Promise (c)	ܫܘ̄ܘܿܕܵܝܵܐ	
Work (p, c)	ܥܒ̄ܵܕܵܐ	
Cross (p, c)	ܨܠܝܼܒ̄ܵܐ	
Together (c)	ܐ̄ܚܖ̈ܵܢܹܐ	ܚ

249

Yesterday	ܐܬܡܠ	ܝ
Last year (c)	ܐܫܢܬܝ	
From that time (c)	ܡܝܢܝܠ	
My sword (c)	ܣܝܦܝ	
Go (c)	ܙܘܠܐ	ܠ
We go (c)	ܙܘܠܢ	
Waves (c)	ܓܠܠܐ	
People (c)	ܥܡܡܐ	ܡ
Seas (c)	ܝܡܡܐ	
Medicines (c)	ܣܡܡܢܐ	
Year	ܫܢܬܐ	ܢ
Short period (c)	ܘܫܢܬܐ	
Your (p, c)	ܐܢܬܘܢ	
Giants	ܓܢܒܪܐ	
Get out (p, c)	ܡܦܩܩܢ	ܩ
Clear (c)	ܡܕܩܩܢ	
Set her free, Liberated (f, c)	ܚܪܪܗ	ܪ
Regret (c)	ܐܬܬܘܢ	ܬ

Note: The letter "ܘ' as vowel "ܘ݁" short "o", unlike the above, it does not write but pronounce in the following words: "all" ܟܠ and pronounces as ܟܘܠ, and "because" ܡܛܠ and pronounces as ܡܛܘܠ.

Appendix F

Rules of how to apply هنقد in the word if the word has no ܗ letter.

Rule 1: every noun ends with **Sqapa** Ö vowel and letter **Alap** ܐ without **Taw** ܬ, the plural is made by changing the final vowel **Sqapa** to **Zlama Qishya** Ọ and place the two dots on the second letter from last, like:

  Wood: ܩܝܣܐ
  Woods: ܩܝܣܹܐ
  Farm: ܚܩܠܐ
  Farms: ܚܩܠܹܐ
  Sparrow: ܨܸܦܪܐ
  Sparrows: ܨܸܦܪܹܐ
  Angel: ܡܲܠܲܐܟ݂ܐ
  Angels: ܡܲܠܲܐܟ݂ܹܐ

This rule applies on masculine noun too except what in rule 2, like

  Honest man: ܘܕܝܼܨܐ
  Honest men: ܘܕܝܼܨܹܐ
  Teacher: ܡܲܠܦܢܐ
  Teachers: ܡܲܠܦܢܹܐ
  Learner: ܝܠܘܿܦܐ
  Learners: ܝܠܘܿܦܹܐ

Rule 2: Every adjective starts with a **Pthaha** vowel Ọ on first letter and ends with ܐ then the plural is by moving the Pthaha to second letter and place the two dots on first letter, like:

  Blind: ܣܡܝܐ
  Blinds: ܣܡܹܝܐ
  Pure (Class Syriac): ܘܗܐ

251

Pure: ܩܢܕ̈ܐ

Except:

Lion: ܐܪܝܐ

Lions: ܐܪ̈ܝܘܬܐ

Note: If the first letter has **Sqapa** ◌̇, the plural is by having **Pthaha** ◌̇ on second letter and placing the plural two dots on the second letter from last. Like in:

Infants (c): ܝܠܘܕܐ

Infants: ܝܠܘ̈ܕܐ

Except:

Doctor: ܐܣܝܐ

Doctors: ܐܣ̈ܘܬܐ

King's wine servant (c): ܫܩܝܐ

Servants: ܫܩ̈ܘܬܐ

Rule 3: Every name made of two syllables and ends with ܬܐ, it plurals by having Sqapa ◌̇ on silent letter before ܬ. Like in:

Friday: ܥܪܘܒܬܐ

Fridays: ܥܪ̈ܘܒܬܐ

Picture: ܨܘܪܬܐ

Pictures: ܨܘܪ̈ܬܐ

Queen: ܡܠܟܬܐ

Queens: ܡܠ̈ܟܬܐ

If the letter before ܬ has Sqapa ◌̇, it plurals by adding ܘ after the letter, like in:

Sacrifice(c): ܕܒܚܬܐ

Sacrifices: ܕܒ̈ܚܘܬܐ

Rule 4: Every name made of three or four syllables and ends with ‍ܗ, it plurals by adding Sqapa ◌ on the letter before ܗ like in:

Stupidity: ܗܸܓܠܘܼܬܵܐ

Stupidities: ܗܸܓ݂ܠܵܬ݂ܵܐ

Grace: ܒܸܣܬܸܡܬܵܐ

Graces: ܒܸܣܬܵܡܵܬ݂ܵܐ

Teacher (f): ܡܲܠܦܵܢܝܼܬ݂ܵܐ

Teachers: ܡܲܠܦܵܢܝܵܬ݂ܵܐ

Rule 5: Each feminine adjective in masculine form plurals by adding ܗ at the end of the word, like in:

Pure, Sober(c): ܢܲܟ݂ܦܵܐ

Pure, Sober: ܢܲܟ݂ܦ݂ܵܐ

Appendix G

The following images are from the Biology textbooks that is being used at the Syriac schools in Iraq.

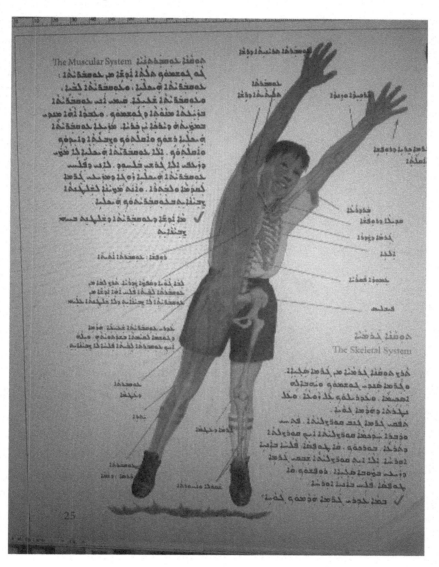

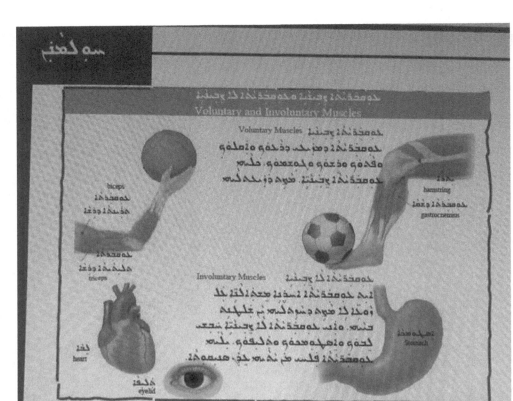

ܟܘܡܚܕܢܐ ܘܚܢܬܐ ܡܟܘܡܚܕܢܐ ܟܐ ܘܚܢܬܐ
Voluntary and Involuntary Muscles

Voluntary Muscles ܟܘܡܚܕܢܐ ܘܚܢܬܐ

ܟܘܡܚܕܢܐ ܘܚܢܬܐ ܒܪ ܟܐ ܕܟܕܥܘ ܘܐܡܠܘ
ܡܩܕܥܘ ܘܕܥܘ ܘ ܟܘܥܥܘ. ܟܠܝܢ
ܟܘܡܚܕܢܐ ܘܚܢܬܐ. ܗܘܗ ܕܪ ܟܚ ܟܝܢ

biceps
ܟܘܡܚܕܢܐ
ܗܕܢܟܐ ܘܕܥܐ

ܢܐܟܝ
hamstring

ܟܘܡܚܕܢܐ ܘܥܡܐ
gastrocnemius

ܟܘܡܚܕܢܐ
ܗܟܢܟܐ ܘܕܥܐ
triceps

Involuntary Muscles ܟܘܡܚܕܢܐ ܟܐ ܘܚܢܬܐ

ܐܝܗ ܟܘܡܚܕܢܐ ܐ ܣܕܢܐ ܡܚܐ ܟܬܐ ܟܠ
ܘܗܟܐ ܟܐ ܗܘܗ ܕܢܘܗ ܟܝܢ ܒܪ ܥܠܝܟܝܢ
ܟܢܝܢ. ܘܐܝܬ ܟܘܡܚܕܢܐ ܟܐ ܘܚܢܬܐ ܝܚܥܥ
ܟܚܘ ܘܐܗܟܗ ܡܚܕܘ ܘܗܟܢܟܘ. ܝܟܢܝܢ
ܟܘܡܚܕܢܐ ܦܠܝܢ ܡܢ ܢܐ ܣܘ ܝܟܝ ܗܣܡܗܐ

ܟܒܐ
heart

ܐܣܟܘܡܚܐ
Stomach

ܗܟܢܘܐ
eyelid

ܢܥܝܟܘܗܐ ܟܗ ܘܡܢܐ ܟܘܡܚܕܢܬܐ
Caring for Your Muscular System

ܘܘܕܢܐ ܝܟܝܕ ܟܘܡܚܕܢܐ ܗܘ ܗܒ ܝܝܠܝܕ
ܘ ܟܗܘܐ.

ܝܟܥܝܢܐ ܘ ܟܘܥܥܘܗ ܚܢܝܟܐ
ܕܟܘܡܚܕܢܬܐ ܗܘ ܟܗܘܐ ܡܚ ܢܐ ܘ ܝܥܡܚܐ ܗܘܕ
ܝܟܘܕܐ ܘܝܡܝ. ܝܟܘܝ. ܟܕ ܚܢܘܗܐ ܘܡܚܕܟܐ
ܘܝܝܢܢܐ.

1. ܣܘܒ ܠܗܣܘܒܟܐ ܘܡܚܗܥ ܣܘܐ ܡ
ܝܝܢܝܘ. ܝܟܘܗ ܚܟܗܐ ܟܗ ܝܝܢܐ ܐܣܘܢܟܐ.
ܘܝܝܚ ܥܝܠܩܐ؟ ܐܘܐ ܥܡ ܣܠܩܠܝܘ
ܚܘܝܟܢܝܘ؟

2. ܢܨܚ ܟܐ ܘܝܝܕ ܗܟܝܟܘ ܚܕܐ ܘܗܘܗ. ܗܘ
ܚܘܕܐ؟

3. ܢܨܚ ܘܝܟܗܐ ܘܚܟܐ ܘܐܡܠܘ ܟܗ ܘܗܟܐ.
ܗܘܗ ܘܝܝܟܗ ܗܟ ܘܚܟܐ ܟܣܘܘܘ؟

Spine, Skull, and Pelvis

skull

vertebrae

pelvis

Caring for Your Skeletal System

239

Appendix H

The International Numerals

The lack of zero in the Syriac language makes it more difficult to deal with. Therefore, in 643 AD, the international numerals, known as the English numerals, were born in the Quinacrine monastery nearby Aleppo in Syria. Based on the number of angles, the monk Sawira 575 - 667 (known by Sebokht, also translated the Indian Numerals to Arabs), a Syriac mathematician and scientist from Nisibin City put the outline of the numbers. Then followed by his disciple and a monk from the same monastery called Merdas, in 663 AD, Merdas made for each number a symbol based on the mathematical base to achieve using sharp and right angles. For example, number one (1) has one angle, number (2) has two angles and so the number (0) has no angle.

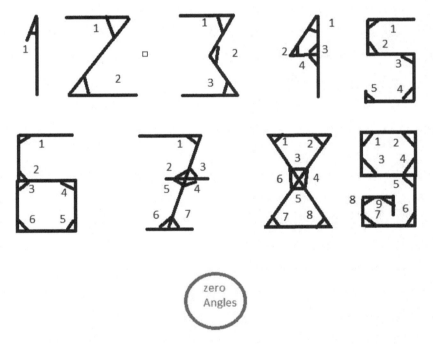

Figure 4-1: International Numerals

257

Appendix I

Ordinal Numbers Beyond the Tenth.

The following ordinal numbers are same for masculine and feminine.

12th	ܗܕܥܣܝܪܝܐ	11th	ܚܕܥܣܝܪܝܐ
14th	ܐܪܒܥܣܝܪܝܐ	13th	ܬܠܬܥܣܝܪܝܐ
16th	ܫܬܥܣܝܪܝܐ	15th	ܚܡܫܥܣܝܪܝܐ
18th	ܬܡܢܥܣܝܪܝܐ	17th	ܫܒܥܣܝܪܝܐ
		18th	ܬܡܢܥܣܝܪܝܐ

20th to 90th

30th	ܬܠܬܝܢܝܐ	20th	ܥܣܪܝܢܝܐ
50th	ܚܡܫܝܢܝܐ	40th	ܐܪܒܥܝܢܝܐ
70th	ܫܒܥܝܢܝܐ	60th	ܫܬܝܢܝܐ
90th	ܬܫܥܝܢܝܐ	80th	ܬܡܢܝܢܝܐ

258

References   ܪܝܫܐ

Bazzi, M. J., & Errico, R. A. (1989). *Classical Syriac. Assyrian – Chaldean*. Irvine, California: Noohra Foundation.

Beth Mardutho: The Syriac Institute, (1992). *About the Syriac language*. Retrieved January 3, 2009, from Beth Mardutho: The Syriac Institute Web site: http://www.bethmardutho.org/aboutsyriac

Caruso, S. *What is Galilean Aramaic?* http://aramaicnt.org/what-is-galilean-aramaic/

ܕܝܠܢ ܡܠܟܐ

http://www.malikyadilan.com/forum/viewtopic.php?t=11136

Edmondson, R. (2005, August 15). What animal sounds are called? Retrieved January 29, 2009, from Did you know? Web site: http://www.myuniversalfacts.com/2005/08/what-animal-sounds-are-called.html

Gary, D. P., & Miles, V. V. (2007). *NEW basics of biblical Syriac grammar*. Grand Rapids, MI. Zondervan.

Haido, Y., & Yousif, J. (2014). *Assyrian Grammar For Advanced Adults – Book 2*. Chicago, Illinois: Assyrian National Council of Illinois

Haido, Y., & Yousif, J. (2012). *Assyrian Reader For Advanced Adults – 2ⁿᵈ Ed.* Chicago, Illinois: Assyrian National Council of Illinois

Jammo, S. (1996). *Chaldean language: Elementary course*. Troy, Michigan: Saint Joseph Chaldean Catholic Parish.

Hebrew For Christian. A Brief History of the Hebrew Language. http://www.hebrew4christians.com/Grammar/Unit_One/History/history.html
Hozaya, Y., & Youkhana, A. (1999). *Bahra. Arabic-Assyrian dictionary*. Erbil, Iraq: Assyrian Aid Society of America.

Lishani (2016). قاموس اشوري متعدد اللغات www.lishani.com

Lo, L. (2005). Syriac. Retrieved January 5, 2009, from Ancient Scripts Web site: http://www.ancientscripts.com/syriac.html

المطران طيماثوس ارميا مقدسي (2004). قواعد اللغة السريانية. منشورات جمعية الثقافة الكلدانية. عنكاوا\العراق

Murphy, R. (1989). *Grammar in use. Reference and practice for intermediate students of English.* Cambridge University Press

Namato, L. (1996). *Teach yourself modern Syriac for windows version 1.1.* Round Lake Beach: Esarhaddon Productions, Inc.

Purland, M. (2004). *Big grammar book.* http://www.englishbanana.com/books/big-grammar-book/big-grammar-book.pdf

Thackston, W. M. (1999). *Introduction to Syriac.* Bethesda, Maryland: IBEX Publishers.

Younan, Paul D. (2000). History of Aramaic. Peshitta.org. http://www.peshitta.org/initial/aramaic.html

Younes J. Fr. & Sadek, I. (2008). *The Syriac Language.* http://www.namnews.org/pdf/pres/sl.pdf

AppleScript®

Mark Conway Munro

WILEY

Wiley Publishing, Inc.

AppleScript®

Published by
Wiley Publishing, Inc.
10475 Crosspoint Boulevard
Indianapolis, IN 46256
www.wiley.com

Copyright © 2010 by Wiley Publishing, Inc., Indianapolis, Indiana

Published by Wiley Publishing, Inc., Indianapolis, Indiana

Published simultaneously in Canada

ISBN: 978-0-470-56229-1

Manufactured in the United States of America

10 9 8 7 6 5 4 3 2 1

For general information on our other products and services or to obtain technical support, please contact our Customer Care Department within the U.S. at (877) 762-2974, outside the U.S. at (317) 572-3993 or fax (317) 572-4002.

Library of Congress Control Number: 2010925705

To my father,
Philip Conway Munro,
for teaching me the difference between
hardware and software at an early age.

Credits

Acquisitions Editor
Aaron Black

Executive Editor
Jody Lefevere

Project Editor
Katharine Dvorak

Technical Editor
Rob Vanderwerf

Copy Editor
Lauren Kennedy

Editorial Director
Robyn Siesky

Business Manager
Amy Knies

Senior Marketing Manager
Sandy Smith

Vice President and Executive Group Publisher
Richard Swadley

Vice President and Executive Publisher
Barry Pruett

Project Coordinator
Lynsey Stanford

Graphics and Production Specialists
Andrea Hornberger
Erin Zeltner

Quality Control Technician
John Greenough

Proofreading
C. M. Jones

Indexing
WordCo Indexing Services

Media Development Project Manager
Laura Moss

Media Development Assistant Project Manager
Jenny Swisher

Media Development Associate Producer
Doug Kuhn